Shapeholders

SHAPEHOLDERS

BUSINESS SUCCESS
—— IN THE ——
AGE OF ACTIVISM

MARK R. KENNEDY

Columbia Business School
Publishing

Columbia University Press
Publishers Since 1893
New York Chichester, West Sussex
cup.columbia.edu
Copyright © 2017 Mark R. Kennedy

Library of Congress Cataloging-in-Publication Data
Names: Kennedy, Mark, 1957– author.
Title: Shapeholders : business success in the age of activism / Mark Kennedy.
Description: New York : Columbia University Press, [2017] |
Series: Columbia Business School publishing |
Includes bibliographical references and index.
Identifiers: LCCN 2016046846 (print) | LCCN 2017003119 (ebook) |
ISBN 9780231180566 (cloth : alk. paper) | ISBN 9780231542784 (e-book)
Subjects: LCSH: Social responsibility of business. | Corporations—Public relations. |
Corporations—Moral and ethical aspects. | Corporate governance. | Strategic planning.
Classification: LCC HD60 .K48195 2017 (print) | LCC HD60 (ebook) |
DDC 658.4/08—dc23
LC record available at https://lccn.loc.gov/2016046846

∞

Columbia University Press books are printed on permanent
and durable acid-free paper.
Printed in the United States of America

Cover design: Jordan Wannemacher
Cover art: Neil Webb

This book is dedicated to Debbie, my true life partner,
and our children—Charles, Emily, Sarah, and Peter,
of whom we could not be more proud.

Contents

Contents

Preface

SOMETIMES THE SIMPLEST OF habits have the most profound impact.

In my family, every school year began with my six siblings and me lining up in front of the front door of our home and taking a first day of school photo. Perhaps this is a tradition in your family. After the photo my mother shared one piece of advice with us, the same advice every year. Her counsel was to be on the lookout for new students, those who were different from the others, and help them fit in.

This habit not only helped new kids in town, but it has been immensely beneficial to me. It led me to meet lifelong friends like Joe San and Ken Sun from Hong Kong. I have also found that cultivating a habit of perceiving differences and integrating those who are different into your circle is a good foundation for success in any walk of life.

When I was twenty-one, both my mother and I were delegates to the 1978 Minnesota Republican Party Convention. My mother was a single-issue voter. When deciding who we should vote to endorse, I was surprised that my mother decided against the candidate most zealous on her key issue and instead favored another candidate who, while affirming support for my mother's issue, also had a broader platform and therefore would have wider appeal and a greater chance of winning the election.

My mother's motivation was narrowly focused, but she took a very broad view in her approach. She instinctively understood that a candidate's fixation only on her single issue would not lead to success, that advancing her one issue was more likely to be achieved by someone who perceived and embraced other concerns while pursuing that goal.

My father reinforced this idea of constantly seeking to bring others into your circle by teaching every child, grandchild, and mentee to look someone straight in the eye, give him or her a firm handshake, and say, "I'm _____, glad to meet you."

While I suspect many parents modeled the simple and easy to understand idea that good things happen from finding ways to unite with others for mutual benefit, my experience has been that this lesson is often left behind when people suit up for business or pursue politics.

Believing to my core that business can be a positive force for good, after two decades working in business I ran for Congress under the banner Kennedy Means Business as a businessman who was skilled at perceiving differences and finding a path to unity, of taking in the concerns of others as I advanced my own.

My mother's focus on attracting broad enough support to achieve results, not simply heated rhetoric to excite narrow interests, stuck with me. I understood that achieving desired outcomes in an electoral campaign required crossing the fifty-yard or midpoint line. Dancing in your own end zone or goal may be fun, but it achieves nothing. I focused on understanding the differences among voter segments and crafting an appeal that united them in support of my campaign.

During my campaigns I prohibited my staff from using the words "Democrat" and "Republican" in press releases. I counseled that if we can't explain the advantages of my position without resorting to partisan labels, we clearly are not explaining it in a way that will capture the swing voters who are essential to electoral success.

In the end, I beat the one in a hundred odds of defeating a four-term incumbent. I won by 155 votes out of a total of more than 290,000 votes. I would have lost if I had left the lessons of my youth behind.

As a congressman, I explored all sides and sought actionable consensus. A whole series of Hill rags automatically showed up in bulk at my office's front door each morning—*Politico, Roll Call, The Hill, CQ Weekly*, and the *National Journal*. To understand competing views, I supplemented these by ordering not only the *New York Times* and the *Wall Street Journal* to get the view from the left and the right, but also the *Washington Post* to get the broader Washington view, *USA Today* to get the mainstream America view, the *Minneapolis Star Tribune* to get the home-state view, and the *Economist* and the *Financial Times* to get the non-U.S. view.

My day began then as it does now with reading each publication, paying special attention to the contrast in how each topic was covered. What was the top story in one was buried in the middle of the B section in another. Competing newspapers' headlines for the same event would give one the impression the papers were covering different topics. This habit helped me identify how I could frame my messaging and form my coalitions in ways that would push beyond agitation to achieve action.

To my dismay, I discovered that both parties were driven by talking points that consisted of little more than the best poll-tested phrases as to why they were right and the other side was wrong. Republican talking points emphasized how the tax cuts proposed by President George W. Bush benefited all taxpayers. Democratic talking points blasted the cuts as benefiting only the rich. Neither talked about the impact of the cuts on future debt levels. I discovered that congressional life gave little heed to the lessons of our youth.

Every Tuesday morning, members of each party caucus meet separately. Members are implored to support the team. In this case the team is the party, not the nation. Yet the idea that the opposing sides would line up to shake hands with the other side at the end of each political contest, as I had experienced playing sports, was frequently absent.

Those who delude themselves into thinking that only the other party acts this way, not their own party, betray their own myopia. There is no monopoly on partisanship in politics. Unfortunately, citizens of all ideologies have narrow political vision.[1] It is citizens with one-sided views of the world who have molded the Congress we have today.

Congress is even more narrowly focused than it was during my service a decade ago. Congress's approval rating during my service peaked at 84 percent and was regularly above 50 percent.[2] It often struggles to maintain double-digit approval ratings today. This is not good for those who serve or those who are not being served.

As a congressman I found businesspeople little better when it came to integrating the views of those not directly involved in the marketplace.

Jonathan Swift said, "Vision is the art of seeing what is invisible to others." In Congress I saw a whole other world that had been clearly within my line of sight but was previously invisible to me. I had never thought much about who made sure that when you flushed the toilet the right thing happened, that everyone had access to clean water, or that the transportation infrastructure was optimally designed. These concerns escape the view of many in business. Few see these and other social concerns as market needs they could profitably address.

I saw how elements of society with no stake in a company's success can foment hysteria, turning their attention to one particular corporation, making it the personification of some hot-button issue, and giving it little chance to alter the proclaimed judgment imposed by agitated elements of society. I saw my former employer Arthur Andersen become essentially extinct even before final judgment of its guilt was reached. I saw Stanley Tool nationally demonized and hounded to abandon plans to reincorporate in Bermuda, Dubai Ports forced to forgo expansion in America, and China's CNOOC oil company blunted in its proposed purchase of Unocal.

I saw how the fault lay primarily with the businesses involved. These businesses would blame the reaction on politics. Yet doing so is an admission that they do not understand politics. I hope to help you understand that blaming something on aggressive activists, sensationalistic media, or meddling politicians is an admission that you have forgotten the lessons of your youth. This is not their problem. This is your deficiency as a businessperson.

These business leaders didn't think of social concerns and did little to prepare for the debate their proposed actions would spark. Nor did they engage in advance with those whose findings would be decisive in achieving their aims. They were surprised by the reaction of Congress, even though anyone who understood the mood of the moment could have predicted the ensuing political response.

On the House Agriculture Committee, I saw industry participants challenged by environmentalist criticism of farming practices, health activists agitating to alter the dietary guidelines, and protectionists pushing to impose national labeling laws in violation of global trade agreements.

On the Transportation Committee, I saw those pursuing funding for road maintenance and expansion confronted by those seeking funding for mass transit and beautification projects instead.

During deliberations on the Financial Services Committee, I saw companies scrambling to contain activists' efforts to constrain their ability to charge market rates of interest and to ensure that a slew of proposals under the banner of "consumer rights" actually benefited consumers, not just trial lawyers.

When businesses were trying to defend their interests from attack or move their own priorities forward, they often failed to acknowledge or address legitimate outside views. I was regularly shocked by the naïveté of their requests to me as their representative. I am not promoting the sophistication of a crony capitalist, but of discernment that displays an understanding of competing points of view, an accommodation of their valid concerns, and the ability to clearly articulate how positions are good for society, not just for business.

As a packaged food association was making the case for their position on the government's dietary guidelines in 2001, I could not help but think that their pitch assumed I was unaware of or unsympathetic to the concerns of organic food enthusiasts (though today all food companies are now sprinting to address those preferences). It was clear that most businesses viewed such challenges as a sideshow, an appendage of the market, not matters that they tightly integrated into their overall strategy. They often compartmentalized public affairs as a staff function and failed to integrate market and nonmarket dynamics into a unified strategy.

In both business and politics I found far too many of my fellow travelers with a narrow focus on short-term profits or winning reelection and not on delivering long-term value or governing. Too few really embraced the belief that long-term success requires ensuring others share in your victory.

Too few in politics and business try to understand the motivations of others, to embrace a full-spectrum view. They are less likely to achieve the kind of lasting accomplishments that would make their labor personally fulfilling. Society suffers because of their ineffectiveness. Businesses stumble from one explosive confrontation to another. Politicians are trapped in partisan gridlock.

Businesspeople must think about and care about the kind of footprint our commercial operations leave. This requires perceiving both unmet needs that our businesses could profitably address and the prickly parts of our operations that we can reform to avoid missteps that will torpedo our reputations. We must actively engage with society to enhance the accuracy of our self-perceptions and prospects for mutually beneficial collaborative actions. We will find those irrevocably opposed to our organizations, necessitating the ability to form broad coalitions to win political or public opinion contests. Most of us learned these skills in our youth. Reteaching them from a commercial perspective is the focus of this book.

Acknowledgments

THIS BOOK CLEARLY WAS a team effort for which many are to thank.

My first thoughts go to my family, who are always my source of inspiration. Each family member played a role—my parents and siblings, together with whom I first learned the importance of incorporating the aspirations and concerns of others; my wife, Debbie, for her patience and review of countless drafts; my son Charles for coming up with the word "shapeholders"; his fiancée, Alison, for her cover critique; my daughter Emily and son-in-law, Josh Kempf, for their thoughtful critiques at many stages in the book's development; my daughter Sarah for her constant encouragement; and my son Peter and daughter-in-law, Tara, for injecting helpful insights.

My friend and fellow author Joe Pine has been a constant source of encouragement and advice. The basic framework came together with multicolored sticky notes on the Newton, Massachusetts, porch of Barry Horwitz with the help of Matt Shaffer. Matt and Galen Danskin both helped in writing cases that contributed useful input.

The concepts and frameworks that formed the basis for this book advanced greatly as I developed an article for the *Strategy and Leadership* journal. The guidance of Robert Randall of Emerald Publishing was very helpful, as were those who reviewed my article. Thanks to John Brandt and Kerry Moore for their helpful edits in developing this piece.

Another advance in formulating my seven steps came with the introduction of my massive online open course through the George Washington University. Thanks to Tom Kelly, Camille Funk, John Brandt, and Paul Berman for supporting this effort.

Without the confidence and counsel of Leah Spiro with Riverside Creative Management, my agent, this book would never have happened. She was always uplifting and insightful. I am indebted to John Taft for introducing us. Herb Schaffner's edits directed my book proposal and framework in a constructive direction. His comments were always helpful. His interest in the content was contagious.

The input of Myles Thompson from Columbia Business School Press made this book immeasurably better. Myles has a passion for communicating ideas that can shape the world in a manner that delivers the maximum impact. Stephen Wesley's sharp eye was instrumental in honing my writing. This thoughtful attention to each word, paragraph, and chapter has made this book easier to read and richer in content.

Thanks to the many people who reviewed drafts of part or this entire book, including Ken Cohen, Matt Dallek, Hüseyin Gelis, Mark Green, Barry Horwitz, Steven Kennedy, Helen Kennett, David Rehr, Matt Rhoades, Brent Robbins, and Jeff Weber.

In many ways the ideas in this book spring from experiences in four spheres of my life—business, politics, academia, and community. Many in each field deserve credit for shaping the insights shared in this book.

So many during my extended business career have taught me useful life lessons. Special thanks to those bosses who set me on a path to success—Jerry Levin, Ralph Thrane, George Mileusnic, Jim Leahy, Russ Davis, Ron Tysoe, Jim Zimmerman, Dale Kramer, and Susan Engel; to close colleagues who taught me so much— Ray Lee, Susan Storer, Susan Robinson, Bob Graves, Tim Schugel, David Weiser, and Brett Heffes; and to those who kept me organized and productive, especially Thelma Noonan.

Thanks to Jeff Smith, who brought me to Accenture after my service in Congress. Not only did I meet so many wonderful people during my time there, but I felt as though I received a second MBA by gaining the many insights the firm has to share with its clients. The strong support and prescient insights of Andy Parker and Dan Rosen contributed to the completion of this book.

I am indebted to the voters of Minnesota for entrusting me as their servant in Congress and to the many volunteers, supporters, staff, and advisors who contributed to my victories. Without the experiences I gained in public service this book would not be possible. My congressional staff, especially Pat Shortridge and Lonny Leitner, provided both insight and encouragement for this book. My good friend and former congressional colleague Mark Green has long been my touchstone and was very helpful with his input.

My ideas have been battle-tested in many classrooms, initially the ones I sat in as a student, later in ones where I had the opportunity to engage with students. I am grateful to the many teachers who inspired me, from Mrs. Loken, who drove me to excel, and Mr. Monical, who taught me math at Pequot Lakes High School, to Professor Thomas Murray, who set me up for my first step up the career ladder at Saint John's University. Three professors at the University of Michigan are worthy of note here: Professor Ray Reilly, whose final class counsel was to be multinational and multifunctional and to choose increasing revenue over cutting expenses. Professor Aneel Karnani was very helpful in guiding my early entry in academia. Perhaps there is no one whom I more sought to emulate in my academic career than C. K. Prahalad.

Special thanks for the guidance and confidence of Paulo Prochno at the University of Maryland's Robert H. Smith School of Business; Oksana Carlson at Johns Hopkins Carey Business School; Mauro Guillen, director of the Lauder Institute at the University of Pennsylvania; Zeynep Gürhan Canlı at Koc University's Graduate School of Business; Pierre Dussauge and Corey Phelps at HEC Paris; Bruce Buchanan at the NYU Stern School of Business; Fr. Ollie Williams at Notre Dame's Mendoza College of Business; and Julia Marsh at the London Business School.

Special thanks to the many people at George Washington University who nurtured me—President Steve Knapp, Provost Steve Lerman, and Dean Ali Eskandarian for hiring me; professors Chris Arterton, Steve Billet, Lara Brown, Michael Cornfield, Matt Dallek, Roberto Izurieta, Dennis Johnson, Luis Raúl Matos, Gary Nordlinger, Larry Parnell, and David Rehr; my staff led by Sarah Gunel; my board of advisors; and the many public affairs professionals who shared their insights with me and my students.

My journey in founding and leading three speaking programs bonded me to wonderful lifelong friends and exposed me to a wide range of thought leaders. Perhaps nobody modeled the idea that life is a game of addition for me better than Craig Shaver, who, together with my brother Steven, Gregg Peterson, and Bill Guidera, helped me found the Minnesota Rough Riders and kept it thriving after my election to Congress. Matt Lindstrom has been a dedicated partner with St. John's University Frontiers of Freedom Lecture Series. Thanks to the exceptional leadership of Kristin Robbins, Tim Penny, and Steve Sanger, together with the early support of Dave Frauenshuh and Sid Verdoorn, I benefited greatly from the many insights I gained as Founder and Chairman of the Economic Club of Minnesota.

A final and special thank you for the extra efforts and wise counsel of Angelique Foster, without whom I could never have juggled the competing demands on my time to finish this book.

Shapeholders

Introduction

From the Heart of a Businessman

THERE IS A NEW BREED of constituents that businesses are ignoring and treating haphazardly. They do so at their own peril. Twenty years ago a business could get by just appealing to stakeholders with a true stake in its success (customers, suppliers, employees, local communities), but today's more political age of social media, twenty-four-hour news cycles, activism, and hyperregulation has bred organizations that have no stake in a company's success but intense passion for pressing businesses to mend their ways, to change the de facto rules of commerce.

Some consider political, regulatory, media, and social activist actors as stakeholders in an organization's operating environment. Yet these actors' lack of a stake in a company gives them greater ability to constrain or expand a firm's opportunities and risk. They demand a different engagement approach than those benefiting from a company's success. They demand their own name.

This book defines the social activists, media outlets, politicians, and regulators who have no stake in a company but a powerful ability to shape its future as *shapeholders*. It identifies effective strategies for engaging them.

Greenpeace had little concern with the impact on Peabody Coal of its efforts to leverage media attention to persuade President Barack Obama to issue an executive order leading to regulations of power plants that reduced the demand for Peabody's product. Peabody's resulting bankruptcy confirmed the ability of these actors to shape its future.[1]

John Mackey showed how having common cause with these same categories of actors can have a powerfully positive impact on both the planet and profit. His company, Whole Foods, working in tandem with healthy food activists, has significantly altered food-consumption patterns as a growing share of the population seeks organic foods. Doing so greatly benefited the bottom line of Whole Foods.

The advent of social media and smartphones a mere decade ago has greatly amplified the ability of shapeholders to alter the tune to which commerce must dance. Tweets by President-elect Donald Trump influenced the actions of United Technologies, Boeing, Lockheed Martin, and Ford even before he assumed the Presidency.[2] Citizens now expect companies to address not just market needs but social concerns like clean air, clean water, skills training, affordable health care, and opportunities for those left behind.

The challenge facing business today became clear to me when, on the way to a George Washington University Board of Trustees retreat as the head of their Graduate School of Political Management, I chatted with a fellow professor from our policy school. Trying to explain the essence of what makes this book unique, I suggested that it was written from the heart of a businessperson, someone who had not just studied business but was in the commercial trenches for decades. Trying hard not to snicker, she said, "Hmm, 'heart of a businessperson'—I never thought of that before."

After the 2008 financial crisis and a presidential campaign whose centerpiece was reining in commercial misdeeds, the public view of business went toxic, and people like my colleague are unsure whether businesspeople actually have hearts. In his final State of the Union address in 2016, President Obama spoke to the public's distrust of business when he posited that the country had not done enough to make "sure that the system is not rigged in favor of the wealthiest and biggest corporations" and was still "letting big banks or big oil or hedge funds make their own rules at everybody else's expense."[3]

As senior vice president and treasurer of today's Macy's from 1987 to 1992, a tumultuous period for the company, I witnessed the brash face of capitalism on Wall Street up close. As a business executive turned congressman, I saw vividly how the low regard for business has hurt not only commerce but society, too. Hasty regulations spurred by the crisis often hampered competitiveness.

Few people focus on the benefits that business delivers to society. Contributing to this myopia is the fact that many businesspeople have a narrow view of their own social contributions. Most are disciples of Milton Friedman, who insisted that "the business of business is business"—that business benefits society plenty by providing jobs while supplying products and services that deliver consumers value greater than the price paid. Yet digitally empowered social agents have the power to force companies to do more.

Friedman also said, "The social responsibility of business is to increase its profits."[4] The essence of this book is to reveal where businesses are violating the spirit of Friedman by neglecting their long-term profits. Not collaborating with society is a costly misstep. By not widening their lens to capture the social needs businesses could profitably meet, they forgo profit opportunities. The animosity toward businesses that seem to overlook these opportunities has bridged the partisan divide. Consider this 2016 *Wall Street Journal* headline: "Republicans and Democrats Agree: We Hate Wall Street."[5]

In *Give and Take*, Adam Grant makes the case that givers are more likely to succeed than takers. Grant writes that too often we don't "stretch the time horizons out far enough. It takes time for givers to build goodwill and trust, but eventually, they establish reputations and relationships that enhance their success."[6] In this book, I make the case for a corollary: that integrating social concerns into business strategy gives us the best chance at business success.

Back inside the school van, maybe my colleague didn't consider what we owed to businessmen like Henry Ford, who produced the first affordable car to enhance the mobility of the masses. Before Ford, the rich had automobiles, but not the average person. Ford saw fortune at the bottom of the pyramid long before my professor C. K. Prahalad (who taught at the school Ford nurtured, the University of Michigan) identified that phrase to define the business opportunities in serving less advantaged consumers around the world.[7] We see selling cars to Americans as purely market focused. At the start, Ford was responding to social demands.

John D. Rockefeller, who refined the oil for Ford's invention, broke into the big time by addressing a social issue. Rockefeller's Standard Oil brand started as kerosene for lighting, produced to exacting standards to reduce the risk of fire when two out of five fires in New York City were caused by the burning of kerosene for lighting.[8]

Google's Project Loon[9] aims to girdle the world with balloons floating in the stratosphere, twice as high as airplanes, that will deliver an aerial wireless network to the bottom of the pyramid: remote huts and villages across the planet. Many see this as a social investment today. But if it works, if it helps hundreds of millions emerge from poverty and becomes as ubiquitous as Ford cars and Exxon gas—everyone will forget it was born to solve social challenges and consider it purely as meeting market needs. People need to understand this.

It is not just my fellow professor who forgot about the benefits that emerge from the hearts of businesspeople. Too many of us in business fixate on a drive for efficiency in current operations instead of observing unmet social needs that could be profitable to address—or costly to ignore.

Business complains that the standards society imposes on business are sometimes legitimate and sometimes not. The same is true of the actions of businesses. As early as 2000, Rainforest Action Network's executive director Kelly Quirke demanded that Citibank "cease funding . . . mining or oil exploration,"[10] two of its most significant lines of project finance. Crazy? Martin Shkreli's Turing Pharmaceutical acquired a drug for cancer and AIDS sufferers and increased the price from $13.50 to $750 a pill.[11] Any less crazy?

Business responses to activism often undermine their cause. Some business leaders see social demands as an existential threat to the survival of their businesses. So they gird for battle. They often seem more intent on electing a blocking minority to stop further tax hikes or regulations than on attracting broad enough support for a governing majority. This may help them in the short term. But their approach is easily painted as self-serving and harmful to the effective conduct of democracy. This not only makes this strategy hard to sustain in the long run, it fuels animosity toward business.

Some businesses sidestep social concerns through internal action. They may find, like Volkswagen, that efforts to manipulate compliance with emission standards cost dearly.[12] The president of Mitsubishi Motors, who reportedly manipulated emission reports for twenty-five years, said, "This is a problem that threatens the existence of our company."[13] Starbucks found overly creative tax policies could harm your brand in places like the United Kingdom.[14]

Some seek to avoid external action by manipulating external actors. Bribing officials in emerging markets may accelerate growth in the short term. But it can cost you your job, as Avon's CEO found out, and tarnish your company's image.[15] Or consider Tokyo Electric Power (TEPCO), which cozied up to its regulator, Japan's Nuclear Safety Commission (JNSC), such that JNSC became "a watchdog with neither bark nor bite."[16]

When the Fukushima disaster happened, JNSC was unprepared and TEPCO suffered not only national shame, it was also banned from nuclear power operations in Japan and faces criminal investigations.

In stark contrast are businesspeople who take a broader view, one that genuinely addresses public concerns. Though it may cost more in the short run, these enlightened actions can be profitable in the long term.

Levi Strauss & Company set high standards for its Asian factories, sidestepping condemnation over labor abuse and setting industry standards. GE retooled its product line by applying Ecomagination, profitably enabling its customers to achieve their sustainability goals. Danny Wegman—whose family's third-generation grocery business enters each market by first engaging the local community before opening a store offering unmatched service, quality, and ongoing commitment to the community—shows a more enlightened view.

Wegman's approach not only charts a path of sustainable profits for his business, but does so by lifting up society as his company profits, endearing him to multiple social actors. His strategy incorporates the concerns of not just those directly tied to its business, like its customers and employees, but the broader public as well. And that has propelled its profitable expansion from a single store in Rochester, New York, to a presence throughout the Northeast. Danny Wegman reflects the heart of a businessman.

Engaging to Win

The path to effectively engaging shapeholders is based on the principle that life is a game of addition. Understanding the concerns of others and attracting people to our side are essential whether we collaborate or compete. The inability to listen, a "my way or the highway" approach, hurts our long-term success.

It is precisely this engagement that enables an organization to develop new paths, products, and initiatives. Recognizing, attacking, and solving social problems before others helps our organization succeed. Success comes from engaging in a proactive, positive, solution-oriented manner. This approach avoids costly missteps and captures differentiating opportunities.

Chapter 1, "Shapeholders," will introduce you to the idea that long-term sustainable business success requires a full-spectrum view of those forming the environment of business—shareholders, true stakeholders (employees, suppliers, customers, and local communities), and social activist, media, political, and regulatory shapeholders who have little stake in a company's success but great ability to shape the opportunities and risks it faces.

Just as traditional color printing involves unifying three separate color plates—red, yellow, and blue—with black, so business success requires integrating the concerns of shareholders, stakeholders, and shapeholders. Businesses that address one or two categories but not shapeholders miss opportunities and end up in battles they would not have had to fight or lose battles they could have won.

The chapter also considers how what I and others call the paradox of profit[17] turns normal ideas about the focus of business strategy on its head—the surest path to losing money is to be preoccupied only with profit; the surest path to profit is a preoccupation with addressing consumer needs and social concerns.

Chapters 2 through 5 provide background on the categories of shapeholders—social activists, media, politicians, and regulators. We explore what makes them tick, how they have evolved, and their impact on the environment within which business operates.

Chapters 6 through 12 consider each of the seven steps for shapeholder success. Chapter 6, "Align with a Purpose," addresses the imperative to embrace a purpose that benefits both society and the bottom line. This is how the three dimensions of shareholders, stakeholders, and shapeholders are melded into a unifying focus. The subsequent chapters address anticipating shapeholder opportunities and concerns and engaging in anticipatory actions that position you to unify (chapter 7, "Anticipate"), assessing both the legitimacy of opportunities and concerns and the results that would ensue from alternate company responses (chapter 8, "Assess"), how to avert worse outcomes when a legitimate concern cannot be beneficially addressed (chapter 9, "Avert"), how to acquiesce if an illegitimate demand is either not worth fighting or cannot be denied (chapter 10, "Acquiesce"), and how best to unify in collaboration (chapter 11, "Advance Common Interests") and in competition (chapter 12, "Assemble to Win").

The final chapter considers how business as a whole could do a better job of making the case for the free enterprise system upon which it depends (chapter 13, "Pope Francis, a CEO Worth Emulating").

I hope with this book to prove that your business can help itself while helping others. My goal is to convince you that it is critical to add another dimension to your strategic planning and execution—the nonmarket, or what I define as shapeholders, those social actors with little stake in your organization but a significant ability to shape your future. I hope to make you appreciate that it is narrow-minded for a business to focus only on the market.

The key to success in today's political age is to unbundle shapeholder actors who have no natural stake in a company from those who do, true stakeholders. The primary motivations of stakeholders and shapeholders are different—one seeking monetary reward and the other seeking to change business behavior. Each must be understood and addressed. We will discover that while effective stakeholder engagement can smooth your path to engaging shapeholders, there are more steps required for effective shapeholder engagement.

I want you to think about business strategy not just in the context of board meetings, but also in light of what is said on television or in blogs, the social problems in the shadows, the legislation passed in capitals, and the protesters outside those capitals. I want you to see those things are your business and to understand how they shape you and how you can shape them.

In today's political age, we share a common imperative to align our market strategy with a nonmarket strategy that benefits both society and the bottom line. Does your business have the expertise to solve social problems in a way that aligns with your market strategy? Can you communicate better with the media and interest groups so you don't become an innocent victim, but find a way to be the hero? Can you sidestep every confrontation possible and win those you must? Can you reveal the heart of a businessperson?

Who Are the Shapeholders?

Shapeholders

Talent perceives differences; genius, unity.
—WILLIAM BUTLER YEATS

I SPEND A LOT of time in taxis. I find the chitchat between the driver and me to be a great source of insight on local sentiment. Each place has its unique perspective. Walking into your first meeting in a foreign city with fresh intel is invaluable.

I was lucky enough to get an English-speaking taxi driver in Beijing around the time of the 2008 Summer Olympics. He explained to me how the Chinese viewed the games in gold medals won, where they excelled, while Americans focused on the total medal count, where we prevailed. Arriving at my meeting, I congratulated my Chinese hosts on their gold medals. They especially appreciated hearing that from an American. It cost me nothing, but it gained their affection.

One sunny afternoon in Minneapolis on my way to Washington, D.C., I struck up a conversation with my cabdriver. He was not particularly chatty. He was in his fifties, polite, and earnest. I noted that he had been reading the *New York Times*. I asked why. He said that the last passenger had left it. Perhaps in an effort to repay the many insights I had received from other cabdrivers,

I told him that I was going to give him a piece of advice that he might remember when he was lying on his deathbed as one of the most meaningful he had ever received. My secret for success? To read not just the *Times* but also the *Wall Street Journal* every day.

How on earth could reading two newspapers daily qualify among the most meaningful advice one could give? After all, neither paper does a particularly good job of covering entertainment, fashion, or sports, the really important things in life. Was it just for the crosswords?

After all, doesn't everyone keep up with the news? Doesn't everyone seek out multiple sources? How unusual would he be if he followed my advice?

Perceiving Differences

So why did I tell him that? At the beginning of classes I have taught at leading business schools and George Washington University's Graduate School of Political Management, I ask students to write down their "go-to" sources for news. Take a second and record yours.

If you quickly define one or more sources of news that you have a regular habit of accessing each day to be "in the know" on major business, political, and geopolitical events, you are already among a small subset of humanity. I have found that many of my graduate students are not. A recent Pew Research study revealed Facebook as the leading source for political news for the baby boom, Gen-X, and millennial generations, even though less than a third said they "liked" news organizations to add content to their Facebook page.[1]

How can business school graduates earn a payback on their investment in an MBA unless they read not just an industry paper or a weekly business news source but a comprehensive daily paper like the *Wall Street Journal* every day? How else can they stay current on what is happening in commercial affairs and consider how it affects their company, applying the knowledge they learned in B-school?

If MBAs leave what they have learned on the shelf, their schooling will have little impact. If a senior executive finds them unaware of a recent development that has captured the imagination of the C-suite, their chances of promotion are limited. Yet this concern only begins to touch on the underlying basis for my advice to the taxi driver.

My next activity in class is to show a photo of dispensers for *China Daily* and *Politico* alongside each other on a Washington, D.C., street corner. I offer my students extra credit if they can find anything negative about Chinese government leaders on the front page of *China Daily* or anything positive about the U.S. government leaders on the front page of *Politico*. Many of my students have tried unsuccessfully to earn extra credit. I do this to emphasize how every news source has a slant.

The *Journal*'s editorial page showcases how the intelligent right thinks. You might say, "I am no conservative. I prefer the *New York Times*." Fine. Its editorial page plays a comparable role on the left. But do you read the editorial pages of both? Few do.

As the head of a school that appeals to all political persuasions, I attended both the Democratic and Republican conventions in 2012. The *Times* was stacked high for all to read at the Democratic convention in Charlotte, but the *Journal* was AWOL. At the Republican convention in Tampa, the *Journal* was widely available, but the *Times* absent.

Knowing that each presents a differing point of view, do you read both to compare and contrast, to ascertain the bias of each, to provide feedstock for developing your own informed view? Do you quiz cabdrivers to further supplement your effort to gain a complete picture of the state of affairs?

When I was in Congress, constituents regularly approached me to complain about some item in the news that gravely concerned them. Many were shocked when I correctly predicted from which news outlet they were quoting, and they were unaware of rebuttals from competing sources. For instance, the *Times*, MSNBC, or the *Nation* may have just released a story about the complicated nature of the new Medicare prescription drug coverage that rolled out during my time in Congress. Their audiences complained about the complexity of the multiple plans from which seniors *had* to choose. At the same time, the *Journal*, Fox News, or *National Review* may have recently detailed how the competition among the multiple plans helped to drive down the cost of this coverage. Their readers and viewers were happy about the choices from which seniors *could* choose but complained that the cost was still too high for taxpayers.

The loudest voices in public debate are rarely familiar with counterpoints. I have found few have the talent that Yeats referred to of being able to see differences. How could they? So few people read the news regularly, even fewer deliberately seek out competing views.

Even among the better-informed people who read these prestigious newspapers, most fall prey to what is called *confirmation bias*, "the tendency to search for, interpret, favor, and recall information in a way that confirms one's beliefs or hypotheses, while giving disproportionately less consideration to alternative possibilities."[2]

Alexis de Tocqueville intuitively understood this tendency when he observed in *Democracy in America*: "Though different men may sometimes find it their interest to combine for the same purposes, they will never make it their pleasure."[3]

If you are one of the rare birds who regularly reads both papers (or their counterparts in your country) in depth, searching out competing views, you are part of the most important fraction of the 1 percent club on the planet. If you are a taxi driver, you won't be in that position for long, unless it is a job you really enjoy. Unless business leaders belong to this exclusive club with a full-spectrum view, their companies and careers are increasingly at risk.

Seeking Unity with Shapeholders

The penalty for business leaders who fall prey to a black-and-white perspective that doesn't consider other points of view has increased as the power of what I call "shapeholders" has risen. These actors make it essential that executives overcome confirmation bias and not only follow Yeats's advice to perceive how shapeholders are different but take the next step to find points of unity.

Shapeholders shape a business's opportunities by either making new options available or taking them off the table, but they are not themselves helped or harmed by a business's success or failure. The activist, media, political, and regulatory forces I define as shapeholders may lack a stake in an organization, but they will profoundly shape the opportunities and risks it faces. The rise of social media and smartphones has magnified their impact.

Many scholars lump shapeholders, who have no natural stake in a company, with stakeholders, who do have a stake in a company's success, but I disagree with that categorization. The two have remarkably different motivations and measurements of success. They demand unique approaches.

Stakeholders are motivated by rewards defined in monetary terms that reflect the stake they seek in a company—salary, benefits, invoice price, taxes paid. They understand that their ability to share in a company's profits depends on its success.

Shapeholders measure their success in petition signatures, media mentions, public opinion polls, bills sponsored, votes, laws enacted, regulations issued, government agencies created, and in the end, businesses mending their ways. Being guided by the desire to change corporate behavior, even if it hampers a company's ability to succeed or puts it out of business, unleashes shapeholders to engage in a much wider range of activities than stakeholders. Shapeholders can be a company's best friend or worst enemy.

The shapeholder actors who have the power to propel or disrupt the best-laid plans of the biggest names in business are an altogether different breed than stakeholders. One spokesperson for London-based Globalise Resistance, a group that defines its mission as opposing "the global growth of corporate power,"[4] told the media that they aim to rid the world of corporations and that they welcome the destruction of corporations.[5] Ask many CEOs or public affairs executives and they would say such groups are stakeholders. Treating them as such is part of the disguise that has kept shapeholders invisible.

Too many executives are stuck in the stakeholder time warp, not realizing that we have entered the more political era of aggressive shapeholder actors. This leaves companies poorly prepared to play defense and lacking the agility to capture opportunities presented by social changes or to present their positive contributions in a convincing manner.

Ever-expanding arrays of social activists prod businesses to address myriad issues, inventing innovative ways to capture attention, like intercepting Shell's Artic-bound drilling platform in the middle of the ocean.[6] Today's 24/7 news cycle and blogosphere, hungry for juicy content to capture audiences' attention, eagerly seek to report tales of corporate misdeeds. Political actors, anxious to avoid being painted as corporate stooges, jump on every opportunity to prove they are defending the "little guy" against business behemoths.

The Occupy movement, the Arab Spring, and the increased populism of political parties on both the left and the right reflect a growing angst over income inequality. Companies such as

McDonald's take center stage in campaigns as progressive politicians push for, and in many American cities succeed in setting, a $15 an hour minimum wage. Conservatives paint the Export–Import Bank as corporate welfare and seek to terminate it, putting at risk the competitiveness of companies like Boeing, Caterpillar, and General Electric in global markets.

Expectations for businesses to direct their activities in a way that benefits not just their bottom line but also society have escalated. Business leaders like John Mackey of Whole Foods press for practicing *conscious capitalism*, and Paul Polman of Unilever advocates for businesses to set higher sustainability standards. The unanticipated political and cultural crossover popularity of the Pope Francis pressing this point further compels businesses to broaden their focus.

Society is also increasingly asking business to fill the void resulting from political gridlock. When pressing for government action hits a roadblock, activists attempt to leverage public opinion to press businesses to solve societal challenges that were previously the purview of government. Many businesses accommodated LGBTQ demands for benefit changes long before being required to do so by the courts, much less by legislative action. Activists coaxed businesses to oppose legislation they view as contrary to LGBTQ rights.[7]

All these pressures make it imperative for businesses to engage with shapeholders, not out of charity, but to avoid costly conflicts, capture new opportunities, and perhaps just to survive.

Achieving the genius of unity of which Yeats speaks is essential in this more political age. It takes two steps. First, we must understand what motivates different opinions. Second, we must constantly seek paths to positioning our approach in a way that appeals to the aspirations of those different from us.

Unity among differences—sounds good, but confusing. An example may help. When delivering an article for the Watertown Willing Workers 4-H Club in the later 1990s to the small main street offices of our local paper, the *Carver County News*, I noticed that they had several color plates laid out to print that week's edition. While black-and-white monotone printing takes just one plate, printing in color in a predigital world required blue, red, yellow, and black plates. You can make out some of the story by looking at any one of the color plates, but it only becomes clear when you combine all four.

Just as printing in color requires integrating black with three categories of color—blue, red, and yellow—so effective strategy requires integrating all three dimensions of the environment in which businesses operate. That means driving profits in the marketplace to reward *shareholders*; effectively engaging true *stakeholders* like employees, suppliers, and communities; and engaging the social activist, media, political, and regulatory *shapeholders* who have little stake in a company but great power to mold its prospects. Just as Yeats achieved greatness by seeing three seemingly unrelated loves of literature, philosophy, and Irish nationalism as "a discrete expression of a single conviction," effectively engaging society requires seeing each shareholder, stakeholder, and shapeholder layer distinctly, and then melding them into a single conviction. Failing to integrate a single layer can distort our prospects. While the literature addressing shareholders and

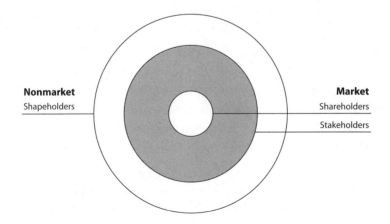

stakeholders is extensive, the appropriate approach to shape-holders is still opaque because of the fatal flaw of treating them as stakeholders, even though they have no stake in a company's prosperity.

Resolving differences between companies and shapeholders requires appreciating whether shapeholders present a legitimate concern with one's operating methods. It also requires understanding, regardless of the underlying legitimacy, whether the perceived benefits of collaboration can be captured or whether shapeholder demands to alter our operations can be cost-effectively parried.

The absolute imperative to effectively engage shapeholders is driven by a reality that turns any normal idea about strategy on its head, the *paradox of profit*. Simply put, the surest path to losing money is for a company to be preoccupied with profits. The surest path to profit is for that company to be preoccupied with benefiting society. Let us consider the contrasting examples of Arthur Andersen and Starbucks.

Paradox of Profit: The Surest Path to Losing Money Is Preoccupation with Profit

As a freshly minted small-town college grad in 1978, I was thrilled to land a big-city job with a public accounting firm—and not just any accounting firm, but arguably the best in the world at the time, Arthur Andersen & Co. Its advisory arm was the envy of every other firm. Its partners consistently out-earned their peers. Positions there were highly sought after.

What impressed me most was its reputation as a disciplined, stand-up firm that held itself to ethical by-the-book accounting standards. I was proud to be an Andersen certified public accountant.

Andersen's new recruits were indoctrinated in what it meant to be part of this esteemed firm at its training center in St. Charles,

Illinois, which we called Camp Andersen. Andersen saw itself as the best in the profession and expected its accountants to conduct themselves accordingly, both in their actions and their appearance.

Our required uniform was a business suit, not a sport coat and slacks. During training, I was asked by the cafeteria staff to put my coat back on at lunch. Andersen professionals wore their suit coats whenever they were outside the office, including during lunch. I wore a short-sleeved shirt to work one hot summer day and a partner asked me when my shirt was going to grow sleeves. Andersen was the last firm to stop requiring its accountants to wear hats—felt in the winter, straw in the summer.

At the end of my two-week orientation at Camp Andersen in January 1979, a partner delivered the famed "Professionalism Speech." Beginning with recounting how Arthur Andersen responded to a request to approve a client's bad bookkeeping by saying there was "not enough money in the city of Chicago" to make him do it, the partner recounted the firm's long history of abiding by the founder's motto to Think Straight, Talk Straight.[8]

On the job, I witnessed that professionalism and commitment to high standards firsthand. As one example, our unit refused to issue an opinion on an audit I participated in because we had doubts about the client's internal controls.

Imagine my dismay when two decades later, during my first term in Congress, I watched the firm's demise. Now Arthur Andersen is remembered as the firm that shredded documents to conceal its involvement with fraud at Enron. The company was convicted on obstruction of justice charges. And it was guilty. Yet many of its 85,000 worldwide employees who found themselves out of work had nothing to do with Enron, nor were they engaged in dubious accounting. The once-heralded firm became a company with few assets other than Camp Andersen, which it rented to others and eventually sold.[9]

Initially Andersen's demise was merely a personal nuisance. My opponent for reelection had taken to referring to me as

(R-Arthur Andersen) instead of (R-MN) to tie me to the Enron scandal. But over the years I struggled to understand how a firm that I was proud to have as a part of my pedigree, that was once known as the "gold standard" and "Marine Corps" of the profession and the "conscience of the accounting industry," could lose its way, at great harm to itself and society.[10]

Arthur Andersen executives had drifted from the ideals that were drilled into me at Camp Andersen and that had made me proud to be a member of the firm. The partners were fixated on the bottom line, chasing after consulting revenue that created tensions with their reason for existing—to uphold the integrity of financial reporting. The firm's leadership had stopped adding the concerns of key segments of society into their summations.

Arthur Andersen remained diligent in addressing the concerns of its *shareholder* partners and its *stakeholder* employees, suppliers, communities, and clients (it was a bit too good to its clients). Its demise came when it did not respond to the legitimate concerns of *shapeholders* with little stake in its success but great power to shape its future—the media, the Securities and Exchange Commission, the Justice Department. When the Enron scandal seemingly affirmed shapeholder warnings that pursuit of consulting profits would compromise an impartial assessment of a client's books, these actors led to Andersen's downfall.

What is the difference between stakeholders and shapeholders? Stakeholders are those who suffered from Andersen's fall. Its employees lost their jobs, suppliers lost a client, customers had to incur expense switching auditors, and local communities (particularly Chicago) had to find new employers and tenants. Conversely, the activist, media, political, and regulatory shapeholder actors that ushered Andersen to its grave hardly mourned its loss. They celebrated their role in bringing it down.

When Andersen's leadership narrowed their view, they lost sight of the fact that each business must preserve its license to operate. Private property is only private if government says so and defends this right. Corporations themselves are a political invention. Business must have the consent of society to operate. Andersen's license was dependent on its role in ensuring accurate reporting. When it abandoned that purpose and ignored the entreaties of its shapeholders, society revoked its license.

Paradox of Profit: The Surest Path to Profit Is Preoccupation with Benefiting Society

In contrast, I have also witnessed companies that really understand the power of adding others into their consideration. While I was spending a semester studying abroad in Delft, the Netherlands, in 1981, my wife and I explored the wonders of Europe, including discovering its choices in coffee, seemingly endless variations.

Unknown to me, Howard Schultz, then working for a small Seattle purveyor of packaged coffee named Starbucks, was in Europe at the same time. Enchanted by a visit to espresso bars in Milan that same year, as Schultz describes in his book *Onward*, he became determined to "bring world-class coffee and the romance of Italian espresso bars to the United States . . . [an experience he] fervently believed could enrich people's lives" (xii–xiii). He returned from his travels dedicated to bringing consumers the choices that delivered not only a European minivacation and morning jolt, but did so in a manner that was "good for people . . . good for the planet . . . part of [its] DNA" (18).[11]

Schultz's idea to enrich people's lives focused on creating over and over again the experience he felt in Milan of "the hum of community and a sense that, over a demitasse of espresso, life slowed down" (10). Besides being fixated on the actual process of serving coffee, Schultz sought to create a "third place," "a social yet personal environment between one's house and job, where people can connect with others and reconnect with themselves" (13). Starbucks's purpose was delivering refreshing customer experiences and an environment that bolstered relationships. Starbucks's benefit to society was inextricably intertwined with the market differentiation that delivered profits. Starbucks's focus on benefiting society opened up a highly profitable customer niche.

The collaborative approach Starbucks took addressing concerns about habitat destruction resulting from coffee production embraced shapeholders as allies, not opponents, the opposite approach of Arthur Anderson. Beginning in 1997, Starbucks began its collaborations with Conservation International (CI), an activist group that "empowers societies to responsibly and sustainably care for nature, our global biodiversity, for the well-being of humanity,"[12] working to improve the environmental impact and economic health of farmers producing coffee in the buffer zone of the El Triunfo Biosphere Reserve in Chiapas, Mexico. In 2001, in partnership with CI, Starbucks created its "own sourcing guidelines, setting out a comprehensive procurement process to ensure that the coffee [it] bought was ethically grown and responsibly traded".[13]

This clearly benefited society, but it also benefited Starbucks. In working with shapeholders, Starbucks is pressing for establishment of sourcing standards that competitors like J. M. Smucker's Folgers brand cannot easily match. As I visit Starbucks around the world, I see their counters and stores are adorned with stories of their responsible sourcing, adding to the justification in the minds of its customers for Starbucks's premium pricing.

Starbucks also benefits from its shapeholder-friendly focus, giving meaning to the work of its associates. Because of this it attracts, retains, and motivates quality talent. A worker who thinks about his or her job's contribution to the improvement of society will feel personally invested in the company's activities, making him or her more enthusiastic and attentive to the work—and more likely to stick with the company, even when it's difficult. A worker who thinks about nothing but his or her paycheck is more likely to be bored and watch the clock, eyes glazing over. The brightest people want to be a part of something bigger.

Very few companies have proactively mastered shapeholder engagement. Companies like General Electric, Procter & Gamble, Starbucks, Wegmans, and Whole Foods excel here. Others, like CVS, Nike, and Walmart, have responded to the poke of the tine and found paths to profitable engagement. Yet too many business leaders still treat this shapeholder commotion as a sideshow until it's too late.

Understanding Shapeholders

How can businesses pivot early to avoid Andersen's fate and collaborate with shapeholders to advance their mutual interests like Starbucks? The answer in both cases is to truly understand shapeholders and how to engage them uniquely, not as stakeholders dependent on your success, but as actors whose freedom from needing to worry about your prosperity empowers them to undermine or enhance it in pursuit of their own aims.

Many shapeholders are passionate and political. Anyone who starts a boycott or runs for office is motivated by something, and heavy partisanship runs through every category of shapeholder.

Diagnosing and responding appropriately to activism can be difficult for business leaders who don't spend much of their time with activists, reporters, and politicians. These shapeholders may be unfamiliar and even distressing to business leaders. As a citizen, it is your personal choice whether to support, oppose, or ignore any shapeholder's cause. As a business leader, understanding which shapeholders offer opportunities for mutually beneficial collaboration is a fiduciary obligation. If you don't genuinely understand shapeholders, you can't act judiciously in your company's best interest.

It is perhaps instinctual to believe that organizations with which you are familiar share your company's values and to distrust organizations outside your purview. This is naïve—maybe even dangerous. We must not oversimplify our classification of any organization; instead, we must identify where our priorities collide and where they align. General managers ought to be as familiar with their shapeholders as they are with their top customers and employees.

The most notable examples of shapeholders are social activists, the media, politicians, and regulators. They offer us opportunities, but also risks. We must understand when to collaborate with them, when to compete, and how to succeed in both approaches.

Shapeholders compete in two arenas: public opinion and government—administrative, legislative, judicial, multilateral, federal, state, and local. In these arenas shapeholders have succeeded in changing corporate actions. For example, Greenpeace coerced Mattel to change its packaging sourcing by unfurling a banner over Mattel's headquarters with a picture of a Ken doll that read, "Barbie, it's over. I don't date girls that are into deforestation."[14] And anti-obesity activists persuaded Boston's city government and school board to limit the sale of sodas like Coca-Cola in public buildings and schools.[15] Most market activity takes place in the arena of the marketplace, but these two nonmarket arenas are becoming increasingly important. With the attendant rise in social media, the need to engage public opinion in real time is increasingly important.

The next four chapters look at who shapeholders are and how they behave. We will take a closer look at the key categories of shapeholders, their interests, and their techniques. In the section that then follows, we will define effective strategies for engaging these shapeholders.

In today's political age, the skill that is both in shortest supply and the path to the most impactful differentiation is understanding shapeholders and how to effectively engage them.

- In today's political age, business leaders unable to overcome their own *confirmation bias* (favoring information that confirm one's beliefs) put their companies and careers at risk.
- Leaders must hone a full-spectrum view that perceives differences and constantly looks to unify as many actors as possible in pursuit of common goals.
- This begins with distinguishing between shapeholders who have no natural stake in a company's success but are motivated by a desire to change its behavior and stakeholders who rely on a company's success and seek to increase their share of its profits.
- Shapeholders shape a business's opportunities by either making new options available or taking them off the table, but are not themselves naturally helped or harmed by a business's success or failure.
- Being guided by the desire to change corporate behavior, even if it hampers a company's ability to succeed or puts it out of business, unleashes shapeholders to engage in a much wider range of activities than stakeholders.
- Activist, media, political, and regulatory shapeholders can profoundly shape the opportunities and risks a company faces.
- Just as printing in color requires integrating three categories of color—blue, red, and yellow—so effective strategy requires integrating all three dimensions of the environment in which business operate—shareholders, stakeholders, and shapeholders.
- The absolute imperative to effectively engage shapeholders is driven by a reality that turns any normal idea about strategy on its head: the *paradox of profit*. Simply put, the surest path to losing money is to be preoccupied with profits (Arthur Andersen). The surest path to profit is to be preoccupied with benefiting society (Starbucks).
- Shapeholders compete in two arenas: public opinion and government.
- The rise of social media and smartphones has magnified the impact of shapeholders.

2

Social Activists

Sometimes being a business executive feels like the javelin thrower who won the toss and elected to receive.

—ANONYMOUS

IN 2007, TWO ELEVEN-YEAR olds, Madison Vorva and Rhiannon Tomtishen, wrote a report on endangered primates for their Girl Scout Bronze Award. During their research on orangutans, they discovered that the harvesting of palm oil, an ingredient in most Girl Scout cookies, contributed to deforestation and orangutan habitat loss in Indonesia. They decided to take a stand against the use of palm oil by the Girl Scouts of the USA (GSUSA).

Vorva and Tomtishen first convinced their troop in Ann Arbor, Michigan, to stop selling cookies until the Girl Scouts removed palm oil or switched to a more sustainable source that wouldn't contribute to deforestation in orangutan habitats. But their cause really got a boost when they attracted the support of the Rainforest Action Network (RAN) in the fall of 2010. RAN is an activist group that has a strong history of running hard-edged PR campaigns against rain forest deforestation.

In addition to RAN, the Union of Concerned Scientists joined in a campaign called Project ORANGS (Orangutans Really Appreciate and Need Girl Scouts). Madison and Rhiannon even got their hero, Jane Goodall, the famous English primatologist and UN Messenger of Peace, to sign on to their efforts.[1]

In the spring of 2011, RAN sent an email petition to the CEO of the Girl Scouts and launched an unofficial "Rainforest Hero" Merit Badge. Change.org, a petition tool that hosts sponsored campaigns for organizations, soon picked up on the story, sending an alert to its 1.38 million members and motivating more than 70,000 emails of protest to the CEO of the GSUSA.

Articles soon appeared in mainstream media outlets, including *Time*, CNN, the *New York Times*, and the *Wall Street Journal*. Vorva and Tomtishen also had live television appearances on ABC, CBS, and Fox News.

Soon after, the Girl Scout leadership pledged to move to a certified sustainable supplier of palm oil by 2015. In addition, Kellogg, the manufacturer of cookies for GSUSA, announced that it would require its suppliers to trace their palm oil back to sustainable plantations by 2015.

How did two teenage girls force the Girl Scouts and Kellogg to change their business practices? The simple answer: the power of activists in leveraging media to amplify their message and activate the force of public opinion.

The more actionable insight is that the Girl Scouts and Kellogg left out a color plate in their color printing by not fully considering the shapeholder activists involved in their space. That made them ideal prey for RAN. If the Girl Scouts are at risk of being a target, so is your organization. That is why it is necessary not only to understand social activists but to see the differences among them. In this chapter we will examine social activists and their techniques. Later chapters will address how best to engage them.

The Civil Rights Movement, Saul Alinsky, and Greenpeace Give Birth to Activism

Upton Sinclair's book *The Jungle* provoked public outcry over food quality to get Theodore Roosevelt to advance the Safe Food and Drug Act in 1906.[2] Women's rights broke through when women received the vote under the Nineteenth Amendment in 1920. Yet perhaps because these occurred before the advent of television news, their efforts did not spark widespread activism the way the civil rights movement did. Initial actions on civil rights first targeted the government—Rosa Parks refusing to give up her seat on a public bus (1955) and the drive to desegregate Little Rock High School (1957), but then came the focus on the conduct of businesses. In 1958 the National Association for the Advancement of Colored People (NAACP) Youth Council organized sit-ins at drugstores. Protesters sat at the counter of Dockum Drug in Wichita, Kansas, before the store finally relented and agreed to serve black patrons. A sit-in at Katz Drug in Oklahoma City, Oklahoma, soon followed.

The 1960s saw unprecedented protests in America with Martin Luther King's March on Washington, race riots, and anti–Vietnam War demonstrations. But it was 1971 that demarcated the launch of professional activism. In that year Saul Alinsky published his landmark book *Rules for Radicals*, providing an operating manual for activism, and a group of activists set sail for Amchitka Island, Alaska, to protest nuclear testing; that group would become Greenpeace, the first major activist organization.

Alinsky wrote of his book, "*The Prince* was written by Machiavelli for the Haves on how to hold power. *Rules for Radicals* is written for the Have-Nots on how to take it away."[3]

Alinksy advised that activists must first establish credibility before agitating: rubbing resentments, fanning hostilities, and searching out controversy to get people to participate. "The first step in community organization is community disorganization," Alinsky wrote. By combining hope and resentment, the organizer should create a "mass army" by attracting as many recruits as possible.

But building a team is just the first step. According to Alinsky, the main job of the activist is to prod the target to react. Alinsky advised, "The enemy properly goaded and guided in his reaction will be your major strength."

Greenpeace followed Alinsky's prescription in 1985 when the French foreign intelligence purportedly bombed their ship, the *Rainbow Warrior*, to prevent it from interfering with a nuclear test. It was a boon to Greenpeace, which today boasts 2.8 million supporters worldwide who fund an annual budget in excess of a $100 million and offices in fifty-five countries.[4]

Even if Greenpeace's first focus was on governments and nuclear testing, like the civil rights movement, it quickly pivoted to target business. Its agitation in the commercial space began with bans on fishing techniques like large-scale fishnets (1989), mineral exploration in the Arctic (1991), the disposal of radioactive or industrial waste at sea (1993), and the disposal of Shell UK's Brent Spar platform at sea (1995). It then turned to the chemicals used in refrigerators (1997), clear-cutting in British Columbia (1998), harmful phthalates in polyvinyl chloride toys (1999), and international trade of genetically modified organisms or GMOs (2000).[5]

Business techniques that were commonplace are unimaginable today. The success of Greenpeace has encouraged the formation and growth of many other activist organizations across dozens of causes. Activism is now a global nonprofit sector. Groups compete with one another in searching out business practices to redefine and the innovative tools that can bend business behavior to their will.

In 1998, in response to the impeachment of Bill Clinton, MoveOn.org added an activist dimension to the political arena, sparking a new type of organization not directly affiliated with a political party, but like a party devoted to public education and activism. Similar organizations on the left and right driving a multitude of issues from a dizzying array of angles have mushroomed since then. Business interests now face a more crowded field and political agenda when engaging political matters.

Mark Zuckerberg and Social Media
Put Activists on Steroids

If you believe the story line of the 2010 film *Social Network*, Mark Zuckerberg was not seeking to change the world when he invented Facebook in 2004, he was just trying to break into the Harvard social scene. Facebook was the first software that expanded people's connections with one another and connected activists with people who shared their concerns.

YouTube followed in 2005, allowing activists to capture powerful videos that could compel viewer action. Twitter launched in 2006, with its 140-character tweets allowing real-time communication (including video links) among the masses. The launch of Apple's iPhone in 2007 escalated the adoption of smartphones, allowing activists to easily capture those videos and distribute them to other smartphone users instantly.

The ever-expanding panoply of social media techniques and digital power has put activist groups on steroids, expanding their reach and quickening the tempo of agitation. It has leveled the playing field between the Goliath corporations and activists.

The effects of an activist group's spotlight are long-lasting and severe. In the late 1980s, activists targeted Nike in their campaign focused on workers' rights in Asia. Even though Nike has behaved admirably in the two decades since becoming the symbol of child labor, people young and old around the world can immediately recall this unfortunate chapter in Nike's history. The activists who outed Nike nearly three decades ago did so at a time when the world was much less wired than today. Today, activist groups have more powerful tools at their disposal. What once took a costly mailing now happens almost instantly and can be effortlessly forwarded in a cascading expansion. Activists have learned to weaponize Twitter to galvanize political change (though Twitter remains more capable of taking down institutions than building them).

In our hypernetworked world, businesses operate in a fishbowl. Videos shot on a smartphone can go viral, exposing misdeeds by a wayward manager or a long-ago transgression in a distant plant.

In 2013 Brandon Huber, a restaurant worker at the Golden Corral in Port Orange, Florida, exposed his manager's practice of hiding piles of raw meat, including pot roast, bacon, baby back ribs, and burger patties, outside and unrefrigerated in the Florida heat next to the dumpster to avoid inspection, later bringing the meat back in and serving it to customers.[6]

In 2015 Sofia Ashraf left her job as creative supervisor at the global advertising agency Ogilvy & Mather and months later launched a YouTube rap video titled *Kodaikanal Won't* criticizing Unilever, one of her ex-agency's largest global clients.[7] The video supporting residents affected by mercury poisoning fourteen years earlier at Unilever's plant producing thermometers in Kodaikanal, India, went viral and pressured the company to agree to a brokered settlement.[8]

Sometimes this scrutiny is well deserved—some bad business operators deserve to be demonized. Yet even well-meaning, reputable organizations with countless employers and far-flung operations increasingly are called to account for deviant employees or transgressions incurred far away and long ago.

Stick and Carrot Activists Groups

All activists highlight an issue for the public consciousness, seek to drive the conversation, and effect change in the world. Some seek to force change by punishing wrongdoers. We'll call them *stick* activist groups. The goal of other activists is to entice companies to embrace more responsible behavior either by shining light on good behavior or by applying their expertise to collaborate on positive results. These we will refer to as *carrot* activists.

Stick Activists

RAN, Greenpeace, and the Sierra Club are prime examples of stick activist groups. Their tactics are to attack companies and bring public pressure to bear rather than collaborating with companies to solve problems. They frequently use confrontational tactics and have less interest in engaging in serious dialogue or compromise.

Stick activists judge their own performance based on headlines, petition signatures, retweets, protesters arrested. Their press releases focus on what they have stopped a business from doing rather than new collaboration with a business. Take recent Greenpeace release headlines as examples—"Duke Announces 2015 Closing of Beckjord Coal Plant"[9] and "Success: Mattel and Barbie Drop Deforestation."[10]

Timberland CEO Jeff Swartz faced Greenpeace "guerilla tactics—accuse first and engage later" that activated 65,000 emails from its followers with an implied boycott threat alleging that Timberland's shoelaces came from cows grazing on converted Brazilian rain forest. He lamented that he would have welcomed a call and been willing to reach a solution. He observed that besides caring about its environmental aims, Greenpeace "also cares about recruiting new members and collecting membership fees. Making headlines by attacking companies helps it do that."[11]

Unions sponsor organizations that advance their push for higher wages or against trade liberalization by embracing stick activist techniques. The SEIU, the Service Employees International Union, launching the Fight for $15 campaign in late 2012 is just one example. Unlike traditional union drives advancing toward a secret ballot vote, organizations like Fight for $15 seek to generate publicity to provoke public pressure in an effort to force employers to accede to their aims.[12]

Celebrities engage in stick activism by harnessing their ability to capture media attention to name and shame wayward behavior. Sophia Ashraf is now a celebrity after pressuring not just Unilever to settle mercury claims but also criticizing Dow's response to the Bhopal disaster in 1984 with her video *Don't Work for Dow*.[13] It took Taylor Swift, acting as the champion of innovation and starving artists, less than a day to get Apple to reverse course on its proposal to not compensate artists for their music during the free trial period of its new audio-streaming service.[14] I will defer to your judgment as to whether Pamela Anderson modeling for a People for the Ethical Treatment of Animals advertisement was sincere activism or just opportunistic good exposure.

Carrot Activists

Carrot activists entice businesses into more responsible behavior by offering companies positive incentives to collaborate. Such activists have the same goals as stick activists—more responsible corporate behavior—but they catch their flies with honey, not vinegar.

Some carrot activists seek to alter public opinion and motivate action without resorting to naming or shaming or other forms of punishment of specific organizations. They prod all businesses to be more sensitive to social concerns and laud companies that do. Examples of activists focused on spotlighting specific issues include First Lady Michelle Obama, with her campaign to reduce childhood obesity; the Human Rights Campaign National and the NAACP, which focus on human and civil rights; the National Council of LaRaza, which focuses on inclusiveness in America;

and the Children's Defense Fund and the AARP Public Policy Initiative, which address demographic segments.

Other carrot activists offer access to expertise on achieving results on social concerns. This encompasses Bono's ONE campaign, focused on extreme poverty; Conservation International, the Nature Conservancy, and the World Wildlife Fund, focused on the environment; and Doctors without Borders, addressing health care in embattled regions.

Carrot activist group metrics and press releases focus on progress achieved, not harms halted. While Greenpeace hit the big time when its *Rainbow Warrior* was mysteriously bombed, Conservation International celebrated its first major accomplishment as signing the first ever debt for nature swap agreement with the Bolivian government in 1987, "purchasing a portion of that nation's foreign debt in exchange for the protection of 3.7 million acres in and around the Beni Biosphere Reserve."[15]

In 1990, while Greenpeace was banning fishnets and Arctic mineral exploration, Conservation International was inking its first corporate partnership, a seven-year deal with McDonald's that stipulated the restaurant giant would fund "local farmers, community groups and businesses to make existing farms more profitable—preventing encroachment into the La Amistad Biosphere Reserve, which stretches between Costa Rica and Panama."[16] Many more partnerships followed.

Hybrid Activists

Some activists have a carrot in one hand and a stick in the other. When Human Rights Watch (HRW) begins an investigation, as they did with alleged gang rapes by Barrett Gold's security forces in Papua New Guinea, they tell the company upfront. Unlike the surprise ambush that Timberland experienced from Greenpeace, HRW's tactic is to encourage companies to work with them. Even though they are open to collaboration like carrot activists, they focus on uncovering and reporting misdeeds like stick activists.[17]

Individual activists, like Pope Francis working on behalf of the poor and the planet, and organizations, like Black Lives Matter, are not yet focused on singling out companies either positively or negatively. Yet clearly they still have an impact on the overall environment within which business operates. Companies must be sensitive that they could be affected by such activists' efforts to drive messages. Facebook CEO Mark Zuckerberg scolded employees for crossing out "black lives matter" on signature walls at the company's headquarters and writing "all lives matter" instead, calling such acts insensitive to free speech.[18]

Associations and chambers of commerce also have a hybrid nature. These organizations provide a variety of services for their members, but most also engage in ongoing advocacy programs. They are often key components of campaigns organized around a specific issue or legislative action.

Think tanks and policy institutes also play an active role in shaping public opinion. These idea factories help formulate solutions to social concerns. They guard their editorial or academic independence carefully, to avoid being charged as "views for hire." Yet nearly all embrace overarching ideals that align on one side of an issue or the other. The Heritage Foundation and Stanford University's Hoover Institute are filled with scholars promoting market-based solutions. The Progressive Policy Institute scholars often have a different focus. With the addition of Heritage Action under CEO Jim DeMint (former U.S. senator and my former colleague in the House), Heritage has moved beyond just studying issues and more affirmatively into the advocacy space.

When Pepsi promotes its True brand with no high-fructose corn syrup and Chipotle criticizes other restaurants' use of GMO ingredients, these companies behave as activists.

Stick Activist Techniques

Stick activists are confrontational by nature. Alinsky referred to volunteers as a "mass army" and their target as "the enemy." The introduction to his book begins by quoting Job 7:1, "The life of man upon earth is a warfare. . . ."

Business executives rarely enjoy their contact with stick activists as they prod commercial conduct to a higher level. A good way to understand the techniques of stick activists is to consider the campaign waged against Walmart in the early 2000s, in the early days of social media.[19]

Obtain Funding

Stick activists must first obtain funding from concerned individuals, foundations, or politically active organizations like unions.

In December 2004, six unions announced a $25 million campaign against Walmart, a company they had failed to unionize and a competitive threat to unionized grocers. In 2005 the SEIU established Walmart Watch with a staff of thirty-six. The Union of Food and Commercial Workers funded the Internet-based organization WakeUpWalMart.com with a staff of six.

Collaborate with Others

Activists seek out broad-based public support. Forming a campaign to coordinate the efforts of many disparate actors allows them to swarm a company once an initiative has commenced.

Fifty groups, including unions, environmental groups, and community organizations, formed the Center for Community and Corporate Ethics to force Walmart to change its ways.

A broad-based campaign permits coordination with diverse "doers" and a wide array of "funders," including businesses with aligned interests—like small-town banks worried about the expansion of Walmart's financial services offerings.

Attract Attention with Dramatic Action

RAN's slogan is Environmentalism with Teeth. Activists are dramatic to attract donors and volunteers, while agitating a company's customers, investors, and political supporters. Their techniques include protest rallies, petitions, boycotts, divestment drives, and documentaries. The advantage to activists of protesters being arrested is that it prolongs the story and gives it a personal dimension.

Teachers' unions picketed Walmart stores across the nation. "Wake Up Walmart . . . . recruited sixty-five ministers to sign a letter to CEO Scott, the letter stated, 'Jesus would not embrace Walmart's values of greed and profits at any cost.'" A documentary film, *Walmart: The High Cost of Low Price*, extended the campaign to theaters.

Support Assertions with Research

Stick activists submit policy studies highlighting the poor performance of a company on a specific social attribute. They may prepare this analysis themselves or commission it. The core activity of some activist groups is to produce such policy studies.

Wake Up Walmart commissioned Zogby International to conduct a national survey of people's attitudes toward Walmart. The poll revealed that "56 percent of Americans agreed with the statement 'Walmart was bad for America. It may provide low prices, but those prices come with a high moral and economic cost.'"

The Labor Research Association, a labor statistics bureau established by members of the Workers (Communist) Party of America, advanced unfavorable comparisons between Costco and Sam's Club (a Walmart subsidiary) wages.

Engage Politically

Stick activists often invoke political action—pushing specific legislation or advocating with regulatory decision-making bodies through scorecards for politicians, advertising, or aggressive lobbying efforts. Given political gridlock, advancing legislative aims is rarely the primary thrust and is always done in tandem with efforts to sway public opinion. It is easier to apply public pressure on businesses to change their behavior than to enact legislation.

The California legislature passed a bill that only applied to Walmart, but the governor vetoed it. "In April 2005 Walmart Watch ran a full-page ad alleging that Walmart wages forced thousands of its employees to use food stamps and Medicaid for healthcare. . . . The AFL-CIO developed a model bill to be introduced in state legislatures, and their efforts were directed at over 30 states." The Maryland General Assembly passed a bill that only impacted Walmart and overrode its governor's veto.

Leverage Partners in Government

It was social activist agitation that created the Environmental Protection Agency (EPA), Consumer Finance Protection Bureau, Consumer Product Safety Commission, and Occupational Safety and Health Administration. Once these agencies are authorized, staffed, and funded, they can be highly advantageous to activism.

The overall campaign against Walmart also included charges from the EPA. In 2001 Walmart settled with both the EPA and the Department of Justice on Clean Water Act violations in seventeen locations. Though these only represented a small sliver of Walmart's many stores and the civil fine was only $1 million, this result provided fodder for activism.

Seek Legal Action

Walmart faced a wide array of lawsuits, including a class action suit alleging discrimination against its female employees that went all the way to the Supreme Court.[20]

Promote Shareholder Resolutions

It is common for both investors and stick activists to advance shareholder resolutions to promote their goals.

Activists introduced resolutions at Walmart stockholder's meeting addressing executive compensation, environmental reporting, and a requirement to appoint more women to their board.

Target Prey to Achieve Maximum Return

The types of targets stick activists find attractive are:

- *Products* with a brand name to protect and low switching costs. Girl Scouts rely on the attractiveness of their brand of cookies, but consumers have multiple other cookie choices in the marketplace.
- *Operating environments* that produce harmful externalities on the physical or social environment, multinationals operating

in developing countries, or decentralized operations and supply chains. The cookie controversy emerged not from Kellogg's operations in Battle Creek, Michigan, but from a supplier who sourced from Indonesia. Activists will follow the supply chain to find its most sensitive point.

Different Types of Companies Face Different Risks

Companies producing products that are harmful, like tobacco, are easily demonized, and inspire sin taxes or sales restrictions. For those companies whose products are hazardous but helpful, like chemical companies, activists stand ready to pounce on any misstep to strengthen regulations and restrict activities.

Industries that are unavoidable but unpopular among segments of the populace (energy, financial services, and pharmaceuticals) face constant pressure from activists in the areas of cost, environmental impact, or access for those in need. Activists often use retail locations to press their points.

Resource and agricultural companies that operate in remote places far from the glaring eyes of the media are normally just nodes in the supply chain for branded companies. Activists will typically target higher-profile customers or, as with the Keystone pipeline, contend the case (opposition to Canadian oil sands) in the locale that is most environmentally sensitive (Nebraska's Sand Hills).

Wholesome, branded companies are often held to a higher standard and are constantly at risk because of the conduct of their suppliers.

Besides targeting companies, stick activists can also target specific company officials. In a campaign against Citibank, RAN went to the CEO's hometown and "plastered grocery stores with 'Wanted' posters [and] delivered campaign information to [his] neighbors and son."[21] Protesters also showed up "at the doorstep of [a] Google self-driving car engineer."[22]

Walmart has a brand name and competitors with a very extensive supply chain, making it an ideal target.

Leverage Credibility and First-Mover Advantage

Activists generally have more credibility with the general public than do businesses. That is because we naturally see activists as more authentic, pursuing common interests, unlike business executives fixated on preserving their compensation.

Activists also have the first-mover advantage. They decide who to target, on what issue, and when. Their first-mover edge has become even more powerful in today's digital age.

Attract Those with Experience and Entrepreneurial Drive

Stick activists often start out working on a political campaign or a campaign committee. Political staffers have motivation for moving on because political campaigns inevitably end. The migration from political staff to activist group is most pronounced whenever there is a large electoral swing. As the tide shifts, political staffers are put out on the street. Many move to activist groups. Leading a successful activist group can pay more than a political campaign and can provide employment for years, not just months.

It's no coincidence that the coordinated campaigns against Walmart began in December 2004, the month after George W. Bush won reelection and Republicans picked up seats in Congress, leaving hosts of Democratic operatives without employment. The Wake Up Walmart and Walmart Watch efforts were headed by staff from the Howard Dean, Wesley Clark, and John Kerry presidential campaigns.

Extract Victory from Less than Stated Goals

Stick activists shoot high and therefore can win with less. They make seemingly outrageous demands of companies but can claim victory with *any* movement a company makes in their direction. Such partial victories attract more money and volunteers.

The activists wanted Walmart to increase unionization, reduce its effects on small merchants, and expand health-care coverage. These efforts were largely unsuccessful, though Walmart did change its environmental sourcing. Despite going one for four, the activists still declared victory.

So how did Walmart survive?

Among Walmart's more effective responses was to blunt the main thrust of attack: that its wages were too low. Walmart CEO Lee Scott urged Congress to raise the minimum wage in 2005.[23] Since Walmart's average wage was nearly twice the minimum, and its competitors relied more heavily on part-time workers, a higher minimum wage only improved Walmart's competitive position.

By upgrading environmental standards it set for suppliers and working more actively with nongovernmental organizations (NGOs) in this area, Walmart splintered the coalition opposing it.

Walmart survived, adapted, and in many ways is a better company for it. It substantively beefed up its capabilities to engage with shapeholders. From Walmart we can learn that, to avoid the rod of stick activists, develop extensive cooperative relationships with carrot activists.

Carrot Activist Techniques

The techniques used by carrot activists overlap with the stick activist techniques outlined earlier, but they are less confrontational.

Carrot activists rely on outside funding and collaborate on campaigns. They may engage in campaigns that include stick activists, like when Jane Goodall joined with efforts as part of the ORANGS campaigns against the Girl Scouts. They are less likely to do so if already collaborating with a business. This is just one reason why engagement with a broad array of carrot activists can defuse the threat of stick activists.

Carrot activists' activities may include advancing research supporting their aims and promoting legislative solutions. When I was crafting that farm bill in Congress, Ducks Unlimited and Pheasants Forever actively lobbied for specific legislative provisions and ran advertisements in support of their positions, but they refrained from more hostile acts, which puts them in the carrot activist category.

I outline in the following sections the techniques unique to carrot activists.

Expertise on Addressing Social Concerns

Walmart's environmental push received vital guidance through its partnership with a wide range of environmentally focused activists who provided new insights and complementary skills, allowing everyone to achieve more together. Carrot activists see partnership with businesses as a potent force to achieve shared goals by harnessing businesses' resources, supply chains, and expertise to their pursuit of worthy goals. They are right. When Walmart, with the unmatched scale of its supply chain, rolled out new sustainability-focused sourcing standards with the help of carrot activists like the Marine Stewardship Council, the Organic Exchange, and the Green Electronics Council, it likely did more for the environment than could have been achieved by the collective efforts of all NGOs combined.[24]

Standard Setting

Activists both set standards and audit to affirm compliance with such standards, thereby providing a valuable service for sourcing organizations and suppliers alike. There is strategic competition among shapeholders to establish their metrics as the benchmarks for business activity. It is important for companies to develop strategies that addresses standards that affect the industries and activities in which they engage.

Gregory Unruh and Richard Ettenson, professors at the Thunderbird School of Global Management at Arizona State University, suggest that how you respond depends on the degree to which standards have coalesced and your capabilities for taking the lead in defining the standards. LEED (Leadership in Energy and Environmental Design) standards are an example of widely recognized standards that most adopt. Examples of companies applying their extensive internal experience to define industry standards include Starbucks for its sustainable coffee sourcing and Walmart for its supply chain.[25]

While some standards promulgate more rigorous criteria than the companies may have set for themselves, they at least provide a safe harbor to avoid disruptive surprises. Be aware of the standards applicable to your operations and carefully determine whether to hitch your wagon to those standards or establish alternative standards that have comparable credibility.

Quality Control

During a recent course I led in Beijing, our class met with an NGO called the Institute for Public and Environmental Affairs. Its role was to monitor the exception reports of Chinese government agencies on a range of matters, environmental and otherwise, and to report to those companies' customers, normally large multinationals. While companies like Apple were at first hesitant to collaborate, they soon properly assessed that this supplier information was highly valuable for two reasons. Supplier transgressions could wash up on their shore either as a hit to their reputation or, if the Chinese government proceeded with an enforcement action against the supplier, as a supply disruption.

Policy Development/Engaging Legislators

Think tanks and policy institutes investigate policy solutions that reflect the complex nature of issues facing companies. They develop model legislation, offer educational opportunities for legislators, and create opportunities for engaging legislators.

As the source of key ideas that can influence a policy debate, it is often helpful for your organization to be part of the conversation. An example of this is the Chevron Forum on Development at the Center for Strategic and International Studies: "A high-level speaker series exploring new ideas and innovative approaches to global development, with a special focus on the role of the private sector." Such programs allow full independence on the part of the scholars. At the same time, they benefit Chevron in multiple ways—scholars are focused on the private-sector role and Chevron gets the halo effect of being seen to be on the cutting edge of such activities while keeping its ear to the ground to identify both best practices and areas of dissent regarding this topic.[26]

Businesses must carefully screen such organizations so they don't find themselves tangled up in controversial issues unrelated to commercial issues. The American Legislative Exchange Council, a forum for state legislators focused on free markets, strayed from its market focus to partner with the National Rifle Association to make the "stand-your-ground" law one of its model bills. Following the outrage over the shooting of Trayvon Martin, an unarmed black teenager, in Florida in February 2012, progressive groups pressured companies like Amazon, Coca-Cola, General Electric, Kraft, McDonald's, and Walmart to cut their ties with the council.[27]

Highlight Good Works

Carrot activists can shine the light on your efforts that benefit society, as when Nike committed $50 million in 2013 to promote increased physical activity of kids in schools and communities as part of Michelle Obama's Let's Move campaign.[28]

Buyer's Guide

A buyer's guide is a particularly powerful form of spotlighting for an organization with extensive membership focused on a particular issue. The Human Rights Campaign (HRC) advances such a guide, rating companies on whether their benefits and policies meet standards the HRC prescribes or are of interest to HRC's members focused on workplace equality.

Showcase Awards

Activist groups often define hard-to-achieve goals and encourage companies to pledge to accomplish them, complimenting those who do and criticizing those who don't. At the New York Climate Week in 2015, Johnson & Johnson, Procter & Gamble, Starbucks, Walmart, and Goldman Sachs committed themselves to eventually converting entirely to renewable energy.[29]

As consumer or services brands with limited physical footprints, mostly in advanced economies or central cities, agreeing to these commitments is much easier than it is for more asset-intensive companies with far-flung operations. This creates special challenges for companies that are often set up for unfair comparisons by activist groups in need of a foil to contrast with those they deem "best in class." At a minimum, such companies should seek other external affirmations on the issue in question.

Sales Campaigns

Consider the (RED) campaign developed in 2006 by Bono and Robert Sargent "Bobby" Shriver, the head of the public-private partnership the Global Fund. Profits from the sale of merchandise are split between the participating companies and the Global Fund in support of AIDS relief. Companies like American Express, Apple, Coca-Cola, Gap, Nike, SAP, and Starbucks participated. Though the energy behind the campaign has waned, and it came under criticism for how much it spent on marketing relative to the amount collected, the campaign reports raising $315 million for AIDS in Africa.[30]

In summary, business leaders should be aware which activists are engaged in their industry and whether they are holding a carrot or a stick. Business leaders should always be on the lookout for opportunities to collaborate with carrot activists with common interests.

KEY TAKEAWAYS

- If the Girl Scouts are at risk of being targeted by activists, so is your company!
- Saul Alinsky wrote his 1971 classic *Rules for Radicals* for the Have-nots on how to take power away from the Haves. Alinsky

advised activists to combine hope and resentment to create a "mass army" to goad the target to react.

- The introduction of Facebook in 2004, YouTube in 2005, Twitter in 2006, and Apple's iPhone in 2007 amplified the voices of activists.
- Activists highlight an issue for the public consciousness and seek to effect change in the world.
- Stick activists (Greenpeace, RAN, the Sierra Club) seek to force change by punishing wrongdoers.
- Carrot activists (Conservation International, World Wildlife Fund) seek to entice companies to embrace more responsible behavior either by shining light on good behavior or applying their expertise to collaborate on positive results.
- Stick activist techniques included obtaining funding, collaborating with others, attracting attention through dramatic action, supporting assertions with research, engaging politically, leveraging partners in government, seeking legal action, promoting shareholder resolutions, targeting prey for maximum impact, leveraging their creditability with the public, taking advantage of being a first mover, attracting those with campaign experience and entrepreneurial skills, and extracting victory from less than stated goals.
- Carrot activists provide expertise to jointly address social concerns, recognized standards for acceptable behavior, quality-control support, and policy development while highlighting good works through buyer guides, showcase awards, or sales campaigns.
- Business leaders should be aware which activists are engaged in their industry and whether they are holding a carrot or a stick.
- The best way to avoid the wrath of stick activists is to always be on the lookout for opportunities to collaborate with carrot activists with common interests.

3

The Media

History will be kind to me for I intend to write it.
—WINSTON CHURCHILL

HAROLD WILSON, THEN SHADOW chancellor of the United
Kingdom, was complaining that the Swiss bankers were manipulating the British currency. He coined the phrase "the gnomes
of Zurich," suggesting that Swiss bankers ran the world from a
smoke-filled back room in Zurich. The conspiracy theories of my
youth suggested that the gnomes decided who should be president
or whether to commence or conclude military action. The most
paranoid would have you believe that the gnomes put John F.
Kennedy into office and assassinated him when he stopped taking
orders.

When I first visited Zurich in 1982 I got a picture of myself
in front of the Swiss Bank Corporation to prove that I had been
near the throne of power (the gnomes). Yet while reading *House
Mouse, Senate Mouse* to an elementary school class in Minneapolis in 2006, I realized I was looking in the wrong place.

The teacher was trying to help the students understand who I
was as a congressman. She asked whether anyone could name one
of the three branches of government. One student rightly said the

president. Then the teacher asked if anyone could name another branch of government, hoping that a student would suggest Congress so she could proceed with her introduction. After a long pause, one student said, "The media?"

To most people, government is the president against the media. Those who report the news have leapfrogged from being the fourth estate in early-modern times (after the clergy, nobility, and commoners) to the second position.

With the communications revolutions sparked by Facebook and ever-increasing forms of mass expression, the idea that any small group of people is manipulating the world seems fanciful. This multiplication of choices has placed intense pressures on the business model of traditional media outlets. It is harder for them to make money, forcing them to target specific audience segments (read: become biased) and focus on headlines that capture attention (read: business stumbles). This fragmentation makes every slant on news available for prospective audiences, but media outlets that appeal to the full spectrum are few and far between.

During a panel discussion of presidential press secretaries and White House correspondents hosted by my school in 2015, Joe Lockhart, senior advisor and press secretary for former president Bill Clinton, recounted a story from his volunteer work with the John Kerry presidential campaign in 2004. He had been tracking how they were faring with the traditional networks. By this measure, Kerry was cruising to victory. Doing a postmortem on his analysis, Lockhart discovered that he mistakenly assumed that as goes network television, so goes the nation. Closer analysis showed that network television's share of audience had dropped by a third since Clinton first ran for president. It continues to fall.[1] Just look at the D.C. press corps, where reporters for niche outlets now fill more seats than reporters from daily newspapers.[2]

While there are challenges to engaging a more dispersed media landscape, the tools available to spread your targeted message are more plentiful and potent. New monitoring tools allow real-time feedback on what the world is saying about you. A company's website, social media channels, and digitally available expressions of itself, its performance, its purpose, and its beneficial acts applied in a vigorous manner can help it withstand the buffets that the gales of media agitation may stir up.

Media Today

The arena of public opinion is the focal point of nearly all shapeholder face-offs. Shapeholders either leverage the weight of public opinion to directly force corporate action or influence the behavior of political shapeholders to regulate a company or industry. It is essential to understand the state of media today and the effect of the media on public views.

Censoring Lives On

They may no longer ban books in Boston, but what you can read is certainly censored in many ways and places around the globe. This occurs under authoritarian rulers and those who aspire to authoritarian rule and, in more limited ways, in democracies.

Sometimes these media restrictions catch you by surprise. I avoided trouble when giving a guest lecture for HEC Paris Business School in Doha, Qatar, by discovering just in time that I could not show a slide of me toasting with a pint of Guinness. The trouble? It is illegal to show a photo of alcohol consumption in Qatar.

During a briefing for my class in Hong Kong in 2014, a reporter for the *South China Post* shared with our students that when he worked as a reporter in China, he and his colleagues received a list every afternoon from a government ministry excluding certain topics from the day's allowed reportage. How I would love to get that list. This is why I feel so confident I will never have to worry about giving extra credit for students finding bad news about the Chinese government leadership on the front page of *China Daily*.

Yet censorship occurs in countries generally considered democracies. An easy way for a would-be dictator to capture the media is to get his captive business cronies to purchase the leading media outlets. As part of conglomerates that rely heavily on government business, they are much less likely to be critical of government action. The local CNN affiliate owned by a Turkish conglomerate ran a documentary on penguins instead of reporting the brutal crackdown by the government of Recep Tayyip Erdogan on Gezi Park protesters in Istanbul in 2013.[3] CNN Turk aired Erdogan live via FaceTime on his cell phone to thwart an attempted coup in 2016.[4] The owners of CNN Turk can be more certain of the favor of Erdogan than its viewers can be of the evenhandedness of its broadcasts.

Companies must be vigilant in environments of media restriction. As much of a pest that the media can be at times, never forget that an autocrat unbridled by media scrutiny is much worse.

Nothing Stays Secret Forever

It is foolish to believe anything other than that all things knowable will become known to the public. Julian Assange's WikiLeaks has influenced foreign affairs and business. For instance, anti-GMO activists in Europe used U.S. diplomatic cables discussing its strategy to overturn the EU's restrictive measures as a way to exhort adherents to redouble their efforts.[5] HSBC's chief executive, Stuart Gulliver, and his bank found themselves in an awkward spot when it was revealed in the Panama Papers that he had set up an offshore bank account.[6] Definers Public Affairs exposed a potential conflict for an insurance commissioner whose approval is required to affirm the merger between the Anthem and Cigna insurance behemoths.[7]

Nothing Travels Faster than Bad News

The media never reports safe landings, only crashes. One of the most honest reporters I ever met was a reporter from the UK's *Guardian* who told me at a Washington press gala that his role was to "problemize issues."

This is because media outlets are businesses and must appeal to their target customers. For most media outlets, their audience is bored by stories of businesses doing something good but enthralled by stories of corporate misdeeds. With stick activist groups competing with one another to advance their causes by catching businesses out of step, reporters don't have trouble finding such stories. It is only the most business-focused publication that finds an audience who wants to read good news about business conduct.

Social media turbocharges the speed at which news travels. During an appearance I made on Bloomberg TV, my daughter's college classmate saw me on television in Guatemala, took a picture of me on her iPhone, and sent it to my daughter's fiancé in London, who emailed it to my daughter in North Carolina, who emailed it to me in New York. I received her email before I got to the elevators after the interview.

The reality that media can accentuate corporate missteps and spread the bad news at warp speed requires companies to develop robust direct channels to get their side of the story out with the audiences important to them ASAP.

Biased? Of Course! Deal with It

Compare coverage between Fox News and CNN any given evening if you don't believe in media bias. It's like they broadcast from different planets.

Here's a tip I picked up on the campaign trail for determining the bias of a reporter. Daryl Thul, the editor of the *Redwood Falls Gazette*, advised me, "You can tell a writer's bias by which side they present in the last sentence of an article." While an article may include the most important information at the beginning, I always began reviewing an article by reading the last sentence so I know through which lens this information is provided.

As the competition among the endless sources of news makes finding a profitable business media model harder, outlets target the wants (instead of the needs) of customers. Even traditional news outlets change the placement of stories on their websites during the day based on the amount of traffic they receive. This self-reinforcing tendency of modern media makes its bias toward a particular customer viewpoint even more pronounced. A Japanese app called SmartNews goes a step further, feeding its subscribers the top stories trending on social media that second.[8]

As each target customer base shrinks, news sources naturally sharpen their bias. Businesses must accept this and deal with it. As with all attributes of shapeholder engagement, we must observe differences and search out opportunities to add others to our team. Determine which outlets will be receptive to which topics and which can reach your targeted audience segments. Keep them close as you execute your media relations strategy.

Modern-Day Muckrakers

Social media has accelerated the speed of news, but it has also empowered activists. They can profile your misdeeds, real or imagined, using facts or fantasy, and reach a wide audience in the blink of an eye. Remember also that they have the first-mover advantage.

Anyone can be a blogger today. The creative ones with a point of view attract large followings. The smart ones make your missteps or corner-cutting into headline news. These independent writers and bloggers, many of whom are writing as a sideline to successful careers in a variety of fields, are becoming increasingly influential.

Powerline is the creation of three lawyers who attended Dartmouth College together—John Hinderaker, Scott Johnson, and Paul Mirengoff. In 2004 they helped expose fabricated documents that were featured on *60 Minutes* criticizing President George W. Bush's service in the Air National Guard. The blog's investigations eventually led to the resignation of anchor Dan Rather and several others at CBS, directly impacting CBS's business.[9] If independent bloggers can bring down a fellow muckraker at *60 Minutes*, no business should feel immune.

Many stick activists take their inspirations from the heralded investigative reporters that embraced the muckraker traditions of turning up hidden stories of abuse, corruption, or misconduct. Upton Sinclair's *The Jungle* targeted the meat-packing industry, Rachel Carson's *Silent Spring* targeted pesticides and DDT, Ralph Nader's *Unsafe at Any Speed* targeted the auto industry—each of them had a transformative effect on businesses.

The muckraker tradition is alive and well in the twenty-first century. The 2013 documentary film *Blackfish*, directed by Gabriela Cowperthwaite, profiling an orca held in captivity named Tilikum, forced SeaWorld to abandon its use of captive killer whales in its shows.[10]

It is easy for businesspeople to ignore these rumblings, to dismiss them as unrelated to their market success. But that's dangerous. I found out the hard way. Perhaps you have seen or heard about the 2004 documentary movie *Fahrenheit 9/11*? I ended up in the movie and the trailer and featured in the cover of the promotional video trailer for the movie.

Returning from the Capitol to my office after a vote, I was confronted by Michael Moore with a camera in my face. He told me, "I'm trying to get members of Congress to get their kids to enlist in the army and go over to Iraq. Is there any way you could help me with that?" My response was, "I'd be happy to . . . I have a nephew on his way to Afghanistan."

In the movie Moore showed himself questioning me, but skipped my answer, adding clips of other congressmen refusing to talk with him, followed by the statement, "Of course, not a single member of Congress wanted to sacrifice their child for the war in Iraq."[11]

With the facts on my side, I went to the airwaves on every major broadcast and cable network and starred in the subsequent film, *Michael Moore Hates America*,[12] exposing the fallacy of Moore's allegation. I was able to turn this attack on its head. Not all are so fortunate.

Michael Moore's purposely narrow view was ready-made for audiences with similarly narrow views—a profitable example of target marketing. He made a bundle on the film. Yet its deliberately slanted depiction distorted the real picture. It is vital to realize that your business could well be next on a sensationalist producer's hit parade. Moore has already taken on the auto, food, and health-care industries with arguably misleading movies. How can you avoid being the star in a muckraking documentary and prepare to respond if you are unlucky enough to be?

Internet Trolls

Having gone from major news networks that, though biased, value fact-checking, to so-called documentarians with even deeper biases that require digging to expose their lies, we now confront Internet trolls, whose obvious bias, dishonesty, and promotion of fake news constitute their stock-in-trade. In Internet slang, a troll is a person who sows discord, starts arguments, and inflames conflict.

Leslie Gaines-Ross, Weber Shandwick's chief reputation strategist, recounts how "after the explosion of BP's Deepwater Horizon drilling platform . . . Leroy Stick (an alias) began publishing the tweets of a totally made-up representative of a similarly bogus BP public relations division. While crude oil spilled into the Gulf of Mexico, devastating the regional ecology and economy, the satirical Twitterer (@BPGlobalPR) tweeted about the division's lunch menu and other inane matters. Tens of thousands followed his updates—far more than the number who followed the real BP Twitter account."[13] This only inflamed public anger toward BP.

Exaggerating the power of the insidious trolls is our old nemesis: confirmation bias. Recent studies of the Internet by Michela Del Vicario of Italy's Laboratory of Computational Social Science suggest that confirmation bias has caused division of the Internet into virtual communities where "baseless conspiracy theories spread rapidly." When others affirm one's views within these clusters, group polarization ensues, causing everyone in the group to become more confident, more extreme.[14]

Social and Traditional Media: Vying for Credibility

Surprising to some, research has suggested that blog outlets and social media have significant credibility with readers. In Edelman's 2015 Trust Barometer, 64 percent of the respondents trusted online search versus 62 percent for traditional media, 53 percent for hybrid (dot-com versions of traditional media and digital outlets like *Huffington Post*), and 48 percent for social media.[15] Those that appear "just like me" have great credibility. The impact of Internet trolls should not be underestimated. A robust and responsive social media presence is the best response.

Effective Media Engagement

You cannot change any of this. Rather, effective media engagement requires actively listening to what the world thinks and says about your organization. It requires sustained and penetrating messaging of the news the company wants widely known and vigilance to promptly address bad press. The fact that owned media outlets are trusted by 47 percent of respondents in Edelman's survey suggests that you can credibly communicate your own story to great effect.

Let's review a few key factors vital to effectively communicating.

Active Listening

Measure Public Opinion. Stay informed of the public view of your company and the issues important to your company. Understanding how opinions vary by demographic and geographic segments, which messages would alter those views, and the credibility attached to various sources of information are valuable inputs into one's communications strategy.

Monitor Media Real Time. In days gone by a company executive could stay informed by reading a few newspapers and watching the nightly news. Now, with the explosion of bloggers, pundits, and trolls, we need more robust monitoring. Several companies offer media-monitoring tools that can provide real-time awareness of what people are saying about you. They incorporate every mention not only through traditional outlets like television (drawn from closed-captioning) and newspapers but also from Facebook posts, tweets, and the like. Global companies need this not only in the languages of their home offices but in the language of all their major publics, translated for consumption by senior management.

The best tools allow you to pinpoint not only how much volume is behind each word or phrase associated with the company but also a rough sense of whether the sentiment is positive or negative and which outlets are driving the debate. When responding to an issue, these monitoring tools are essential input into assessing whether your response is calming the waters or stirring the pot.

Retain Research Capability. You must have investigative capabilities to uncover any clandestine attacks against your company. With the heightened credibility of "someone just like me," those undermining your siting of a facility or business practice may put the face of "concerned local resident acting unprompted" on their message, an activity referred to as "astroturfing." If such a person is really being fed talking points from a large NGO, and if a corporate competitor is funding that NGO, those facts could prove vital to neutralizing an attack. In the information age, information is king. You cannot afford to be behind the information curve.

Test Messages. Digital communications allow you to constantly test your messaging by sequentially comparing iterations of a message with different audience segments to see which draws the most favorable response.

Target Communications

Begin with Informing Stakeholders. How critical it is to keep even your closest allies informed was clear to me during my first congressional reelection campaign. My wife and I sat down with our four school-age children to give them a preview of the campaign ahead. I explained that this would be one of the top races in the country and that there would be a lot of negative ads on television. I warned them that the ads would say things like "he poured poison down your sinks, threw grandmas into the snow in the winter, and was completely responsible for Enron" (the top business scandal of the day). My sixteen-year-old daughter asked me, "What did you do with Enron?" I explained that I had done absolutely nothing with Enron.

To quote Yogi Berra: "Half the lies they tell about me aren't true." Perhaps he was trying to communicate that even your friends will half-question whether lies about you are true. The fact that my own daughter felt compelled to ask about my involvement with Enron highlights that you must ensure you get out your side of the story, including directly to those who already know you the best.

For companies, it is essential that you ensure that your own stakeholders are well informed. It is a tremendous threat if they can either be turned against you or lose confidence in the company. They could become key components of your coalition in a shapeholder skirmish. Your messaging to them should communicate in terms that address their specific concerns as employees, customers, suppliers, and communities, but those messages should have a constancy of purpose that unites their focus.

Cultivate Dialogue with Opinion Leaders. None of us can be an expert on everything, though we all know people who think they are. People look to others whose views they value for cues on specific issues. These could be journalists, bloggers, activist groups, associations, think tanks, government representatives, perhaps even politicians and the rare business leader willing to speak out. The views of these opinion leaders are magnified.

A regular dialogue with key influencers, sometimes referred to as grass-tops advocacy in contrast to a broader-based grassroots approach, is an essential element of any strategy to succeed in the arena of public opinion. If your team has built and maintained close relations with key media reporters, you have a better chance of providing your side of the story. If you develop broad-based carrot activist relations, you can direct the media toward them during your company's equivalent of a plane crash.

As much as a company may want to cultivate a relationship with a key opinion leader, there is a fine line to tread. It is essential to be transparent about your relationship. The Justice Department assessed a $3 billion (yes, billion with a *b*) criminal and civil fine against GlaxoSmithKline over illegal drug marketing, including not disclosing a payment of $550,000 to radio personality Dr. Drew Pinsky, who spoke favorably about their antidepressant Wellbutrin on his program.[16]

Spread the News That's Fit to Print

Center on Purpose. An organization's broader communications strategy should align toward communicating its purpose, its reason for being that drives its economic engine and benefits mankind. Your purpose is the reputation you strive to earn. Achieving it requires more than just slick communications—it requires aligning the whole company to deliver on the promise of a company's purpose.

Talk Straight. A key element of the global immersion residencies I have set up for students in capitals around the world include meetings with leading political figures. The question I always ask them is this: "As an advocate, what would it take for me to get a second meeting with you?" The answer is always the same: Be a reliable source of credible news that helps them make difficult decisions.

While every organization will frame a message in the way that puts it in the most favorable light, if you do not also address uncomfortable details, you may leave behind your credibility. The fact that the anesthesiologists' claim that nurse anesthetists could not be adequately supervised by general practitioner medical doctors in rural hospitals was refuted by many other medical professionals caused me to classify their testimony as self-serving and therefore less useful to me.

Don't Overreach. One of the few functions I retained in my campaign was to review most press releases. A campaign is always tempted to position its candidate as the one who would go the furthest to fix the country's problems. I often struck draft language obliging me to positions I could not execute if elected. Being devoted to balancing the budget, I could not commit to every spending priority or tax cut. As a greener-than-average Republican, I was not always comfortable with the party line on environmental regulations.

Just as some politicians will say anything to get elected, some communications professionals may not fully understand what is required to execute a promise and can overreach a company's capabilities. It is important to keep the need for follow-through foremost and to give clear guidelines about when public commitments can be made.

Show Them the Fire. I have stood at the center of high-profile events in business and politics and found that the media accounts often report only the smoke. You must fill this void by showing them the fire. Telling the parts you want understood in an engaging way allows you to write your own history.

The U.S. Navy took a CNN reporter along for the ride in May 2015 when flying a reconnaissance mission over the disputed South Pacific islands where China was building an airstrip.[17] In such disputes, the United States would have to gain not only the support of its own citizens but the support of other nations. Letting a network with global reach see firsthand what the navy sees helps to advance that aim.

Fill Vacuums in Real-Time Through Direct Communications Channels. In the political age, you must bypass mass media and reach key populations directly in real time. When your media monitoring identifies an emerging issue, you must be able to respond in minutes, not days or weeks. This can be done through your company's website, social media channels, and stakeholder email lists.

Churchill said, "When the eagles are silent, the parrots begin to jabber." Do not leave vacuums for the parrots to fill. Lean forward into matters of importance to the company. Take center stage in a crisis.

When passengers in the Washington Metro saw smoke in a 2016 incident along the Red Line, many riders feared a repeat of a 2015 smoke incident that left one rider dead and more than eighty injured. They begin crying and climbing over seats to escape. The train operator offered no information, only admonishing passengers in a panicky voice to "please close all doors between cars." One passenger, Chuck Holmes, squeezed "the barest of a 3G signal" from his cell phone looking for any information but found nothing from @Metrorailinfo—the official Metro account. Luckily, he found a tweet on a user-sponsored site that relayed that Metro was in the process of pulling the train back to the platform.[18] The Metro Authority was fortunate that while they were silent the parrot was helpful, forestalling panic. It would have been far better for them to rely less on good fortune and to speak out immediately during a time of crisis.

Communicate Through Multiple Channels. To reach a wide audience, you must communicate through multiple channels. Bolstering a blog post with a related video and news release through distribution lists and social media has been found to multiply viewership by a factor of fifteen. With more channels, the message is exposed to more eyes. There is an increased chance it will be deemed relevant, since each outlet serves different interests, and the multiple content elements elevate its ranking in search engines.[19]

Media engagement is critical. But whether the press is unfettered is a function of the political shapeholders, those who set the rules for us all.

KEY TAKEAWAYS

- The media landscape has become more fragmented, disrupting the business model of media outlets and forcing them to serve more tightly defined segments, heightening their bias toward the preferences of their unique audience slices.
- In today's media landscape, censoring lives on, nothing stays secret forever or travels faster than bad news, and social media vies with traditional media for credibility.
- Companies must learn to engage many more-narrowly focused media outlets, modern-day muckrakers, and Internet trolls.
- Firms must be active listeners—measuring public opinion, monitoring media in real time, maintaining robust research capabilities, and testing messages.
- Organizations must target communications by keeping their stakeholders well informed, cultivating dialogue with opinion leaders, and spreading the news that's fit to print by talking straight, avoiding overreach, showing the fire by providing first-hand accounts, filling vacuums in real time, and utilizing multiple direct-communication channels.

4

Politicians

Just because you do not take an interest in politics doesn't mean
politics won't take an interest in you.

—PERICLES (430 B.C.)

IN A MEETING WITH businesspeople in Syria during a congressional delegation visit I participated in to Damascus and other
regional capitals in 2004, the local General Motors dealer complained that U.S. sanctions were preventing him from getting
replacement parts. When I mentioned that Syria was designated
by our State Department as a state sponsor of terrorism,[1] the
businessman said, "Now, let's not let politics interfere with this."
Wishful thinking for him, and for any business.

Legitimate businesses must be familiar with the political players, the terrain they occupy, and how to effectively (and ethically)
navigate its contours.

A cliché when speaking about nearly any capital is that it is so
many square miles surrounded by reality. But politicians live in as
structured and disciplined a reality as business—it's just a different
kind of reality, one that varies by jurisdiction, one that often is at
odds with the business reality.

Those who ignore the calculations of political actors face huge
obstacles, as Uber found out in Paris when they brashly spread

their disruptive car-for-hire service in the face of stiff resistance from entrenched taxi drivers. Taxi drivers burned tires, blocked the Paris ring road, smashed windshields, and attempted to overturn cars in opposition to Uber being allowed to operate.[2] The government pressed criminal charges that resulted in Uber's executives narrowly escaping prison time[3] but still being found guilty of "misleading commercial practices" and "complicity in the illegal exercise of the taxi profession." Uber was fined €800,000 and two executives faced personal fines of €30,000 and €20,000.[4] The French parliament also introduced legislation to block the use of a permit that allowed drivers to affiliate with Uber.[5]

In stark contrast, General Electric (GE) secured approval in 2015 to acquire most of the assets of Alstom, one of France's largest private-sector employers that was viewed as central to France continuing as a major manufacturing power. After a year and a half of active engagement, GE deftly overcame determined resistance from President François Hollande and his industry minister Arnaud Montebourg that included attracting Siemens to make a rival bid in an attempt to keep Alstom in European hands and Hollande personally meeting with the heads of GE and Siemens, seeking to play one off against the other.[6] GE made the necessary arrangements to secure approval by the European Union, the United States, and twenty other global regulators, which included selling some Alstom assets to an Italian rival.[7]

So what is the political math by which politicians, governments, and regulators govern? Political math determines who they pay special attention to, how they interact with one another, how they make decisions. Political leaders factor individual businesses and other shapeholders into their equations. They have your number. Do you have their number?

Having been both a corporate financial officer and a congressman, I can tell you that business math is easier. You sell for more than you paid and you profit. It's straightforward.

The easiest way to explain political math here is to break it down into four levels (there are five, but the fifth level, *regulatory* math, is the subject of the next chapter). *Yes-no* math is a primary factor fueling corruption at all levels. *High-level* political math determines who really makes the decision—authority, community, or liberty. *Elected official* math determines who politicians include in their calculations. *Government* math is the algebraic equation necessary for the wheels of governance to turn.

Yes-No Math

In the 1976 movie *All the President's Men*, when reporter Bob Woodward was trying to get to the bottom of the Watergate scandal, Deep Throat advised him to "follow the money."

The difference between *yes* and *no* on key political decisions can mean millions or billions of dollars to an industry. The difference between *yes* and *no* on key commercial decisions can mean thousands of jobs, along with their associated economic activity, pivotal to the success of political agendas. Both make it worth spending a lot for the preferred outcome—businesses on lobbyists to influence political decisions, governments to influence commercial outcomes. These stakes create conditions ripe for corruption.

In later chapters we will consider strategies for political contributions, policy development, grass-roots engagement (chapter 7), and engaging in spirited issues-focused campaigns in which each side wants to build the winning coalition that include political actors (chapter 12). Here we consider who politicians are and how they think. And, most importantly, how *not* to win politicians' affection: bribery, capture, bullying, or tilting the playing field.

Bribery

Yes, straightforward corruption of the sort where politicians receive kickbacks in exchange for their votes or assistance with administrative agencies exists in America. No, it is not endemic. In the end, our system of justice roots out these aberrations.

I was only too pleased to vote to expel Jim Traficant from Congress[8] and never met convicted lobbyist Jack Abramoff or received money from him. Four other members were convicted from my time in Congress: Republicans Bob Ney[9] and Duke Cunningham[10] and Democrats Frank Ballance[11] and William Jefferson.[12] Yet these represented less than 1 percent of Congress.

Even if another 1 percent of representatives were corrupt, the scale of their deceit is unlikely to meaningfully tilt the direction of significant proceedings. I suspect a comparable percentage of business leaders fall prey to greed. So long as we have a free media and independent judiciary, the effect of this type of fraud can be contained.

Capture

While most contributions to rank-and-file members have limited effect, the structure of committees and concentration of power in committee chairs and leadership, combined with the allure of compensation for employment following political service, do create conflicts of interest—and at times even capture. It's hard not to consider who might pay you a six- or seven-figure salary after your term of public service. This is particularly the case for committee chairs and leadership who wield significant power on the detailed wording of legislation upon which the rank-and-file vote.

Besides the prospects of a large future paycheck, committee chairs suffer further temptations. A requirement of obtaining and retaining their chairs is to raise boatloads of money to fuel party campaign committees. They receive most of this money from those who are regulated by their committees, which creates perverse incentives.

Further contributing to this incestuous relationship is that most committee members are from districts with significant interests related to their committees. Farm-state legislators dominate the Agricultural Committee. Those with big energy or technology employment in their districts often sit on the Energy and Commerce Committee. The Armed Services Committee is stacked with members with large defense plants in their districts.

These legislative tendencies create an inherent pressure to set the hen to guard the fox den. But pushing back hard is the threat of populist backlash against any legislative action viewed as too favorable to business. Many in public service are disciplined on this—they don't let thoughts of future employment sway them on a policy matter. But some are influenced by the pressures they receive from contributors, the statements they make in soliciting contributions, or hopes of future employment.

To limit this temptation, U.S. senators and cabinet members are prohibited from lobbying for two years after leaving office. U.S. representatives and senior congressional staff cannot lobby for one year.[13] I proposed a lifetime ban; no one would cosponsor me.[14] I think, over time, this approach would attract elected officials with skills other than political advocacy and diversify Congress. Sadly, even the shorter restrictions are often circumvented.[15]

Term limits on elected officials would only accelerate these revolving-door temptations. They would deprive legislatures of seasoned talent, making lawmakers even more dependent on guidance from outside interests.

Many believe the solution is to ban money in politics. The First Amendment makes this impossible in the United States. Efforts by reformers have made matters worse. Limiting contributions to candidates caused money to instead flow to the parties. Then, when the 2002 Bipartisan Campaign Reform Act (commonly called McCain-Feingold)[16] restricted contributions to the parties, money instead poured into super PACs. The result has been not less money but further movement away from requiring a candidate to say, "I'm Mark Kennedy and I approve of this message" and the balancing nature of the parties. Now political advertisements are more strident and narrowly focused on special interests.

These developments have complicated matters for corporations. Candidates are ping-pong balls buffeted by shrill, special-interest super-PAC advertisements with relatively less money available in their own campaign coffers to set their agendas. Public service has become less attractive for quality candidates, as they not only have less control over their messages but must answer to the public for ads run on their behalf over which they had no say. Electoral outcomes are more unpredictable. In addition, the multiplication of leadership committees and super PACs means more entities holding out their hands for corporate contributions.

This complicates ethical political engagement. As the saying in Washington goes, "If you don't have a seat at the table, you're on the menu." But when does your success in defining what is on the menu constitute crony capitalism, where the company and government officials both benefit, but the public suffers? To be more accurate, let's call it bank-shot cronyism. A legislator did not pocket a bribe, but his or her fund-raising prowess secured a plum political assignment. The legislator's conduct in that position then led to a high-paying, private-sector job.

Soon after I voted for a bill authorizing prescription drug coverage in Medicare that did not have as many cost-containment provisions as I would have liked, one of its chief architects left Congress and became the head of the top trade association and lobby group for the drug industry. Did this committee chairman fight as hard as he could have to ensure the public interest received its full due from the industry? It would be impossible to conclusively prove or disprove that both the chairman and the industry did or did not benefit greatly at the expense of taxpayers and seniors.

Contributions to invest in a seat at the table are perhaps appropriate, but never as a quid pro quo. It's okay for businesses to seek those with prior public service for their skills, which have lasting value, but less so to leverage their transient connections. Businesses should follow the spirit of the law when hiring former officials, not just its letter. When their employees assume public roles, businesses should refrain from any actions that would cause them to be conflicted.

Bullying

Revolving doors lead one to wonder whether a legislator was captured. Bullying occurs when organizations with enough political clout to matter make public threats. No single industry is unified enough or big enough to coerce the votes of any significant number of elected officials (though they may be able to co-opt powerful chairpersons). Any blatant attempt by a business would cause a backlash that would sink it.

While many outside groups have significant influence on specific issues, perhaps only two are considered by Congress members as powerful enough to influence the outcome of a primary. The National Rifle Association's influence caused the recall of two Colorado state legislators in 2013.[17] Unions have threatened retaliation against Democratic officials who support trade, a credible concern in many districts.

Writing on the Trade Promotion Authority (fast-track) in 2015, *Politico* reports, "The AFL-CIO was blunt in the call that went out to Rep. Scott Peters, a Democrat who represents San Diego: Vote yes on fast-track authority and the Trans-Pacific Partnership, people familiar with the conversation recall, and they'd spend a million dollars to knock him out in next year's primary."[18] Representing a port city, Peters felt he could ignore these threats.[19] When fast-track came to a vote in 2002 while I was in Congress, a Democratic member told me that he voted *no* only to avoid the consequences of the union's retribution in the primary.

Tilting the Playing Field

Let's consider conditions in which commercial decisions—adding jobs, embracing sustainability—are important to government, prompting politicians to extend benefits to companies. When does gaining such exemptions for your organization qualify as cronyism? How about gaining special favor for your industry? Did it benefit the public? Some cases are easy to assess, but many are complicated. Clearly these examples tilt the playing field—but do they do so legitimately?

- The National Electrical Manufacturing Association secured a ban on selling low-efficiency lightbulbs, thereby requiring customers to buy high-efficiency bulbs.[20]
- SolarCity designs, installs, and leases rooftop solar systems predicated on homeowners selling any solar energy they don't use back to their local electric company at advantageous rates set by the state.[21]
- The cost for New York City's $4 billion upgrade of LaGuardia Airport is split among public and private entities. Access to slots in such congested airports is restricted, often benefiting legacy airlines instead of low-fare carriers, and "perimeter rules" artificially restrict competition at LaGuardia.[22]
- In 2013 Washington State provided Boeing preferences with an estimated lifetime value of $8.7 billion to entice it to build its 777X plane in the state.[23]

- In the process of developing and selling more high-efficiency turbines, aircraft engines, and train locomotives, GE receives government incentives promoting such efficiencies. GE has received $837 million in subsidies since 2000.[24]

Accepting this government favor involves at least four risks.

Relegation Risk. With government cash comes government shackles. What the government subsidizes, it also regulates. Government largesse extracts much of the value from the commercial activity. Much of the money made from driving a taxi goes to pay off the government-auctioned medallion required to run a taxi—leaving little for the driver.[25] Farm subsidies fuel higher prices of farmland, creating value for investors but increasing costs for farmers who remain in the business.[26] Electrical manufacturers may find the same becomes true with high-efficiency lightbulbs.

Reversal Risk. If the government giveth, the government can also taketh away. In the battle of the billionaires, Warren Buffett's NV Energy utility successfully convinced Nevada's Public Utilities Commission to impose rules that made it uneconomical for those who've already signed up for panels leased from Elon Musk's SolarCity to sell their excess solar energy.[27]

Raise Risk. If you receive a benefit from your government, you provide legitimacy for other governments to support your competitors. What happens if they raise your bid? Government benefits received by Western airlines detract from their push to deny the Gulf's big three airlines—Emirates, Etihad Airways, and Qatar Airways—access to destinations in their regions because they've received excess government subsidies.[28]

Reputational Risk. Accepting government aid leaves companies open to attack. Activists will stir up public resentment if market shifts make it impossible for Boeing to deliver the jobs promised by locating a facility in Washington.

Are these examples of commendable public-private partnerships benefiting the public interest or examples of crony capitalism? Many of the innovations we benefit from today sprang from government-funded efforts like the Manhattan Project and the demands of World War II, the Cold War, and the battle against terrorism. Even M&Ms were invented to support the war effort: heat-resistant and easy-to-transport chocolate to be included in soldiers' rations.

A case can be made that the biggest challenges we face as a society require all hands on deck. Libertarians would answer that businesses should neither seek nor accept any benefits. Liberal environmentalists would say that all sustainability incentives are inherently justified. Who is right? Let me suggest that in addition to complying with standards that level the playing field determined by the World Trade Organization, differentiating between constructive collaboration and crony capitalism is measured by the balance of who benefits most.

Presumably public-private deals deliver benefits to a company's shareholders and to society. One can include social benefits, like reduced pollution, in calculating what society gets. If the net result of the partnership delivers more commercial profits than financial and social benefits to society, I suggest that the company is de facto a crony capitalist and should be sanctioned. If the benefits from the unified efforts tilt in favor of society, companies at least have justification for the incentive they received.

What about governments beyond the United States? How ought we act responsibly in environments where the promotion of crony capitalism is a central feature of the government?

High-Level Political Math: Authority, Community, or Liberty

High-level political math determines whether the media is a watchdog or lapdog of government, whether activists are allowed to exist,[29] whether the courts and regulatory bodies implement the rule of law or the rule of raj. If an authoritarian is in charge, he or she may try to place other shapeholders under his or her thumb. Democratic countries are split among those that incorporate authoritarian techniques, elevate community decisions, or embrace individual liberty.

• *Authority.* Political leaders need only look at Winston Churchill's ejection from office in 1945 after successfully leading the effort to save the country (may I suggest civilization itself) from the Nazis and compare it with the three generations of Kims in North Korea who have impoverished their country while enriching themselves, and they will see that dictatorial regimes are safer perches. These advantages to a leader have attracted those in all but the most mature democracies to employ authoritarian techniques.

Rachel Dawes explained the foundations for authoritarian power to Bruce Wayne in *Batman Begins* when describing crime chief Falcone: "As long as he keeps the bad people rich and the good people scared no one will touch him." Conducting business in authoritarian countries is troublesome—the government controls much of the economy and corruption controls much of the government. Crony capitalism is more the rule than the exception, often in the form of state-owned enterprises (SOEs), where distinctions between business and government are unclear.

Ensuring control of the media is an essential element for authoritarian success, an obstacle for companies the rulers believe to be in conflict with efforts to control public opinion. Don't expect to use Google, Facebook, or Twitter in China anytime soon. Moves to open or close come with little warning or explanation. In February 2016 China issued new rules that ban companies with any foreign ownership from engaging in online publishing. Two months later, Apple suspended its iBooks and iTunes movie services despite earlier accommodations to China in dropping from its Chinese catalog any apps involving the Dalai Lama or free-speech activists.[30] Without public notice, Alibaba's partnership to bring Disney characters to Chinese screens was suspended that same month,[31] even as Disney was in the process of opening Shanghai Disneyland.[32]

Authoritarian countries like China can pressure companies for access to Western technology to facilitate their climb up the economic value-added chain. While the Chinese government did little to police the black market in Microsoft products, it probed Microsoft's software distribution methods and prevented agencies from buying its products. In response, Microsoft set up a joint venture with an SOE that provides technology for Chinese military and civilian use.[33] A U.S. congressional report in 2012 effectively banned the purchase of networking equipment from Chinese telecommunications company Huawei over espionage fears.[34] This added legitimacy to a security justification for reviewing source code. Should a business risk intellectual property theft to comply with government mandates? IBM agreed to let China review some product source code, but only in a secure room.[35]

• *Community.* While the Anglo countries have a history of separating business and government, continental European countries have a history of close cooperation between business and government, and in Asia the roles of business and government have long been combined.

The rapid rise of Japan, South Korea, Taiwan, and Germany as they recovered from war saw close collaboration between business and government, including capacity-building foreign assistance from the United States and a concentrated focus on gaining market share globally in targeted industries. Power in these countries remains centralized in ministries that attract the best and the brightest. Other emerging economies have histories of strong state control of the economy, whether a military dictatorship until 1985 in Brazil or the red-tape Raj that controlled India.

While Anglo governments focus on regulating commercial excesses, community-governed countries unify society to achieve government-directed ends. It is no cultural accident that it was the United States that passed the Foreign Corrupt Practices Act (FCPA) to impose criminal penalties on businesses trying to influence governments. When it passed in 1977, Europeans said it was impractical, while Asians found it incomprehensible.

Navigating the shapeholder currents in community-governed countries requires understanding that the central administration retains significant involvement in economic matters. Legislatures are often subservient to direction from the central administration, and party discipline is exercised over individual legislators. This demands that companies preoccupy themselves with the national administration, act native as much as they can, and exercise care in avoiding FCPA violations.

- *Liberty.* "Money goes where it is treated best." This is why the world's leading financial centers evolved in countries that embrace Anglo standards—London, New York, Hong Kong, Singapore, and the westernized financial markets of Tokyo and Dubai. In liberty-centric democracies, elected officials are more independent from the party. This is why we must understand *elected official math*.

Elected Official Math

Elected officials are good at political math, otherwise, they wouldn't stay elected for long. Their formula is this: My primary voters must be greater than my opponent's primary voters. My general election voters must be greater than my opponent's general election voters. And my campaign money must be greater than my opponent's campaign money. Calibrating the algebraic dynamic between the three sections of this formula is unique to each official. How do officials add up their voters?

Peter or Paul?

When targeting segments of the population for an electoral majority, elected officials first decide whether they will be primarily aligned with Peter or Paul. The Irish playwright (and cofounder of the London School of Economics) George Bernard Shaw observed, "A government with the policy to rob Peter to pay Paul can be assured of the support of Paul." The French philosopher Voltaire wrote in 1764 that "the art of government consists of taking as much money as possible from one party of the citizens to give to the other."

The oversimplified dichotomies of Shaw and Voltaire belie a continuum of views on nearly every issue, yet the fault line between those with more and those with less has and always will be at the center of politics. Irrespective of the individual views of executives, the public often sees business as the classic Peter, a source of increased revenue, a giant to be constrained.

In business, the decision to invest in something—say, a new store or a piece of equipment—depends on whether it has a positive return on investment (ROI), whether the internal rate of return (IRR) exceeds the cost of capital, and whether it has a positive net present value (NPV). In politics, spending always has a positive ROI, IRR, and NPV from the perspective of the total electorate, because only a small percentage of the electorate pays the bills.

Determining how small a percentage pays how much of the taxes is a lesson in politics. As with anything in politics, each spot on the political spectrum will frame the answer in terms favorable to itself. If you are a conservative, you will seek your answer here from someplace like the National Taxpayers Union. If you want a liberal view, seek your answer from the Citizens for Tax Justice.

Taking the answer of who pays what in U.S. federal income taxes from the Tax Policy Center, a collaboration between the Urban Institute and Brookings Institute (both on the left) confirms that the top 20 percent of taxpayers pay 84 percent, while the bottom 60 percent pays 3 percent of the total.[36] Citizens for Tax Justice would say you should be looking at more than just federal income taxes, you should also consider state, local, and payroll taxes. Calculated in this way, the top 20 percent only pays 65 percent of all taxes of all types and the bottom 60 percent pays 17 percent of all taxes.[37]

Depending on how you calculate it, 80 percent of taxpayers pay either 16 percent (versus 84 percent paid by the top 20 percent in federal taxes) or 35 percent (versus 65 percent paid by the top 20 percent in total taxes) of all taxes. This reflects a similar concentration of income, but still proves that an overwhelming majority of the electorate are Pauls. Calculating taxes paid versus potential benefits received would imply that the vast majority of eligible voters would favor more government benefits.

In reality, this lopsided Paul vote is mitigated: while the vast majority of Peters are politically active, many Pauls do not vote. And their voting formula is more complex than simply benefits received minus taxes paid. The party of Peter also benefits from the fact that people are regularly told and to some extent believe that the rich do not pay their share of taxes, that they will somehow find a way to escape higher taxes, leaving the little guy with the bill.

In the United States, most consider Democrats to be the party of Paul. A recent Pew Poll showed an overwhelming majority believed Democrats "too often [see] government as the only way to solve problems."[38] And most view Republicans as the party of Peter. A similarly sized supermajority believed the party "is too willing to cut government programs even when they work."[39]

The Peter versus Paul alignment dictates where conservative and liberal parties align on foreign policy and social issues. If Peter represents the establishment and Paul represents those receiving fewer of the benefits of the current order, it stands to reason that Pauls are more likely to want to change the social order and to be less vested in defending it. Those politicians who garner the support of Paul by offering benefits face pressure not to take away Paul's butter to pay for guns. So the party of Peter generally contrasts itself with the party of Paul by emphasizing a strong national defense and traditional values.

Having aligned with Peter or Paul, elected officials must carefully assemble the remainder of the coalition of voters whose support they seek.

Define your Electoral Coalition

Politicians are like retailers whose store is only open one day every two, four, or six years, and whose currency is votes. Whether a policy is in the elected official's interest is not defined by financial analysis but by voters—and not just any voters, but voters in the official's district. A politician may value your opinion on an abstract, intellectual level but only really cares if you are from that politician's district or can influence that district. Then you have the politician's full attention. What makes sense for a politician is not what's logical or in the best interests of the country as a whole but what will lead to reelection. That is how the electoral system incentivizes politicians to act.

Their decision to align with Peter or Paul implies natural allies. With Paul come unions and certain natural demographic allies. With Peter come small business and different demographic allies. Those in Paul's camp can easily be beholden to the SEIU. Those in Peter's camp couldn't care less what the SEIU thinks, but would have a hard time crossing the NFIB (National Federation of Independent Businesses).

While some districts will tolerate deviation from the norm, the discipline of elected official math nearly always dictates positions on issues like life and guns. Each adds an increment to an official's electoral base. In most congressional districts in the United States, the party's primary contest is more threatening to an elected official than a general election. This imposes a discipline of its own not to stray from the party or ideological line too often. Witness how even though President Donald Trump seeks to appeal to both Paul (with his trade skepticism) and Peter (with his stances on corporate taxes and deregulation), he has adopted strong early stances on abortion and guns.

When looking for mutual interests between your business and any politician, it is best to understand a politician's calculus so you can assess whether you can be part of the equation.

Contributor Overlay

An essential element of elected officials spreading their messages to their voting blocks and blunting attacks by their opponents is attracting sufficient campaign donations. Most contributions are given to officials with whom the donors agree. Even so, while small-dollar donors can fuel the early stages of an insurgent campaign, most contributions come from wealthy individuals or companies. In addition to the corrosive effects we have discussed, contributions cause candidates of either party to temper the populist push for higher taxes on the rich and onerous regulation on commerce.

Political Roles

When assembling the coalition to make elected official math work, it is useful to understand how officials calculate success. Business-people who work with elected officials must understand the five roles [40] an official might embrace.

- "The Legislative Insider" focuses on taking committee assignments seriously and works effectively to pass legislation, hoping to someday become a committee chair.
- "The Party Insider" promotes the power and ideology of his or her own party and hopes for a party leadership post.
- "The Ombudsman" establishes a record as champion for local or state interests, perhaps hoping to run for governor.

- "The Statesman" does "what is right" for the country rather than what is politically expedient, and has his or her eye on the presidency, the vice presidency, a cabinet role, or a public policy position.
- "The Outsider" is a critic of the system or advocate of a single issue who seemingly only wants notoriety.

An official's chosen role will determine how receptive he or she is to policy positions and approaches.

Staff Perform Many of the Calculations

Many businesspeople complain to me that, when they attempted to talk to a senator or representative, they were relegated to staff in other offices and couldn't speak to the member. I tell them they are shortsighted. The member must approve significant actions, but staff members have a lot of discretion as to whether the office takes your issue and tries to advance it or not. If you treat staff as unimportant, they will treat you as unimportant.

Government Math

Now let's turn to government math. Each capital has its winning equations for achieving legislative success. Whether you want a bill to become law or not, you must know the numbers necessary for that to happen. For example, in Washington, D.C., the generic winning equation is this: $(2x + 1) + 218 + 60 + 1$.

$2x + 1$. Membership in most committees in the U.S. House and Senate are allocated by the proportion each party holds in the overall chamber, generating a relatively even split. Not so with the Rules Committee of the U.S. House. For the

Rules Committee, the majority has twice as many members as the minority party, plus one for good measure. This is the basis for the saying "Rules run the House." A vote rarely happens unless the Speaker wants it to occur. The committee also controls the time allotted and rules for debate.

218. With 435 members of the U.S. House, it takes 218 votes for a bill to pass. This rarely happens (and rarely does the Rules Committee allow an attempt) unless that 218 includes a majority of the majority party. While 218 members signing a discharge petition can bypass the Speaker and the Rules Committee, this is rare.

60. By tradition, the Senate needs sixty out of one hundred members to support a vote of cloture, an agreement to proceed to voting on the matter at hand, allowing a minority of only forty-one senators to block. This is often one of the most challenging hurdles. In matters that affect revenue, a simple majority can suffice if a disciplined party controls both chambers.

1. The President must sign the bill, or else Congress must have enough support to override a veto—a two-thirds vote in each chamber.

Each party in each chamber has whips who focus on crossing the required threshold or preventing others from crossing. The White House has legislative liaisons who do the same on matters of presidential priority.

The generic winning equation varies from country to country. In parliamentary systems, the executive, in the form of a prime minister or head of government, is always in line with the majority in the primary legislative body, though the role of the head of state varies widely. This may give the executive and the party more control over legislation. In community-governed nations, the bureaucracy has immense power. In dictatorships, the formula is simply 1. In party monopolies like in China, the number is either 1 or another single digit. We had better understand the formula for successfully engaging government wherever we conduct business.

Once the politicians complete their work, regulators put laws into action. Their work is so complicated, varied, and often opaque that it is difficult to summarize as an equation.

KEY TAKEAWAYS

- Political math determines who politicians pay special attention to, how they interact with one another, and how they make decisions. Each political leader factors individual businesses and other shapeholders into his or her equation. They have your number. It is important you have theirs.
- There are four levels of political math.
- *Yes-no* math is a primary factor fueling corruption at all levels.
  - Companies are advised to exercise discipline in: seeking a seat at the table, but never quid pro quo; leveraging former public service skills, not their transient connections; complying with the spirit of the law when hiring former officials, not just its letter; and refraining from any actions that would cause a conflict for former officials who enter public service.
  - Companies that participate in public-private partnership must carefully weigh the risks involved—*relegation risk* when government restrictions squeeze profits from the transaction; *reversal risk* from ebbing political fortunes; *raise risk* from another government being more generous to a competitor; and *reputational risk* if the course of events prevents commitments being fulfilled.
  - Public-private partnerships should benefit society more than the company to avoid charges of crony capitalism.
- *High-level* political math determines who really makes the decision—authority, community, or liberty.
- *Elected official* math determines who politicians include in their calculations.
- *Government* math is the algebraic equation necessary for the wheels of governance to turn.

5

Regulators

The reality is that zero defects in products plus zero pollution plus zero risk on the job is equivalent to maximum growth of the government plus zero economic growth plus runaway inflation.
—DIXIE LEE RAY, WASHINGTON GOVERNOR

THERE IS A LATIN PHRASE, *nam homo proponit, sed Deus disponit*—"man proposes, but God disposes." In Washington, a parallel developed: "the president proposes, Congress disposes." I heard fellow members of Congress say this several times when the president proposed something they disagreed with and intended to alter during the legislative process. But I think the truth goes further: Congress disposes and the bureaucracy transposes, often changing Congress's intention into something completely different. Congress's penchant for kicking the can down the road means that legislation often includes a mere outline for action, which allows regulators to fill in the blanks. This gives regulators great leeway in shaping opportunities available to businesses.

The U.S. Dodd-Frank financial regulation shows the shaping power of regulators. As the *Economist* laments, "At 848 pages, it is 23 times longer than Glass-Steagall, the reform that followed the Wall Street crash of 1929. Worse, every other page demands that regulators fill in further detail. Some of these clarifications are hundreds of pages long."[1]

Multivariate Regulatory Environment

There are so many variables involved in regulatory math that it is impossible to capture it in a formula. Regulations occur at multiple levels of government in every jurisdiction in which a company operates. Each must be attended to.

Carefully construed, prudent regulation can protect responsible businesses from less scrupulous operators in their industries or in other industries. That is why health insurers want tougher rules for medical devices in the United States, "citing regulatory gaps exposed . . . when a tool used for decades in hysterectomies was found to spread cancer"[2] and thus exposing insurers to serious claims.

Federal regulations protect against a hodgepodge of regulations between states or companies. Industry pushed for an update of the Toxic Substances Control Act, administered by the EPA, in hopes of quelling environmental and health-safety activists' efforts to persuade big retail chains and state and local governments to set their own standards.[3]

France's BNP Paribas found out the hard way that you must pay attention to more than your home country's regulations. They incurred an $8.9 billion fine in 2014 from the U.S. Justice Department for violating U.S. sanctions against Sudan, Cuba, and Iran.[4]

Sometimes regulators work against one another. The U.S. Federal Communications Commission (FCC) halted construction for a year on elements required to meet a congressionally mandated deadline for installing positive train control overseen by the Federal Railroad Administration (FRA).[5]

Sometimes they seamlessly coordinate across borders. Five of the world's biggest banks were fined $6 billion for allegedly manipulating foreign exchange markets in an agreement involving multiple regulators in the Switzerland, the United Kingdom, and the United States.[6]

Anyone who has seen the regulatory process close up knows that the regulations can cripple business, especially when crafted by those with animosity toward business or a misunderstanding of commerce.

Adding to the rules crafted by those who don't trust businesses are companies that affirm this distrust by seeking special language to their own advantage. The producer of Netflix's *House of Cards* series secured $11.5 million in unplanned tax credits from Maryland governor Martin O'Malley to film the third season in the state.[7] This was on top of $26 million received for the first two seasons. A study by Maryland's Department of Legislative Services found only 10 cents of benefits to the state for every dollar granted in such tax credits.[8]

And sometimes poorly crafted regulations are rushed through to appease populist rage. The fury of the masses may be transient, yet the effect of the shackles lasts. Big banks can afford the lawyers and accountants necessary to decipher the many provisions of the Dodd-Frank financial regulations passed in 2010 in response to outrage over the financial panic of 2008. Yet it imposes a "too small to succeed" burden on smaller banks, hampering their ability to lend to small businesses, thereby limiting their ability to drive job growth. Dodd-Frank's clumsy effort to address those "too big to fail" by harnessing the Federal Reserve's ability to be a lender of last resort will backfire according to Hal Scott, a professor at Harvard Law School and author of *Connectedness and Contagion: Protecting the Financial System from Panics*.[9] Scott argues that investors will be quicker to panic, knowing the impotence of the Fed, making the repeat of 2008 more likely and more disastrous.[10]

Because of all of the above, active attention to regulators who wield power in your business domain is of the utmost importance.

Regulators' Interests

What do regulators want? Each regulatory body in the U.S. federal government (the EPA, the FCC, the FRA, the Securities and

Exchange Commission) is primarily composed of careerists who are protected from political influence by civil service laws. The civil service was established to abolish the *spoils systems*, under which political victors extended federal jobs to their friends, supporters, and associates. To be overtly political in the civil service is abnormal, even though public-sector employee unions are actively engaged in political campaigns.

Civil service involves a competitive exam and highly prescribed criteria for review and promotion. Those who choose this profession are motivated to follow a narrow and well-described path toward promotion. Regulators get ahead based largely on how well they regulate from a regulator's perspective.

There are a select number of political appointees in each regulatory body in the United States, often requiring Senate approval. Political appointees are less common in other countries. In the United States, these officials are primarily tasked with advancing the president's policy agenda. While appointed officials can navigate the labyrinth of rules and layers in a regulatory body, their influence over the decisions of careerists is purposely limited. This is particularly true in a Republican administration. It is rare to find career bureaucrats attracted to a small-government philosophy. During Republican administrations, their approach is often to "wait out" the political appointees.

Do They Understand Business?

Those who view business as a force for good are more likely to choose business as a career, and those who view government as a force for good are more likely to choose government as a career. It is only natural that those who work in the governmental bureaucracy see more government as beneficial.

Within the bureaucracy, a sense for what it takes to nurture a vibrant business community is uncommon. When I was in

Congress, I attended a reception in 2002 at Johnny's Half Shell restaurant close to the Capitol. I struck up a conversation with someone who had been regulating coal mines for a dozen years. He told me, "Someday I would like to visit a coal mine."

Do not expect regulators to have a detailed understanding of what drives your business, what pressures you face, and the strategic imperatives to which you must respond. They are not likely to carefully balance pursuit of the regulatory intent with the need to ensure a vibrant economy that can generate the types of careers that will sustain and fulfill a country's citizens.

Applying pressure from the administration, legislative action, or the courts has some effect, but it is usually indirect and time-consuming. I have found the best path is normally to bury yourself in the regulations themselves and the regulatory mind-set and work the process as best you can.

Regulatory Capture

What happens when regulators get too close to those they regulate? This is called *regulatory capture*. The paradox of regulation is that the more complex it becomes, the more likely regulatory capture will occur—because industry can afford to hire the most highly skilled, often with regulatory experience.

Consider the 2010 Deepwater Horizon disaster when an explosion on BP's oil rig killed eleven crew members, sank the rig, and caused the largest offshore oil spill in U.S. history. More than 200 million gallons of crude oil were pumped into the Gulf of Mexico. Untold damage was done to the marine, fishing, and tourism industries along the Gulf Coast. In an example of capture, regulators prior to the disaster were "taking oil companies at their word when they claimed to have the capability to cope with worst-case deep-sea drilling catastrophes," thus allowing BP to remain unprepared for massive oil spills.[11]

Getting extremely close to regulators may seem ideal, but over time it always comes to naught. Izzet Garih, chairman of Alarko Holding, a leading developer in Turkey, once told me a story about the relationship between business and political officials in Turkey. His father, Uzeyir Garih, had been a friend of Suleyman Demirel, later the prime minister of Turkey, when they attended Istanbul Technical University. Even though they had known each other since university, Garih maintained a politely distant relationship, visiting Demirel occasionally, but not too often.

At one meeting the prime minister complimented Garih's wise approach toward his relationship with government officials. Demirel said that businesspeople ought to treat government like a fireplace. If you are too far away, you will be cold. If you get too close, you may burn.

This completes our review of shapeholders. Now let's consider how best to engage them.

KEY TAKEAWAYS

- Regulatory math is the most complicated of all, because it occurs at multiple levels of government in every jurisdiction in which a company operates.
- In advanced democracies, regulators are motivated to follow a prescribed path toward promotion based on how well they regulate as judged from a regulator's perspective.
- Regulators often lack detailed understanding of the industries they regulate and are disposed to view more government intervention as positive.
- Pressure from the administration, legislative action, or the courts has some effect, but it is usually indirect and time-consuming.
- It is vital to retain expertise in every jurisdiction with regulatory authority over the company. That expertise must include being informed on the regulations themselves, the regulatory mind-set, and how best to engage in the process without falling prey to regulatory capture.

Seven Steps to Shapeholder Success

WE HAVE SEEN THE dangers of not incorporating the concerns of shapeholders into your strategic decision making. So how is it best done?

Managers have so many responsibilities when they chart the course of their businesses that they often leave out important considerations or delay timely actions. This is particularly the case when engaging shapeholders—they are unfamiliar to many businesspeople, they typically travel in different circles, and business incentives drive a short-term focus that leaves longer-term shapeholder concerns beyond the horizon.

To help, I will outline the "seven steps to shapeholder success," all beginning with the letter *A*—steps that take a long-term view of the best path. The first set of *A*'s—align, anticipate, and assess—define how to position yourself alongside shapeholder actions.

- *Align.* A company must align itself with the goal of delivering profit *and* social benefit. Effective engagement requires credibility with shapeholders. Given the history of businesses engaging non-market forces tactically, even disingenuously, there is understandable skepticism to overcome. So to establish authenticity with shapeholders you must align your company with a purpose.

• *Anticipate.* It is critical to anticipate the concerns of shapeholders and possible nonmarket crises that may erupt. This not only prepares a company to fend off assaults by activists but can often shed light on how to eliminate vulnerabilities and address legitimate concerns. The key is to expect the unexpected. Along with exploring downside risks, a company should look out for upside opportunities to create shared value.

• *Assess.* For each issue that springs up, a company should assess the legitimacy of shapeholder claims and whether activism or collaborative efforts will prevail.

The second set of A's—advance, avert, acquiesce, and assemble—shows how to act in response to an attack from or opportunity offered by shapeholders.

When considering how to pick a strategy for addressing the different challenges and opportunities that shapeholders present, the "shapeholder decision matrix" is our guide. The key metrics come from the assess step: Is the claim legitimate? Is there an upside for the company?

• *Avert*: If we assess that the shapeholder claim is legitimate but there is no upside for the company, we should avert potentially negative outcomes by proposing solutions that address the legitimate claim.

• *Acquiesce*: If we face an illegitimate demand from a shapeholder that we cannot profitably rebut, it may make sense to acquiesce.

• *Advance*: In the case of a legitimate concern in which an upside exists for the company, we should advance shared interests.

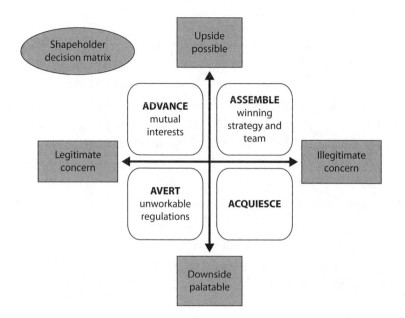

• *Assemble*: If the cost to acquiesce to an illegitimate issue is prohibitive, or the company believes it can prevail, it is best to assemble a coalition of allies with common cause to ensure success if a confrontation results. Succeeding in such face-offs requires optimizing why, what, where, who, how, and when. Businesses should do the same when industries or industry segments are engaged in political contests.

I dreaded coming home with a report card with anything other than straight As. But I will let you in on a little secret: my mother was a kittycat compared to the shapeholders who will call you out when you don't pay attention to each of these seven *A*'s. If you fail to prepare, prepare to fail.

Note that delaying these steps reduces the benefit of company action while increasing the penalty the company would incur if forced to act later. It is often a case of pay me now or pay me more later.

Guardrails, Not Ambulances

Too often businesspeople don't understand how vital it is to avoid conflict with shapeholders. Brian Mattes from the Vanguard Group told me that he advises his fellow executives, "I'd rather put up guardrails than line up ambulances at the bottom of the hill." The seven steps will identify the hills and steep curves in your operations and where to put up guardrails.

I think the challenge Western companies have is that they focus only on the last *A*—assembling for battle. We follow the Carl von Clausewitz approach to conflict: decisive battles seeking conclusive results. Effective shapeholder engagement requires embracing the Eastern thinking of Sun Tzu in *The Art of War*. Sun Tzu wrote, "The skillful leader subdues the enemy's troops without any fighting."

Integrated Strategy

Too often, shapeholder strategy is simply unfocused charitable activities and engaging with shapeholders as a nuisance, reflexively and insincerely. A company would not dream of launching a new product line without a plan that was well thought out and vetted at the highest levels of the company so that everyone knows what the company intends with this new line. But if a company wants to avoid shapeholder disruption, advance a trade agreement, or alter a regulation or debilitating tax, it often has no cohesive plan.

Clearly defined shapeholder strategy is vital in regulated industries, although shapeholders are increasingly active in all industries. And while they may not target your company specifically, they likely have significant influence over your customers or suppliers.

The importance of shapeholder strategy changes over time. The Internet at one time was nearly immune to government influence. Today, issues like privacy, taxation of e-commerce, and the protection of intellectual property have made shapeholder engagement critical to high-tech companies. Anticipating and influencing the direction of change in the shapeholder environment and capturing the opportunities it creates requires an integrated strategy.

We will consider the seven steps sequentially, although we should think of them as iterative. Constantly feeding back results of the later steps to refresh thinking when considering the first steps is essential. The coalition partners you must assemble to win should be included in efforts to build relations to anticipate developments in broader society.

Your strategic planning must include both playing to be remembered in the marketplace and writing the future by effectively engaging shapeholders in the nonmarket arena. The result of your plan to implement these seven steps to shapeholder success must integrate with your plan to succeed in the market. Shapeholder strategy is most successful when it aligns with and supports the market strategy so closely that it is hard to tell when shapeholder strategy ends and market strategy begins. Great power comes from an integrated strategy.

6

Align with a Purpose

If you lose your purpose . . . it's like you're broken.
—HUGO CABRET, THE MOVIE *HUGO*

THE PARADOX OF PROFIT says that if you seek, as Milton Friedman advocated, to maximize profit for your shareholders, you must pursue what benefits society as a whole. That twofold direction, which benefits a company's bottom line *and* society, is its purpose. Society imposes costs on businesses that do not provide social benefits and offers profitable opportunities to those who do. Businesses that ignore shapeholders risk the costly disruption that Nike faced over labor standards and, worse still, the fate of Arthur Andersen. They also miss opportunities to marshal shapeholder energy to propel them forward, like Starbucks and Whole Foods have done to their benefit.

An authentic purpose springs from a company's core competencies that drive its profits. This is the best path for your company—and society. When Nike promotes physical activity to combat obesity and Anheuser Busch InBev promotes clean water, each company and society are better off. As people become more fit, Nike sells more shoes and clothing. AB InBev needs clean water in the many nations around the world in which it operates to produce the beer it sells.

Align for Authenticity

Once your purpose is set, you must be devoted to achieving it by aligning your operations toward its fulfillment. My life has shown me the benefits of authenticity and the penalties of inauthenticity.

After graduating with my MBA from the University of Michigan, I joined the Corporate Development Department at Pillsbury. We gave code names to our acquisition targets so that our fellow workers would not know what company we were trying to buy. The code name for the first acquisition I worked on was "Overrun." Overrun refers to the amount of air that is injected into ice cream as it is being made. Yes, it's true. If you allow most ice cream to melt, the liquid will fill only part of the container. The fact that the entrepreneurial company in New Jersey we called Project Overrun did not inject air into its ice cream gave the product a creamy smooth taste that melted in your mouth. Let the ice cream melt, and it would fill up the container.

Others sold ice air-and-cream. Overrun's authenticity, that it sold *just* ice cream, was the secret to its success. That is the aim every company should strive for. That company's real name— Häagen-Dazs.

The purpose you define for yourself becomes the foundation on which your reputation rests. Do you have a reputation for selling air as ice cream or selling ice cream?

Reputation is earned by authentic actions, not by spin. My young son Charles enjoyed spending time in the toy and sporting goods departments of ShopKo stores after his Little League games while I did unscheduled inspections as an executive of the company. As we drove home one afternoon, Charles said, "You know, retail is just like baseball. Every day you start zero to zero.

Even though the people were happy with you yesterday, if you don't perform today, you do not win. You have to win every day."

Charles's words are true not just about baseball and retail. They apply to how businesses should engage with shapeholders. Every employee, every day, must engage with shapeholders consistent with the company's commitments and purpose. Reputation is like a fine crystal vase—it takes a long time to build, but seconds to break.[1]

BP found this out the hard way. After having unfurled a new global brand motto, Beyond Petroleum, with much fanfare a decade earlier, an explosion on BP's Deepwater Horizon oil rig on April 20, 2010, killed eleven and caused the largest offshore oil spill in U.S. history. The world's attention was fixed on the immense damage inflicted on nature and the fishing and tourist industries along the Gulf Coast.

The year of the spill, the company's brand was removed from the index of the world's hundred most valuable brands. Julian Dailly, director of valuation at Interbrand London, described the ratings fall: "BP failed to execute on the standards they talked so proudly about in the press and the majority of the company's brand value has been destroyed as a result."[2] Its brand deteriorated so far that activists protested the Tate Art Museum in London for accepting contributions from BP.[3]

When a judge approved a $20 billion settlement relating to claims from the spill in 2016,[4] reflecting just part of the $56.4 billion BP had set aside to cover costs related to the disaster,[5] BP's misstep was still hurting its reputation. Reports blaming the spill for baby dolphins dying[6] and a movie entitled *Deepwater Horizon* kept the story of BP's misdeed alive.[7]

What a mess. BP found out the hard way that saying one thing and doing another leads to charges like greenwashing and leaves you worse off. The intense response to the inconsistencies between BP's statements and it actions proves the general public has seen this movie several times before.

Align to Avoid Mission Creep

How can a company's purpose align with its market strategy in a way that delivers social good but keeps it from being society's ATM?

A logistics company's market strategy was to be the best in the world at affordably delivering freight—rain or shine—in a timely manner. Society benefits from the low costs and more reliable access to goods and services this company provides. The company defines its purpose as "improving people's lives through affordable and timely freight delivery."

A global foundation brought together this logistics company and NGOs to map out a strategy for helping people in need during natural disasters. The logistics firm agreed during the meeting that it would help streamline the process by optimizing the logistical flow of relief through available airports and roads—even when damaged or of insufficient scale. By applying its expertise in this area, the logistics firm brought more aid to more people, saving lives.

Even though the logistics firm had agreed to help, a representative from an NGO was angry with the logistics firm, because it would not say that the firm's purpose was to save lives. The logistics company was obviously happy to save lives, but there are many other ways the firm could work toward that goal—funding food for starving children, providing clean water for those without it, or supplying maternal health care in impoverished regions. If the firm were to define its purpose as "saving lives," it would obligate itself to contribute its resources to every such proposal, even if the effort had not even a remote connection to the company's capabilities and strategy.

It makes sense for a food company to have a purpose that includes feeding starving children or for a water systems company to have a purpose that includes providing drinking water to all or for a health-care provider to have a purpose including bringing maternal health care to impoverished regions. But it doesn't make sense to expect any of those things from a logistics company.

Rather, the logistics firm's aim should be to engage with society in ways that mesh with and support its market strategy and purpose. It can improve people's lives by delivering freight (relief) in a timely manner during disasters (saving lives). And because this activity is consistent with the firm's market strategy, it can deliver this benefit to society and keep its shareholders happy. Its good works would also, as Plato wrote, "inspire good actions in others," in five different ways:

- Good press highlighting the company's core capability could generate sales.
- Greater brand loyalty, especially with those prospective future customers in the disaster region it helped, could generate sales.
- Better-trained employees, seasoned by the high-stress challenges of disaster relief, could lead to better customer service.
- Better employee engagement fights turnover.
- Better standing with members of society would make the company a more attractive partner to carrot activists, a less attractive target to stick activists, and a citizen in good standing when seeking government approval for things like the construction of logistics facilities.

And here's the best part: society is better off when each company does good within its own market. This is basic economics—the law of comparative advantage. Each company has specific, local knowledge of its market that other companies, working in other markets, don't have. That knowledge allows it to do good more effectively and more efficiently in its area of expertise. So the greatest good is accomplished when each company focuses its philanthropic efforts on its own market. Why should a company get caught up in everyone else's business?

All these by-products could lead to higher profits, Friedman's aim for businesses. At a minimum, they help the company deliver the kinds of benefits society demands in the most cost-efficient manner.[8]

Defining a Differentiating and Actionable Purpose

Many companies already have statements that describe their market strategies. Some describe how their actions benefit society. Too few companies have a purpose or mission statement that unifies the two—market strategy and social benefits.

In *Made to Stick*, Chip and Dan Heath[9] outline how it is essential to communicate in a way that guides action. That is the role of a purpose statement. The authors contrast Disney calling its employees "cast members" and Subway calling its employees "sandwich artists." The first works, the latter not so much.

Disney auditions its cast members for a role because it wants employees to realize they are *onstage* whenever they are in the park; park visitors are *guests*, not customers; and cast members' jobs are *performances* and their uniforms are *costumes*. This contributes to the magic we know as Disney. Subway really does not want its employees to infuse individual artistic expression into the sandwiches they make.

Volkswagen (VW) took a $7.27 billion charge to earnings and lost $26 billion in market value two days after the EPA alleged the company used software to circumvent emission standards.[10] Both numbers are billions, with a *b*. Ouch. Review the closest thing VW had to a purpose statement[11] at the time of its stumble and you can easily predict the shapeholder calamity.

The first line is filled with platitudes like "beneficial for everyone." The second line says, "As we see it, advancing digitization is not a threat but a major opportunity that we aim to and indeed will leverage." Leverage for what? VW seized the "opportunity" to "leverage" "digitization" to sanitize its EPA reporting and discovered that its idealization of "digitization" could be a "threat." Its statement is well engineered but should be more actionable and directional to VW's employees.

The first three press releases listed on VW's "Sustainability and Responsibility" Web page immediately following the revelation of its digital duplicity on emission standards compliance addressed the company's efforts to expand its digital capabilities. It seems Google wants to be a car company in its drive to invent a driverless car, and VW wants to be Google.

A casual observer could easily get the impression that the VW translation for "purpose" is "digitization." That makes it a bit easier to understand how someone at VW could have even thought about taking a proactive step to deliver compliance with EPA standards through digital deception. Did VW's preoccupation with all things digital distract it from delivering environmentally responsible automobiles?

If VW had better aligned with an actionable purpose statement that focused more on the benefits delivered (sustainable mobility) and less on the process (digitization), it might have avoided this massive blow to its reputation with customers and shapeholders alike.

Crafting a purpose is a three-step process:

1. *Define Market Strategy.* A clear purpose relies on a clearly defined market strategy. This is a vitally important step. The degree to which you seek and actually achieve a position as the best in the world permits a stronger purpose statement. The world is so global and competitive that few can survive without targeting a combination of product offerings, customer segments, geographies, and operational capabilities that allow it to be the "best" choice for someone, somewhere, somehow for something.

Those who rely on government putting its hands on the scales—through subsidies or protectionist measures—have a harder time making the case that they are benefiting society. To be the best at what you do is not only good market strategy, but it improves your credibility with shapeholders, enabling a virtuous circle. A stronger purpose statement based on your strategy to be the best engenders shapeholder support by asking society for less but offering more. This helps you be the best.

2. *Assess Benefits and Harms.* List all of the positive and negative effects that achieving your business strategy has on society and delineate how you can maximize the benefits and minimize the pains. A survey of executives showed that little more than half believed large corporations made a positive contribution to the public good. The other half was divided between believing big companies' effect on the public good was neutral or negative.[12] This starkly demonstrates that companies must do better in identifying and promoting their social benefits.

3. *Purpose Statement.* Finally, reach consensus on which purpose that maximizes social benefits best aligns with your market strategy. That's your purpose.

Once you have the substance of your purpose, you need an effective purpose statement. I am constantly looking out for real-world examples of organizations claiming a purpose, and I have seen four types: (1) platitudinal, (2) pedestrian, (3) a bridge too far, and (4) differentiating, all of which I discuss below.

Platitudinal

These purpose statements are so general that they don't really provide direction, are outside the influence of the company, or both. They are of little value.

Sometimes highly diversified companies struggle to form anything other than a general statement. Samsung's businesses span "advanced technology, semiconductors, skyscraper and plant construction, petrochemicals, fashion, medicine, finance, hotels, and more." It maintains it is "making a better world."[13] It is hard to get more diversified than Samsung, and it is hard to get more platitudinal than "making a better world" (or VW's reference to being "beneficial for everyone").

Whether you consider Apple's goal to "push the human race forward" and Samsung Electronics' goal to "inspire the world, create the future"[14] platitudinal or differentiating depends on whether you believe their products are accomplishing these ends.

When I was dining at the Hard Rock Cafe in Shanghai in 2007, their front entrance was emblazoned with a sign reading: No Drugs or Nuclear Weapons. These are worthy goals, but perhaps too lofty—certainly for Hard Rock Cafe.

Pedestrian

These purpose statements *are* achievable and align with the business strategy, yet they either do not understandably define how society is better off or focus on a benefit the company is not uniquely positioned to deliver. Too often they are little more than advertising slogans, rather than differentiating purposes. Some examples of advertisements I have seen recently:

- Sealy—We Support the Backbone of America. But what is the benefit?
- Pepsi—Every Pepsi Refreshes the World. Perhaps a bit of an overreach, and how does it distinguish itself from Coca-Cola?

- Directski.com—"I want to bring affordable skiing to the people . . . the rest of the world is Bono's problem." A quote attributed to founder Anthony Collins.

A Bridge Too Far

These purpose statements are impossible or extremely hard to achieve and leave the company open to accusations of insincerity, or "greenwashing," as we saw with the Beyond Petroleum purpose statement. If you advance such a purpose statement, you'd better deliver. Expect the purist to pick at any inconsistencies in your actions.

Differentiating

Differentiating statements hit the sweet spot. They articulate a goal of expanding the social benefits that come from achieving a firm's market strategy in a manner they are uniquely positioned to deliver. So how do we suss out a differentiating purpose?[15]

- *Nurturers.* These companies are innovative providers of products or services essential to nurturing society. The big challenge these companies face is competition from nonprofit organizations or charities. This demands especially sharply focused purpose statements.

  UnitedHealth Group: "Helping people live healthier lives and helping make the health system work better for everyone [by embracing] our values of integrity, compassion, relationships, innovation and performance every day, in everything we do." UHG's embrace of innovation has been a source of profits for itself and more affordable, higher-quality healthcare outcomes for society.

• *Accelerators.* These companies help governments deliver public goods better, cheaper, and faster. Or they help companies accelerate their sustainability goals or deliver government-supported services more efficiently.

ABB Group's (a Swedish-Swiss robotics and power automation company) commitment to "power and productivity for a better world" is exemplified by examples of "Cut CO_2 emissions by 180 tons a year? Absolutely" and "Cities that consume 30 percent less energy? Certainly."

• *Transformers.* These companies advance disruptive innovation that empowers individuals and businesses to achieve their personal goals.

Cisco: "Impact X. We give people skills to thrive in a connected world, empowering them to be global problem solvers and speed the pace of social change. That's impact multiplied."

• *Exemplars.* These companies exemplify a specific attribute of social benefit.

Cargill: Food security. "Helping the world thrive."

• *Builders.* These companies focus on building the communities in which they operate.

US Bank: "Actively engaged in developing, strengthening and energizing our communities. Individually and together, we live our brand. It's all of US serving you."

• *Uplifters.* These companies give us a boost, help us think happy thoughts, inspire us to achieve great things.

Disney: "Promote the happiness and well-being of kids and families by inspiring them to join us in creating a brighter tomorrow."

Some companies that could clearly define an animating purpose statement seem content with reciting views on social engagement—ethics, community, compliance, diversity, governance, health, safety, sustainability, and workplace. These are essential components of responsible behavior. But by failing to enunciate a unifying purpose statement, these companies fail to harness the power of such statements to motivate positive behavior by all associated with the company.

Focus Public Affairs on Your Purpose

Any seasoned businessperson knows that working outside your core competencies is suboptimal at best. But businesspeople rarely apply the same standard to their engagement with shapeholders. The acid test of whether your efforts to engage are succeeding is whether those efforts sell more soap. When Unilever sponsors a series of art exhibits at the Tate Modern Museum in London, will it sell a lot more of its Persil or OMO soap?

In contrast, its competitor, Procter & Gamble's Tide brand, contributes to society by sending specially designed trucks requiring little water to do laundry for those who find themselves temporarily homeless in areas of natural disaster. There's no water, but everything is dirty. Will P&G sell more soap because of these actions? I wouldn't be surprised if generations stayed loyal to Tide, remembering how P&G helped grandma and grandpa in their hour of need.

Apple shows how sponsoring exhibits in art museums can "sell more soap." Artistic appeal became even more essential when Apple's product ranges began to include watches in 2015. With the better sales potential for Apple Watch clearly in mind, Apple sponsored the Metropolitan Museum of Art's exhibit at its Costume

Institute entitled *Manus* × *Machina: Fashion in an Age of Technology*. This exhibit showcased that designs can result from craftsmanship and automation alike, handsewn or computer modeled and 3D printed. This established a certain amount of desirability for the new Apple Watch and was one of the Met's best-attended exhibits.[16]

These examples show how public affairs aligned with a company's purpose can benefit a company's bottom line and broader society. To maximize an organization's benefit to society and attractiveness to allies, it is essential that an organization's public affairs be tightly aligned with its purpose.

To say that you should focus your public affairs and corporate social responsibility (CSR) efforts on your purpose does not mean there are good charities or bad charities. Nearly every charity aligns with some company's purpose. Both charities and companies are better off if they have shared interests. Companies are less likely to cut these activities in tough times, leading to stable revenue for the charity. And shared purpose may lead to opportunities for the company and charity to collaborate.

Put Your Purpose Center Stage

A purpose is worthless unless you truly and publicly embrace it. It isn't worth anything if you hide it under a basket. You can give meaning to all of your activities by connecting them to your purpose. This will form a lasting impression of your company, one that connects your company with good works. There is a growing list of standards for CSR reporting. Follow them, but do more. Put it in product. Put it in your advertisements. Most importantly, put it in your actions to ensure you are not subjected to charges of being inauthentic.

Those companies that have put purpose center stage have reaped the benefits. For example, because the design of the Prius shouted out "Hybrid!," Toyota has sold three times as many hybrids as every other manufacturer combined.[17] Many consumers want to be *conspicuously* environmentally friendly and are attracted to the Prius.

I frequently assign my students the task of finding and evaluating a company's purpose statement. One metric I assign them is this: How many clicks from their website's home page did it take to find a purpose statement? The best at this metric, like ABB and Cargill, have their purpose statements next to their company names at the top of every page on their websites. Other commendable companies like Ecolab and Pfizer have their purpose statements on their home pages. But too many companies have a purpose statement buried deep on their websites or totally indiscernible.[18]

Advertisements that ran during the 2015 Super Bowl reflected themes with a social aim. On the surface these ads seem completely altruistic. Deeper examination reveals that they reflect companies embracing purposes for their businesses that benefit both the bottom line and society.

Super Bowl ads are the most expensive of all. That companies let their purpose shine during these pricey ads confirms that engaging society and shapeholders is the best way for a company to differentiate itself.

Consider three examples of companies on offense by showcasing their purpose statements during the Super Bowl:

Coca-Cola   #MakeItHappy. Coke is working hard to associate drinking or sharing one of its products with happiness and happy people. It promoted that image by addressing the negative, often insulting tone of many social media posts. The ad shows the happy consequences of changing the prevailing sentiment on the Internet from "No one likes you" to "There is no one like you."

Microsoft   #Empowering. Estella's Brilliant Bus is focused on giving disadvantaged children the chance to experience how they can use technology "to do more and achieve more." As they learn how to apply technology to improve their own opportunities, their proficiency with Microsoft products improves Microsoft's opportunities.

Procter & Gamble Always #LikeAGirl. P&G took advantage of a heavily male audience to change attitudes toward young women. Empowering women is central to the brand promise of Always. P&G promoting healthier views toward women is highly appealing to women, the primary consumers of their products.

Embrace your purpose and others who share that purpose will embrace you.[19]

Shapeholder Engagement Must Be CEO Led

Lord Browne was clearly enthralled by the creative wordsmith who came up with BP's Beyond Petroleum slogan, but he neglected to align the rest of the company to the slogan. The spill in the Gulf of Mexico made it clear that BP was first and foremost a petroleum company, and an undisciplined one at that. BP is a prime example of how a company that makes a commitment to the public without aligning every function in the company often finds itself two steps behind, rather than one ahead.[20]

Fulfilling external commitments is more easily said than done. It often requires companies to change their operations. Committing without change would be inauthentic. It is essential that a company only make external commitments that have the full backing of a well-informed CEO who avoids the temptation to overreach. Only the CEO can weigh the benefits and costs of shapeholder engagement strategies, ensure their fulfillment, and guide the alignment of social engagement with company capabilities.

Shapeholder engagement is trickier to navigate than the market. Rather than buyers and sellers voluntarily engaging in exchange, you face a multitude of actors, each with different motivations, governed by things like majority rule, due process, and public access—and all can sway public opinion, government, or the courts to force businesses to act. The trade-offs necessary to make sound decisions with this much complexity require general manager leadership.

Effective engagement with shapeholders means integrating the planning and execution of strategies for market success and shapeholder engagement. This requires CEO leadership. The combined strategy should then be applied to the respective market and shapeholder environments with great care to keep them aligned during execution.

Take Walmart, for example. Because Sam Walton only focused on customers and suppliers, Walmart became the prime target of environmental activists. Under Lee Scott's leadership Walmart responded to the assault by outside forces by becoming the environmentalist's hero, enforcing strong environmental standards on its suppliers. The approach toward shapeholders set by Sam Walton was unsustainable, but Walmart's successful engagement with shapeholders under Lee Scott kept it alive.

Uber put shapeholders on edge when, while the company was facing allegations that its drivers sexually assaulted female passengers in New Delhi and other cities,[21] a 2014 article in *GQ* magazine suggested that there was minimal screening of Uber drivers and portrayed Uber cofounder and CEO Travis Kalanick like this:

> Kalanick probably wasn't the first kid in his class to lose his virginity. But the way he talks now—which is large—he's surely making up for lost time. When I tease him about his skyrocketing desirability, he deflects with a wisecrack about women on demand: "Yeah, we call that Boob-er."[22]

It is small wonder that Uber faced pushback from shapeholders as it rolled out around the world.

When managers formulate strategy to engage shapeholders, they may draw on the expertise of lawyers, communications specialists, representatives in leading capitals, and community relations specialists. The complexity and trade-offs require the direct involvement and oversight of general management. It is shortsighted for managers to be hands-off with their government affairs function and view them only as a stopgap to keep bad things from happening. CEOs instead should engage in shapeholder relations with the goal of not only avoiding bad things but also proactively shaping the future in a positive direction through effective collaboration.

Align All Operations Toward Fulfillment of Commitments

Activists will hesitate to commit unless the CEO plants his or her flag on their shared issue. And they will expect follow-through on commitments. Every company operation must align toward fulfilling external commitments.

As General Mills found out, you must not only address every piece of your operations under normal conditions but also consider contingency operations as well. A disruption in rail service to its plant in Lodi, California, necessitated using contract trucks in the fall of 2015. Then a little wheat in a contract truck caused a recall of gluten-free Cheerios. How could they recover and build trust with those highly sensitive to gluten and the activists who cater to them? To General Mills's credit, they caught it early, responded quickly, and the head of their U.S. cereal business personalized their regret for the matter in a company blog post.[23]

Staffing/Resource Implications

Aligning a company toward fulfilling a united purpose under CEO leadership requires the CEO to manage those charged with engaging shapeholders, a tight coordination among all functions interfacing with shapeholders, and a seamless integration of shapeholder strategy with a company's marketing strategy.

It is a mistake to parcel out communications, PR, CSR, community relations, and government relations as disparate functions. Ideally these activities should be unified under a C-suite executive who reports to the CEO.

A dispersion of these functions, burying them lower in the organizational chart or under a function that is not primarily outward facing (like human resources), reflects a company that is not taking shapeholders seriously. When it hits its first major confrontation with shapeholders, leadership will wake up.

Having a communications or PR executive and a government or external affairs executive reporting to different people is equally dangerous. If a CEO views the world primarily through the lens of the news of the moment, there is a heavy temptation to sugarcoat the message or commit to more than a company can deliver. Like BP, you may enjoy a short-term high of public adulation only to crash hard later.

Being authentically aligned toward fulfilling our purpose is just the first step in effectively engaging shapeholders. We next turn to understanding how to anticipate the opportunities and threats they present.

KEY TAKEAWAYS

- The paradox of profit says that to maximize profit for your shareholders, you must pursue this goal in parallel with benefiting society as a whole. That combined direction, which benefits a company's bottom line *and* society, is its purpose.
- An authentic purpose springs from a company's core competencies that drive its profits—Nike promoting physical activity and benefiting from selling more shoes and clothing.

- Promoting a purpose like BP's Beyond Petroleum without the ability to deliver on the expectations of social actors can harm a company's reputation.
- A well-designed purpose can help a company avoid mission creep in its social engagement.
- Crafting a differentiating purpose is a three-step process: (1) define your market strategy; (2) assess how your company benefits and harms society; and (3) agree on a purpose statement that maximizes social benefits in a way that best aligns with your market strategy.
- Seek to move beyond a platitudinal, pedestrian, or "bridge too far" statement to find a truly differentiating purpose that articulates a goal of expanding the social benefits that come from achieving a firm's market strategy in a manner it is uniquely positioned to deliver.
- Organizations benefit from putting their purpose center stage and aligning all their public affairs activities toward that purpose.
- It is essential that a company only makes external commitments that have the full backing of a well-informed CEO who avoids the temptation to overreach.
- General management must oversee the integration of the planning and execution of strategies for market success and shapeholder engagement.
- All functions engaging shapeholders should report through the same general management executive who reports to the CEO to ensure coordinated action.

7

Anticipate

By failing to prepare, you are preparing to fail.
—BEN FRANKLIN

STEVE JOBS ANTICIPATED THE opportunity to "push the human race forward" with Apple. Wall Street was surprised when risky subprime bets came home to roost and the world blamed it, sparking a regulatory response and souring its relationships with the public.

Unsurprisingly, a 2015 Gallup survey of the American public's attitudes toward industries placed the computer industry at the top (69 percent of Americans viewed it favorably) and banking near the bottom (only 37 percent viewed it favorably).[1]

I recall sitting at breakfast in 2012 listening to an executive of one of Wall Street's most prominent banks protesting that there was no way his bank could have anticipated the fallout from its trading in mortgage-backed securities. As the banker went through each step he believed was impossible to anticipate, I kept thinking to myself, "Wow, and these guys are supposed to be the smart ones."

It's a poorly kept secret that innovation on Wall Street means finding creative ways to skirt the costly requirements for capital reserves imposed by regulators to serve as a buffer for difficult periods. If one just considered the volume of innovative (read: risky) packages of subprime mortgages that were sold and the natural cycles in the housing market, it seemingly would have been easy to predict a crash. With huge compensation differences between Wall Street and the average Joe, one ought to have anticipated that the general public would not be thrilled with weak players requesting government aid because their innovation sidestepped the requirement to set aside adequate reserves. Given that bailouts would likely be necessary, one should have expected voter resentment would compel Congress to pass further regulations. I will grant that picking the timing of such a crisis would be hard but anticipating its occurrence was clearly predictable.

If major banks had a brainstorming session to think about the shapeholder risks that might occur and couldn't anticipate something like the crisis that unfolded, they don't deserve their reputation for genius. If they anticipated it, but like the Arthur Andersen partners sought to capture inflated profits for a few more years, they deserve the animosity they got.

The Issues Life Cycle

Shapeholder issues have a natural, even predictable, life cycle. Risks are easier to counter and opportunities are easier to capture if we can identify them early.

The issues of the day change constantly. Sometimes it's because of scientific advances, elevated moral concerns, activist group entrepreneurial actions, changes in institutions, or just reactions to crises.

The further an issue advances, the more difficult it is to influence and the worse the possible damage to a firm. You should not wait until the enforcement stage to realize a regulation is unworkable. You should not delay until interest groups define the issue against the interests of your own business's activities. You must anticipate issues and determine how you can define them in a way that benefits you or mitigates damage.

As obvious as this is, it is remarkable to see how placid so many industries are about issues that are on a glide path to growing into ever more perilous threats to their operations.

Take for instance the anti-GMO movement in America. Nearly all mainline crops—corn, soybeans, wheat—farmed domestically are GMO strains. Efforts to blunt the slow creep of public attitudes against these products have picked up, but they are not even close to the level necessary to counter the negative drift in public opinion. Based on current trends, I predict a forced costly shift in plantings that disrupts farmers and the agricultural distribution system, undermining the ability to feed the planet, despite the fact that a recent Pew survey shows more scientists believe that GMOs are safe than that climate change is mostly due to human activity.[2]

Or consider what steps technology companies are taking to calm privacy fears and prevent the push for initiatives like the European Union's "right to be forgotten" from spreading.[3] These actions seem inadequate relative to how these movements could hurt them.

Companies everywhere are paying too little attention to the rising angst over income inequality. This bubbles into street protests and a toxic populism that pushes up political candidates hostile to free enterprise who embrace popular actions that distort the market against competitive businesses and workers, while pushing out politicians who are sympathetic to genuine pro-growth policies.[4]

If commercial enterprises were to anticipate just how much this will cost them if they don't promptly address issues and act accordingly, they could evade the costs of inaction. Nearly all corporate missteps can be avoided if they are anticipated. Companies miss bountiful opportunities to profitably address social needs because they fail to anticipate the future they could create.

Let us consider the six steps to effectively anticipating opportunities and threat. We will then turn to the ten preparatory steps companies should take to be well positioned to capture those opportunities or mitigate those threats.

Anticipating Opportunities and Threats

Step One: Open Your Eyes

The first step to anticipating is to open your eyes. I have watched one company after another making mistakes so basic you would think they had their eyes closed.

Even though a temporary tax break was well publicized and many companies jumped at the chance, a large multinational company came to me as a congressman looking for accommodation because they had missed the window to capture the benefit. It would have boosted their bottom line significantly and was well known to many, but they weren't paying attention. It took years for this proposal to be discussed, proposed, debated, passed, enacted, and open for action. They still missed it.

It's difficult to anticipate the actions of disparate and opaque activist groups. But tracking and responding to opportunities and risks presented by government as they happen is comparatively easy. Begin by getting the simple things right.

Associations, lobbyists, and public affairs firms can track relevant political developments for a company in the capitals around the world that are significant to its operations. To digest and respond to this information, a business at a minimum needs someone within the company who understands the information received and has the ear of the company's senior leadership so they can marshal a company response quickly. This need for a rapid response is one of the reasons general management must be engaged with a unified public affairs function.

Most companies find it advantageous to establish a presence in major capitals that includes this tracking function. Boeing, Caterpillar, Ford, GE, Google, Microsoft, Pfizer, Procter & Gamble, Toyota, and many others have public affairs offices in Washington, D.C. Many large multinationals have public affairs professionals in a half dozen or more locations. This is the type of role that is ideally performed by someone who knows the elected official math and the government math of whatever capital they are located in. Many companies and public affairs firms legitimately look to hire knowledgeable former Capitol Hill or administration staffers to perform this role.

Here their value is providing insights into the process and players, not because of their connections to pivotal players. It is wise for a company to source staffers from both ends of the political spectrum to ensure it is not getting a slanted view and to avoid being viewed as slanted.

With gridlock in national capitals like Washington, D.C., states or provinces are increasingly becoming the centers of legislative action. This has multiplied the number of venues requiring monitoring. Helping staff manage this complexity are online platforms that track legislation and dialogue in multiple capitals. Tools like Quorum Analytics also apply quantitative analytics to help identify champions for a specific issue position.[5]

Step Two: See 360°

Ralph Waldo Emerson sparked controversies in his day and was adept at addressing those he opposed. As he said, "If I know your sect, I anticipate your argument." It is absolutely necessary to know the sects that can impact a company, to anticipate their arguments, and to peer ahead to understand how trends may change these conditions in the future. As a business leader, you must cultivate what I call "360° vision."

My wife was taught while studying fashion design that you can't see up the fashion ladder. This is true with more than just fashion. We all have blind spots. For businesses, a blind spot with respect to shapeholders can be debilitating.

Examples of companies underestimating shapeholder concerns include Microsoft not taking EU antitrust investigations that began in the mid-1990s seriously enough from the start (resulting in mushrooming multiple large fines and judgments that extended the review until 2013),[6] Nike not initially recognizing that it would be held accountable for how its suppliers treat their workers, and Uber bursting into the market without much apparent planning concerning how best to address the political resistance it would face from entrenched urban political interests.

Most CEOs are pretty familiar with the Fortune 500 world, but to effectively engage society, they must see society. General managers must concern themselves with not just their companies, but how their companies relate to the world.

Truly effective general managers must prepare to address the public on issues, communicate with the media, testify in regulatory and congressional proceedings, lobby government, participate in coalitions and associations, serve on government advisory panels, meet with activists, negotiate with interest groups, and partner with NGOs. To perform these roles effectively, they need a broad perspective.

Just as pressure on businesses to be more aware of social needs is increasing, their connection to communities is decreasing. The reduced attachment of businesses to specific communities is a by-product of market strategies that have enhanced their efficiency and opened new markets but reduced their community attachment in the process. As companies have increased their reliance on specialized outside vendors for a growing array of services, their direct attachment to communities has diminished. As firms have become increasingly global in an ever-increasing constellation of geographies, they have become less attached to any one location.

We are all in many ways like a submarine, submerged in our own experiences—where we grew up, what we studied, what we do for a job, where we live, who we call friends. Just as a submarine uses a periscope to get a wider view of the world around it to avoid bumping into things, so must each of us.

Executives must take concerted action to increase awareness of social needs. You cannot productively engage the broader forces in society if you don't see them. It isn't enough for CEOs to ensure the staff members they hire for shapeholder interfacing roles come from diverse backgrounds. Executives themselves should pay attention to news sources from both the left and the right, international publications, and summaries of activism in their industries.

Step Three: Peer Into the Future

Facebook, Twitter, and social media allow attacks on your reputation to go viral so fast that when it comes to your response, a New York minute is 59 seconds too slow. You must respond in minutes or hours, not days or weeks. This requires you not only to observe different perspectives but to anticipate actions by those with different perspectives—to see around corners.

I was visiting London in the middle of discussions on their congestion-charging program, and I asked several taxi drivers about this new scheme. The first two I asked were dead set against it. The third taxi driver didn't care. I suggested to him that it seemed like a slippery trend. First they limited trucks, then SUVs, then twelve-cylinder Jaguars. I said, "You know, the city of London is a pretty compact place and we could all afford to lose a couple pounds. Why don't they just allow bikes and walking in London or only allow bike taxis?" That woke him up, prompting him to ask, "Why can't they drive SUVs in London?" I don't mean to promulgate transportation policy here, I am just emphasizing that we must see the slopes ahead of us.

Beginning in 2012, China started pricing enforcements against one multinational company after another. In October 2012, Nike was fined for price fixing.[7] In December 2012, one of Carrefour's outlets in northwestern China was fined for charging higher prices at the checkout than were advertised on the shelves.[8] In January 2013, Samsung and LG of Korea were fined for fixing LCD panel prices.[9] Should Audi and Chrysler have been surprised when a year and a half later they were charged in August of 2014 for monopolistic pricing, using their leverage over Chinese car dealers and auto part suppliers to control prices?[10] Did they spend resources on anticipating what these regulators would do?

Step Four: Investigate Your Own Vulnerabilities

Seneca, the Stoic philosopher and advisor to Nero, wrote, "There is nothing so wretched or foolish as to anticipate misfortune." Nero took his advice. How did it work for Seneca? Seneca was named in a conspiracy to assassinate Nero, and Nero ordered him to commit suicide, which he did.

We have all witnessed the last-minute revelation of a political candidate's misconduct altering the course of his or her campaign. Perhaps an opponent hired someone to dig up dirt. That may be, but the more important question is: "Why didn't the candidate identify his or her own vulnerabilities and preempt an attack?" During my congressional campaigns, I always hired someone to investigate me, including the votes I had taken and my public statements, so that I would know anything about myself that my opponent could also discover.

Like a campaign, our wired world requires each business to audit its own vulnerabilities. You want to find the guns pointing at you and look right down their barrels to see what kind of ammunition shapeholders are using. Who considers you an attractive target? Why?

To better understand your vulnerability, perform an independent assessment of your specific susceptibility to legitimate attack. Assess these:

• *Industry.* Evaluate all activity that has occurred in each industry in which you operate. Honestly benchmark yourself against your competitors. How well do you align with the criteria activist groups have promulgated, whether or not you agree with the metrics they use? If you are among the worst performers, watch out. Get out of last place. You don't have to outswim the shark, just the other swimmers. If you are the best in your industry, you may also be a prime target. Activists often target those who hold themselves out as the best and an example to others. Starbucks's renown for being an exemplar in shapeholder engagement has attracted appeals from an endless number of activists, including calls to use only non-GMO, organic milk[11] and to end leases in Trump properties.[12] While it is important to put your purpose center stage, when it comes to social commitments it is essential to follow the adage "underpromise, overdeliver."

• *Company Priorities.* For each issue that the company has identified as important to its overall strategy (GMO restrictions, right to be forgotten), it should create a comprehensive list of actors who may agitate against them. Given that China accounts for a third of Audi's global sales by volume, shouldn't it have had the Chinese government pressing pricing concerns on its list?

• *Company Commitments.* Catalog all public commitments made either in public pronouncements or private commitments by executives to key constituencies. Anticipate whether the company can be assured that it will deliver on these commitments, what actions it must take to ensure delivery, and the degree to which such actions have already been implemented or are likely to be implemented. Starbucks lists inclusion as one of its guiding principles.[13] Does its franchise agreement allow it to order its Saudi Arabia franchisee to remove the sign that reads, "Please No Entry for Ladies Only Send Your Driver to Order Thank You"?[14]

• *Internal Audits.* It is important for companies to have an effective internal audit department. These audits should include not just accountants but operational personnel from different geographies so they can apply their experience to areas prone to shapeholder risks.

• *Brainstorming Dirty Laundry.* A key part of the corporate strategic planning process should include brainstorming the company's vulnerabilities. Too often, a company's strategic planning focuses exclusively on market issues and gives only scant attention to anticipating the nonmarket shapeholder issues from politicians, regulators, reporters, or activists. Certainly more than one person at VW knew of its digital duplicity on emissions standards. If a wide-enough cross section of company employees is included in this brainstorming session, possible social exposures can be identified and defused before they explode.

• *Front Page of the* New York Times *Test.* During a visit to Dubai and Doha in the spring of 2011, just after a major WikiLeaks release of U.S. State Department documents, I saw the impact it had on my business school students' psyches as they expressed how revelations about their own country's dealings with the United States caused them embarrassment. A society that was used to being able to keep certain things under wraps had intimacies exposed in the world press. One Gulf businessman told me that we lived in a "post-WikiLeaks world" and must anticipate accordingly. You may have beefed up your data security, but are you prepared to respond if it leaks?

Step Five: Develop Early-Warning Systems

No matter how well you expect the unexpected, the unexpected still happens. Consider the early-warning signs that were ignored by America before Pearl Harbor. Companies must establish a series of early-warning indicators and develop an expedited decision process for responding to their indications.

• *Be Alert to Irregularities.* A keen eye for spotting irregularities is the first step in an early-warning system. The Economic Club of Minnesota (ECOM) that I founded and chair seeks luminaries with strong points of view to engage in a discussion. Those with incisive views are often magnets for those with contrasting opinions. My crack staff noted that some of the people who signed up online to hear a major CEO address the club did not list an organization. This is unusual for a gathering of leaders. My staff also discovered another person had registered under a false identity. They traced this person back to the Rainforest Action Network and discovered that RAN was bragging about a recent direct action against this CEO's company on its website. This early warning allowed us to deny them admittance and arrange for event security, thereby preventing RAN from disrupting ECOM. Companies need a similarly keen sensitivity to incidents that are out of the ordinary.

• *Employ Media Tracking.* Analytical tools are available to tabulate which words and phrases are most often used in conjunction with your company name in both traditional and social media in real time. This is a valuable tool for determining whether your market communications are effective and an essential early-warning tool for engaging shapeholders.

• *Interact with a Wide Circle of Carrot Activists and Opinion Leaders.* An important process for anticipating shapeholder action includes regular interactions with a broad and diverse group of shapeholders with common interests. As ExxonMobil sought in 2002 to improve its social relations, which had not yet recovered from its 1989 oil spill in Valdez, Alaska, it reached out around the world to environmental and human rights NGOs and others who did not always agree with the company. It arranged several two-day, off-the-record, unstructured get-together sessions with senior ExxonMobil managers each year. The activists and the managers put tough realities on the table to discuss, not with a goal of consensus but seeking to understand each other. ExxonMobil also organized and met regularly with an "external citizenship advisory panel." It had regular conference calls to discuss issues with the broader shapeholder community and created an extensive email list to keep them informed on developments. Such activities are an excellent way to keep the issues in front of you rather than having them sneak up on you from behind.[15]

Developing deeper partnerships with a select group of carrot activist groups with whom you have aligned interests is enlightening. Dave McLaughlin from the World Wildlife Fund takes executives on what he calls "eco-disaster tours" to get a firsthand look at challenges on the front lines in emerging and frontier markets. Businesspeople who are skeptical of the value of such trips always come away saying, "If the world sees this, we're toast." Realizing this early enough that you can fix it will help you avert the fallout.

While you may hire staff from friendly NGOs to execute this role, pay attention to integrating them into the company culture. In the global immersion courses I led in foreign capitals, I assigned students the task of finding opportunities for businesses and NGOs to collaborate. Often the NGO-oriented students did a wonderful job of outlining action a corporation could take to solve a social need but could not pinpoint how the company would benefit. Few businesspeople understand the perspectives of NGOs and vice versa.

Step Six: Shape Your Industry

Given the increasingly dynamic nature of regulatory environments, why not partner with shapeholders to change the rules that shape your industry? The resulting changes can profoundly affect the opportunities and risks you face. Doing so requires being able to anticipate the future you should push to create.

Before 1984, AT&T had a massive monopoly. They not only supplied phone service to nearly every American but were the dominant manufacturer of the phones and their operating systems and the almost exclusive retailer of those phones.

Then potential competitors and a variety of activist shapeholders started agitating for the U.S. Justice Department to file an antitrust lawsuit against AT&T. The courts broke up AT&T in 1984, and Congress passed major telecommunications deregulation in 1996 so that today we not only have AT&T but a host of competitors.

Consumers can choose among Apple, HTC, Huawei, LG, Microsoft, Motorola, Samsung, Xiaomi, ZTE, and many others for mobile phones and operating systems. Without shapeholders changing the telecommunications market environment, you would not have the Apple versus Google Android fight—you might not even have iPhones or Google.

In less than two decades, the world has gone from largely government-owned or government-regulated monopolies controlling phone services, phone devices, phone operating systems, and phone retailing to an explosion of consumer choices. By opening up new competitive markets in these industries, shapeholders have created opportunities for businesses to succeed.

As we speak, shapeholder action is in the process of shaping industries of the future. Privacy and safety activists are complicating efforts by Amazon, Google, and others to seek U.S. Federal Aviation Administration approval to use drones for package deliveries and other commercial purposes. Uber and Airbnb are battling local authorities pressed into action by activist taxi and hotel interests as they rewrite the rules of the hospitality industry around the world. With the U.S. Food and Drug Administration's approval of Proteus Digital Health's chip in a pill, the budding precision medicine industry got a big boost. The nonmarket environment defined by shapeholders changes, and it can dramatically change the opportunities available to businesses. Being a shaper of the industry is better than being shaped by others.

In addition to gaining a 360° view, peering into the future, investigating yourself, developing early-warning systems, and considering opportunities to shape your industry, you must prepare.

The Ten Layers of Mulching

How can we discipline ourselves to be prepared so we capture the benefits or blunt the repercussions of activism?

During my youth I pulled more than enough weeds in my family's garden to know what harm letting them choke off the growth of your plantings could do and how much of a pain it was to pull them regularly. That is why I find mulching so attractive. Mulching keeps noxious weeds from sprouting up and choking your harvest. It also prevents erosion, preserving the soil's moisture and nutrients. This allows what you plant to flourish, blossom, and bear good fruit.

During a discussion with my students in London, Dominic Morris, CBE, then the director of group public affairs for the Lloyds Banking Group in London, described anticipatory measures necessary for good corporate public affairs as "mulching." That's the justification for investing in activities that, while they may not have discrete quantifiable paybacks, do prevent bad things from sprouting up; they nourish the progress of your policy priorities, whether cultivating good political and NGO relations or embracing sustainability standards.

Let's discuss ten mulching activities that organizations should consider.

One: Industry Standards

My basketball coach used to say when trying to teach us the basics of the game, "The lines are your friend, stay within the lines." Some see industry standards as a constraint. They are also protection against aggressive shapeholders who have an unrealistic idea of where the line should be on catching fish, cutting timber, or reporting the terms of government energy contracts. If more than one credible industry standard–setting body exists, it is normally wise to choose to sign on to one or more. It is often advisable to have a company representative join the standard-setting body. If a company has the capacity and credibility to set the industry standard, as Starbucks did with coffee sourcing, this is prudent.

You may consider implementing self-regulation standards through your industry association. Self-regulation may be productive avenues for averting unworkable regulations. Doing so also isolates bad actors within the industry. In any group, there is always someone who flirts with danger. When that company hits a land mine because it crossed the line of industry best practices, you want to prevent that shrapnel hitting responsible industry players. Self-regulating standards not only encourage everyone to raise their game but are a good shield against bad PR backlash.

Two: Supplier Standards

The equivalent of a "run it up the middle" play for stick activists is to find a company that cares more about its brand than its suppliers' standards, to work their way up the supply chain until they find dirt, and to then bring it back to the company's doorstep. Remember the unfurling banners on Mattel's headquarters over the timber that produced Barbie's packaging? Or consider how Greenpeace petitioned Timberland over the leather from which it made shoelaces. It is essential that you have serious supplier standards and rigorous methods of ensuring compliance. Carrot NGOs can partner with you here.

Ill-defined supplier standards can also cause serious problems in meeting the demands of your customers, thereby harming society—something Bridgestone and Ford found out when informal standard-setting contributed to a problem with tire-tread separation and rollovers that were blamed for 148 deaths and more than 500 injuries.[16]

Bear in mind that standards on a wide range of sustainability concerns are constantly tightening. Nearly every supply chain is required to become more transparent. At a minimum, you must keep up. There is a strategic opportunity to differentiate yourself by sourcing your product per your customers' values, which engenders their loyalty and gives you an edge over the competition. Adherence to this core value is what makes Whole Foods, Starbucks, and Chipotle stand out.

Three: Capability to Make Your Own News

Organizations must be able to drive their own news in real time through multiple direct communication channels, especially to their own stakeholders. Maintaining ongoing dialogue with opinion leaders is also essential.

Faced with a slew of rumors about pink slime and the safety of its food, McDonald's launched a communications campaign that directly responded to consumers' questions in 2014 on YouTube, Facebook, Twitter, and its own website. It "hired Grant Imahara, the former cohost of *Mythbusters*, to visit McDonald's restaurants and suppliers around the country."[17]

Four: Insurance Relationships

When a prankster gained access to the intercom system in the store of a major retailer and made a racially offensive statement, the incident could have mushroomed into a negative nation-wide news item. The company's longstanding efforts to cultivate diversity, including strong relationships with shapeholder groups that shared their concern, allowed them to convince the media that this was an isolated incident. Just as the potential of a slip and fall by a customer in your store would compel you to retain an insurance policy, a company should actively work to identify carrot activists who could help it find the danger-prone slick spots in its operation, collaborate on preventing unfortunate occurrences and perhaps testify on their behalf if incidents occur despite of their preemptive efforts. Find the activists in categories important to you who have a track record of credible collaboration.

Five: Potential Coalition Partner Relationships

During the assess step, we will identify which coalition partners could be decisive in setting the direction on an important issue or who may ally with the company if a coalition is formed to assemble to contest that issue. You don't want to introduce yourself to necessary allies in the heat of the battle—you should have already established rapport with them.

The president inviting some of my colleagues and me to the Cabinet Room in the White House to make his case for the Trade Act of 2002 was an effort to assemble to win. His inviting me to return to Washington with him on Air Force One after speaking at Eden Prairie High School in Minnesota earlier that year was anticipating the need to cultivate a potential coalition partner.

• *Stakeholders.* Shapeholders may not have a natural interest in your company's success unless you build a relationship. But stakeholders do, and when building a team to win a political contest, you should begin by ensuring your stakeholders are informed and on your side. This is why it is essential to have robust vehicles and programs for ongoing direct communications with your stakeholders. This is particularly important during a crisis or a heated contest on a policy issue.

• *Associations.* It is best to act as an industry instead of as a single company when a concern is commonly held. This requires relationships with relevant industry or topical associations and chambers of commerce. Oftentimes an association can be the sharp edge of the coalition, playing a needed but uncomfortable role that any individual company would prefer to avoid. Conflicting views between association members may prevent an association from taking the lead on a matter important to a company. This argues for membership in multiple associations—some narrowly focused, others broadly focused. That is why companies belong to broad-based chambers like the U.S. Chamber of Commerce, industry-specific associations like the American Bankers Association, and associations that represent their size segment like the Independent Community Bankers for smaller banks and the Financial Services Roundtable for larger banks. Having your company's executives involved in association advisory committees enhances their own development and better positions the company to steer the association's engagement and overcome resistance to action.

• *Carrot Activists.* Strategizing over how to address potential policy skirmishes will undoubtedly pinpoint valuable carrot activists. These activists must move beyond the "easy to engage" category to include all those "needed to win." Think of effective coalition building as filling out an orchestra.

Companies must identify early which activists can fill these roles and cultivate relationships with them by engaging them in its early-warning outreach activities and finding mutually productive efforts to explore. Just as Coca-Cola found it advantageous to disclose its contributions to NGOs in support of scientific research and health and fitness programs in the United States, a company should ensure that lack of disclosure of its support of carrot activists doesn't undermine the credibility of its collaborative efforts.[18]

Six: Credible Source of Research

One of the most effective tools of advocacy is to be a credible source of information that enables decision makers to make better decisions. Daniel Patrick Moynihan wrote, "Everyone is entitled to their own opinion, but everyone is not entitled to their own facts." You must be a source of facts, not opinions.

Investment Company Institute CEO Paul Stevens says honesty and accuracy in industry analysis can have huge payoffs when building public confidence. He advises that becoming known as an authoritative source for unbiased information is valuable but requires a ruthless dedication to letting the chips fall where they may, even when it puts you in a bad light.[19] The best way to do this is to regularly publish not only statistical aggregations of industry activity and public views of the industry and its practices but balanced and reasoned analysis of the relevant issues of the day. It is perfectly legitimate to have a point of view, but that view is taken more seriously if you honestly lay out its critiques and your response to those critiques.

When a company funds research programs by academics or NGOs, it must disclose its contributions for the results to be deemed credible. It is also important to anticipate attacks on the research findings.

Seven: Combat Corruption: Seven Ps for Purity

When teaching Executive MBA students in Doha, Qatar, about the importance of combating corruption, I told them that when I landed in Doha, the view from my window was cloudy because the plane was covered, like everything in that region, by dust. I explained that where I come from in Minnesota and North Dakota, dust is not our problem. If you live in a place with real winters, your challenge is de-icing.

Before you take off in an airplane during Northern winters they must de-ice the wings to keep ice from building up and causing a plane to crash. Before you embark on business in corruption-prone countries, you need a protective coat of practices that safeguard you against corruption building up and crashing your company.

If businesses engage in corrupt backdoor activities, they have started down a slippery slope. One corrupt payment puts a big "I pay" sign on the company, leading everyone with their hand out to your door, until you eventually get caught. Salespeople for Goodyear Tire and Rubber subsidiaries in Kenya and Angola had become accustomed to paying bribes to government and private-sector workers to secure sales, and in 2015 the SEC fined them $16.2 million for just that.[20]

The heavy penalties from anticorruption law violations elevate the importance of avoiding their snare. America's Foreign Corrupt Practices Act (FCPA), which passed in 1977, caused a sea change in corporate behavior. Now executives can be personally liable for corporate transgressions, and that forces senior management to take the act's provisions seriously. The act prohibits Americans, foreigners acting in America, or certain issuers of securities in American markets from making payments to foreign officials for the purposes of obtaining or retaining business.[21]

Applying these provisions is complicated, especially when your customers are state-owned enterprises (SOEs). The fact that the hand of government in commerce is often more significant outside the United States further complicates matters. How does this relate to asking an SOE executive to attend or a government official to speak at sales promotion conferences in exotic locations? J.P. Morgan was subject to a federal bribery investigation for hiring the sons and daughters of prospective banking clients, including those of financial regulators, major SOEs, and provincial and central government officials.[22]

Forty countries ratified the Organisation for Economic Cooperation and Development (OECD) antibribery convention that requires countries to criminalize bribery of a public official. This allows companies and NGOs a legal platform to prosecute corruption when confronted with it. The United Kingdom passed an antibribery act in 2010 that goes beyond both FCPA and the OECD convention by covering bribery of commercial officials, not just government officials.

Some suggest that the extra restrictions imposed on U.S. and UK companies puts them at a disadvantage compared with companies from countries without similar restrictions.[23] But there is a payoff. Look at the Trust Barometer, published annually by the Edelman public affairs firm, and you'll see that approximately twice as many people around the world trust companies headquartered in the United States, United Kingdom, and western Europe than companies from the BRIC (Brazil, Russia, India, and China) bloc.[24]

My discussions with multinational companies around the world suggest there are essential steps to navigating political frontiers without falling into corruption or ethical traps. I call them the "seven *P*s for purity."

I. PURPOSE.

It is essential to navigate your company's direction by something more than just money-making if you hope to steer your employees from widely varying cultural backgrounds away from the temptations of profiting personally from corruption. Embracing a corporate purpose that delivers profits and social benefits anchors an anticorruption culture throughout the enterprise.

2. PROGRAM FOR COMPLIANCE.

Companies must have a robust code of conduct, actively enforced and widely promulgated, that clearly defines aspirational and prohibited behaviors.

Since many ethical decisions are complex, you should routinely conduct training programs for managers and employees. If your training system is effective, the necessary monitoring can rely less on auditors and inspectors and more on fellow employees applying peer pressure to instill ethical behavior.

Training must be rigorous enough to deter employees from behavior that may be acceptable in one culture but not in others. Indonesia banned Citibank from issuing credit cards for two years and accepting wealth management clients for one year because agents collecting debt on its behalf purportedly fatally beat a Citibank client.[25]

For your ethics program to be effective, it is important that those employees who are found to violate the standards be held accountable for their actions. The board of directors of United Airlines dismissed its CEO in 2015 when investigations uncovered questionable accommodations for the leader of the Port Authority of New York and New Jersey. That dismissal bolstered the credibility of ethical standards at United Airlines and throughout corporate America.[26]

3. CEO AS PROSELYTIZER.

When you create company standards, the leaders at the top must set the tone by testifying to them at every opportunity, to walk the talk, to designate a chief ethics officer and a point of contact to help with ethical concerns. If the top leaders do not take the code of conduct seriously, neither will the employees. That is what made United's board action so effective.

4. PATIENCE.

All companies and senior managers believe they were built for speed, that their hallmark is getting things done and getting them done quickly. This is a recipe for catastrophe in corrupt environments. Even honest governments seem to move like turtles to most businesspeople. Those who profit from accelerating processes to grease their own palms have an incentive to pump the brake every so often to test a company's receptivity to paying for acceleration. If you're in a hurry, they have just the solution for you, but it will cost you one ticket to the slippery slope.

That is why companies must have the patience to say, "If it takes another year to complete this important strategic initiative, I guess we will just have to wait." Establishing a reputation for avoiding corrupt activity takes a while, and can lead to poor short-term results, but is critical for long-term success.

Walmart found out the hard way that even accusations of being in a hurry to establish itself as the leading retailer in Mexico could be costly. In 2011 the *New York Times* alleged that Walmart officials had made payments to government officials in Mexico for approvals like building permits to speed its expansion. This sparked investor lawsuits, a U.S. government investigation, and, according to the *Times*, "nearly half a billion dollars" in costs incurred and at least eight Walmart executives leaving the company.[27] Even though investigations to date suggest these charges may be exaggerated,[28] I suspect Walmart would agree that a patient approach is better.

5. PARTNERS.

It is important to have partners within each country in which you operate who understand how your engagement with the country helps that country, who accept that you will not compromise when it comes to corruption, and who can remove roadblocks that corruption causes.

Take the example of a company that has a ship waiting to unload but is confronted with someone at the port who will not let the ship dock until he or she receives a payment. Even though every day the ship sits idle is costly and the cargo is desperately needed to meet customer delivery deadlines, the company must not bend. No matter how small the amount requested. If it wants to operate in that country, it must conscript someone higher up in the country's power structure who can help.

But if this partner is motivated to help by what is in essence secondhand bribery—you pay your partner, so he or she pays someone else—it is equally corrupt. Many companies have someone from a country's economic development ministry or other government unit who wants those companies more engaged in the country and has assured the company that the government is addressing corruption within the country. This is likely the case if your product or service is needed or adds value to the country.

This is admittedly less likely if you are providing serious competition to a hometown favorite, the social value of your offering is not clear, or your offering undermines government priorities (like Facebook, Google, or Twitter in China). If your benefit is unclear, but you are not a threat, then follow the advice of Emerson: "The only way to have a friend is to be one." An active effort to be a good local citizen by engaging in social responsibility investment can tip the balance. Your company's purpose and the country's own development priorities should direct these efforts.

Cargill raised more than US$3.8 million to build seventy-six schools over its twenty-year history in Vietnam. Building schools benefits 12,000 children, energizes Cargill's employee engagement, and endears it to local communities and community leaders. These efforts involved many ribbon-cutting ceremonies and gatherings in follow-on support of these schools.[29] Ribbon cuttings on good works are magnets for political leaders looking to bask in the reflected glory, allowing opportunities to build relations with both citizens and their leaders.

If you don't even know where to begin, consider William Butler Yeats: "There are no strangers here; only friends you haven't yet met." Perhaps your local embassy, commercial service, or chamber of commerce has advice for you. If these avenues prove fruitless, there are public affairs firms that include partners or associates with prior service in a country's foreign service, military, or other ministries. Your goal should be to get advice on how to establish yourself as a welcome member of the community without stooping to corruption.

6. PROSECUTION.

Talk to any civil servant about the biggest obstacles to addressing corruption concerns raised by corporations and they will include frustration that few companies will go on the record with their complaint, much less participate in pushing legal redress against corruption.

Yes, many countries around the world have judicial systems of questionable independence or have not yet established traditions of prosecuting endemic corruption. That is changing in several countries.

Take, for instance, the corruption scandal that forced Brazil's government-owned oil company Petrobras to write off $17 billion "because of losses from graft and overvalued assets" and landed indictments for not only several government officials but also some of the country's foremost executives. The corruption it exposed was widespread and decades long.[30] Certainly some business must have been passed over in their contract bidding for not going along with their scheme to skim off the top of company contracts. But no business challenged this deceit.

Luckily for businesses, not only do America and Europe export activism to other countries, but we also export legal advocates who aggressively enforce ethical standards. The prosecutors who cracked open the Petrobras scandal, called the Nine Horsemen of the Apocalypse by the local press, were recent graduates of top law schools in the United States, Europe, and Brazil. Jose Vicente Mendonça, a state attorney in Rio de Janeiro, observed, "They're trying to bring some stuff from the U.S. legal system into the Brazilian legal system."[31]

Courts in nations with established legal systems beyond the reach of retribution by the accused have kept up efforts to attack fraud that hurts their countries. It was the U.S. FBI, IRS, and Justice Department, coordinated by the Brooklyn U.S. attorney's office, that uncovered widespread scandal at FIFA, the global governing body of soccer.[32]

U.S. authorities launched a series of wide-ranging investigations into whether Venezuela's leaders used Petróleos de Venezuela to loot billions of dollars from the country through graft and whether its foreign bank accounts were used for black-market currency schemes and laundering drug money.[33]

It is unclear how many honest corporations came forth with information to support these anticorruption efforts. Much more could be done to root out corruption if more businesses and prosecutors withstood the blowback that comes from uncovering dirty laundry.

7. PROMOTING OPENNESS.

There are ample opportunities for companies to promote the kind of openness that reduces corrupt actors' areas of operation. These include promoting formalized government rulemaking, a defined process with open review periods, the opportunity to file public comments, and opportunities for public hearings. This makes it harder for the good old boys' network to slide through provisions that grant privileges to a select few. Joining with other corporations to form an NGO to promote these practices can advance this, as with ETCO in Brazil.[34]

Corruption is one of the most serious challenges multi-national corporations face, but practicing these seven steps mitigates the risks of operating in regions prone to corruption.

Eight: Political Engagement

Businesses have a right to responsibly engage with government. Reputable companies represent and give voice to stakeholders: employees, customers, and the communities in which they operate. We must take great care to ensure a company's activities are ethical, legal, and responsible.

We will consider the optimum approach to issue campaigns in chapter 12. Here we consider anticipatory steps that should occur with no particular campaign in mind.

CAMPAIGN CONTRIBUTIONS: GIVING STRATEGY.

In countries where unions and others advance issue positions contrary to corporate interests, there is a strong case for businesses to support public officials and parties. Whose contributions are deployed to advance the best interest of employees or society at large—unions or corporations? Which side you take largely depends on whether your favorite economist is John Maynard Keynes or Milton Friedman.

IDEOLOGICAL: FREE ENTERPRISE.

Entrepreneurs who fought the hardscrabble fight to make something out of nothing believe to their core that Friedman's prescriptions are not just better for them but better for mankind. They believe the road of Keynes leads to doom. They look for nothing from their contributions other than a philosophical bent that the best government is a small government that imposes fewer taxes and regulations on small businesspeople, a government that doesn't pick winners and losers. These contributors represent the most significant counterweight to the support unions give to parties that promote government intervention.

IDEOLOGICAL: PERSONAL BELIEFS.

While the animating issue for most successful entrepreneurs is a conviction for free enterprise, there are those who believe passionately about a particular issue, be it social, environmental, or in some other arena. Some businesspeople are devoted to a specific party or a particular group that solicits donations and mobilizes members around a particular issue or gender. If their belief is genuinely motivated (not just the focus of their investment portfolios), they can be highly effective and credible contributors.

Given customer sensitivities, it is preferable that business leaders contribute personally rather than contributing from their companies' coffers. Friedman would argue that public companies with multiple shareholders should not be used as a vehicle for personal contributions.

TRANSACTIONAL.

The cynics would suggest that all businesses view contributions as transactional. And when a key vote comes up or an amendment needs to be slid into a bill, the company can call in its quid pro quo. If a company only contributes when in the middle of a specific political battle, it is difficult to rebut this. Businesses, businesspeople, or lobbyists who think like this exist. But they generally lack credibility and are avoided by most politicians.

INVESTMENT.

Many companies think of political contributions as an investment to facilitate good governance. They support legislators who are aligned with their companies' views on many (though rarely all) issues. They also support officials who may agree with their companies' views less often but are in a position of authority on matters where information their companies can bring to the table can inform decisions. A company's goal here is a long-term dialogue and a relationship that does not hinge on any specific vote. While a company's contribution may lean toward one party or the other, there is often a concerted effort to cultivate such relationships with multiple political parties.

The reason I list political engagement under the anticipate step is that shunning a transactional approach and taking a long-term investment approach that anticipates many issues of interest and seeks only to bring useful information to the debate is the most credible and most effective approach for companies with broad interests.

Consider the retailers from Walmart to Speedway SuperAmerica that pushed to enact legislation that limits the amount banks can charge for the use of debit cards. Retailers really had no choice but to accept such cards as payment no matter what banks charged and felt that legislation was the only remedy. In this contest, retailers couldn't count on their traditional Republican allies when opposing banks. Besides, the Democrats were in charge. The retailers prevailed in convincing Congress to pass the Durbin Amendment, which required the Federal Reserve to limit fees as part of the Dodd-Frank financial reform legislation in 2010.

A danger in businesses taking the investment approach is to treat each elected official as just a line on the ledger. The Business Roundtable, an association of the CEOs of America's largest companies, spent nearly $200,000 in support of my opponent in my first run for Congress, a pro-trade Democrat. When I beat the odds to defeat a congressional incumbent in spite of their support for him, no one from the Business Roundtable ever came to my door to establish a rapport.

STAYING ON THE SIDE OF THE BETTER ANGELS.

Whether considering political contributions or hiring former elected officials or government staff, here are five tips for staying on the side of the better angels.

1. *Follow the Law.* The law varies by country, often by industry. Read the law and abide by it. This is an essential but not sufficient step to ensure responsible behavior.

2. *Seek Good Governance.* Too many companies tilt the field in their favor. As an elected official I find this abhorrent, but as a manager I find it naïve. If you obtain favors from the current government, you not only risk long-term loss of reputation when your preferential treatment comes to light, but your benefit is likely only transitory and will be rendered null and void when the new government comes in. Taking the long-term investment approach for a level playing field is preferable.

3. *Practice Openness.* Reporting requirements for political activities vary by country. Follow them all. Many companies have found it helps to be transparent in disclosing the extent and objectives of their political engagement.

Much has been written about "dark money" from undisclosed contributors spent on electoral campaigns or issue campaigns through super PACs, associations, or nonprofit organizations. Organizations like the Center for Political Accountability[35] and Good Jobs First[36] demand transparency of others but offer little of their own. See how long it takes you to find out where their "dark money" comes from.[37] Many businesses suspect such efforts are funded by those hoping that the risk of lawsuits and "name and shame" publicity that disclosure could spark will limit corporate contributions and tilt the partisan balance.

Yet perhaps a bigger challenge businesses have with disclosure is that they are not clear on what political actions are in their interests and align with their corporate purpose. Their most powerful political tool is to communicate directly to their employees what actions will help or hurt the success of the company—and therefore the prospects for raises and promotions for employees. Clarity on a company's political objectives allows it to effectively engage its employees and justify its political activity when disclosed.

4. *Promote Openness.* America has extensive disclosure requirements for campaign contributions and lobbying activities. As with any regulation, these can be made both less burdensome and more illuminating. Yet their general effect is to tilt the scales in favor of engaging only to facilitate good governance. Companies operating in countries with either nonexistent or lax reporting requirements for political contributions often find themselves shut out as decisions are made behind closed doors and only an entrenched elite have a voice—unlike those "not from here."

Take Brazil as an example. Many in Brazil pride themselves on not having lobbyists and believe that no formalized role for lobbying means their political process cannot be so easily manipulated. But even before the Petrobras scandal, the country had its so called Mensalão (Portuguese for "big monthly stipend") scandal when members of their legislature received monthly payments to vote in line with the wishes of the administration.[38] It is tough for legitimate companies to compete against these kinds of distortions.

Supporting rulemaking in every country that follows a formalized process and is transparent and nondiscriminatory toward international players not only delivers the best outcome for legitimate companies, but for a nation's citizens.[39]

5. *Hire for Insights, Not Influence.* It is essential for organizations that hire former officials or staff to do so based on their knowledge of the process and the players, not how well they can influence officials still in office.

Nine: Selling to the Government

Many companies focus on selling to governments. This is best done when companies anticipate a government's objectives and the effect of political actors on the decision making. Helen Kennett of Rolls-Royce advises her sales team to use a TCP (technical, commercial, political) approach. She confirms that the company must perfect the technical and commercial dimensions of a proposal to successfully sell it to the government. But she correctly advises that more is required: the sales team must anticipate the political dimensions of the proposal.

Attuning yourself to the promises a government has made and its plans for implementing them will position your company to submit actionable proposals. What are the motivations of the political players who are affected by or posturing to influence the direction of procurement? You must maintain open and objective dialogues with all relevant players.

As a member of the U.S. House Agriculture Committee, I received several visits from food companies to discuss the makeup of the U.S. Department of Agriculture's official dietary guidelines. You might think these guidelines are only used as an exhibit in high school textbooks. They also influence government purchases for the military; 8.6 million Americans served by the Women, Infants, and Children program; and 31 million children served through the National School Lunch Program.[40] These guidelines have become increasingly controversial, highlighting the political dimension of government purchasing decisions.

Astute companies will define how their products facilitate the efficient and effective delivery of benefits to the public and help address social challenges.

Ten: Country Risk Assessment

A thorough evaluation of country risk is vital before entering a country. Once in a country, keep an eye on emerging risks and be prepared to preempt or mitigate potential harms to your company. This is not just a matter of potential expropriations but also potential financial crises, fiscal adjustments, or significant changes in the regulatory environment.

While few Americans are familiar with the International Monetary Fund (IMF), an international institution established to help countries that overdraw their current account, even random citizens you meet on the street in Brazil or Turkey are familiar with it. For many of them the IMF is a four-letter word associated with the financial hardships coincident with the adjustments a country must undertake to square its accounts with other nations. Companies would do well to anticipate such oncoming crises and act accordingly.

Having considered the necessity to anticipate, let us turn our attention to assessing the opportunities and risks that an organization either anticipates or that arise unexpectedly.

- Shapeholder issues have a natural, even a predictable, life cycle. Risks are easier to counter, and opportunities are easier to capture, if we can identify them early.
- Six steps help organizations anticipate opportunities and threats.

  Open your eyes. Companies must constantly monitor political activity in all jurisdictions that can influence their future success.

  See 360°. Executives must develop a full-spectrum awareness of the social actors and issues engaged within their operating environments.

  See the future. Executives must perceive how issues are likely to evolve.

  Investigate your vulnerabilities. Research contentious issues in the industry—factors that could impact company priorities or challenges that could hamper your company's ability to deliver on external commitments. Perform robust internal audits and active brainstorming exercises.

  Early-warning systems. Be keenly aware of irregularities. Track media mentions. Keep in close contact with a wide circle of carrot activists and opinion leaders.

  Shape your industry. Companies must recognize that if they are not seeking to engage shapeholders to reshape their industries in a more favorable direction, someone else could be seeking to shape them in a direction the companies would find less favorable.

- In addition to anticipating future opportunities and challenges, companies should take preparatory steps that, like mulching, prevent problems from cropping up and nourish positive future outcomes.

  Industry standards

  Supplier standards

  Capacity to make your own news

  Insurance relationships

  Potential coalition partner relationships with stakeholders, associations, carrot activists

  Credible research

  Combat corruption with the seven *P*s for purity

Purpose
Program for compliance
CEO as proselytizer
Patience
Partners
Prosecution
Promoting openness

- Political engagement—take an investment not a transactional approach; stay on the side of the better angels by following the law, practicing and promoting openness, and hiring for insights, not influence.
- When selling to governments, follow the TCP approach: address technical, commercial, and political aspects.
- Do a thorough country risk assessment before entering a country and continue to anticipate risks that can be mitigated.

8

Assess

Officer, to driver: "Wouldn't it help if you wiped off your
   windshield?"
Driver: "I don't think so, I left my glasses at home."

HOW DO YOU SIZE up a shareholder? The value of a diamond is
wrapped up in the stone's clarity. Only an expert eye can see the
inner hues that make the rock worth the price or worthless. Does
it contain hints of pink or blue that are prized by consumers? Or
does a streak of yellow diminish its value?

Similar nuanced skills are required in assessing first of all
whether shapeholder opportunities or claims are legitimate or illegitimate and then whether they offer an upside for the company
or not. The conclusion of these two assessments will guide which
engagement step an enterprise should take next.

Consider the impact from how Levi's and Nike assessed budding concerns over Asian labor standards differently in the 1990s.

Levi's Ducked, Nike Took It on the Chin

Robert D. Haas, then chairman of Levi Strauss & Company and
the great-great-grandnephew of the company's founder, Levi Strauss,

was concerned about worker conditions. Under his leadership in March 1992, Levi's publicly announced new global sourcing guidelines addressing worker conditions, the environment, and human rights. Based on these guidelines, the company made the decision to withdraw from Burma. Facing the difficult decision as to whether Levi's should still source from and invest in China, Haas assembled a China Policy Group (CPG) to consider the question at the end of 1992.

In March 1993 the CPG members reported a division in their group. They all saw "pervasive violations of basic human rights" in China, but while the majority recommended that the company should stay in China if certain conditions were met, a minority advocated total withdrawal. The executive management committee was similarly divided, and so the ultimate decision was left to Haas. In April the board of directors accepted Haas's recommendation that the company should phase out its relationships in China.

Haas had assessed that Levi's customers would find the conditions of workers in China morally unacceptable. He made the difficult decision to follow through on his assessment. This pressured others who faced similar decisions but reached different conclusions. Frank Martin, the president of the American Chamber of Commerce in Hong Kong, called Levi's withdrawal "an isolated incident . . . [that] will have virtually no impact whatsoever on what other companies do in China. . . . It is the decision of one individual chairman of the board of a privately held company."[1]

Neal Lauridsen, vice president for Nike in Asia Pacific, was puzzled. "I can't figure it out. I really have no idea what Levi is doing. . . . Everybody I talk to seems to be going forward."[2] Nike's founding philosophy shaped a different worldview than Levi's. Nike founder Phil Knight devised the strategy for the company in 1962 while at Stanford Business School. His plan was to keep costs lower than competitors by outsourcing all manufacturing, creating one of the world's first "virtual" corporations with no physical assets. By investing the savings into marketing he would create a mega-brand globally.

The labor practices of Nike concerned U.S. labor unions, because they made competition difficult for companies that sourced their product from America. The AFL-CIO created a branch called the Asian American Free Labor Association in 1991. Jeff Ballinger, its employee in Indonesia, devised his own strategy of "one country–one company." Indonesia was that country. Nike was his chosen company. He set about shining a light on the condition of workers in factories from which Nike sourced in Indonesia.

Building on attacks on Nike's labor practices that had begun in 1989, Ballinger published a piece in *Harper's* in 1992 that documented workers who were paid only 14 cents per hour, far below Indonesia's minimum wage.[3] This opened the floodgates, including protests at the 1992 Barcelona Olympics.

The strategy upon which Nike was founded influenced its early response to attacks. As summarized by Harvard's Debora Spar,[4]

> Despite the criticism, Nike insisted that labor conditions in its contractors' factories were not—could not—be Nike's concern or its responsibility. And even if labor violations did exist in Nike's contracting factories, stated the company's general manager in Jakarta, "I don't know that I need to know." Nike's company line on the issue was clear and stubborn: without an in-house manufacturing facility, the company simply could not be held responsible for the actions of independent contractors.

Ballinger and those who joined his cause steadily turned up the heat on Nike. Nike became the archetype for the corporate exploitation of child labor. With public opinion agitated, manufacturers had no choice but to work with shapeholders to form more robust standards for production in emerging markets. Reaching more of a social consensus on these standards allowed Levi's to eventually return to China under these criteria.

Because of Haas's astute early assessment, Levi's sidestepped the frontal assault Nike faced. I have found that people everywhere remember this chapter in Nike's history. Like most companies caught in the crosshairs of shapeholder action, Nike changed course and became in many ways a model corporation. The optimum path for corporate action is to learn from Nike's stumble without stubbing your own toe.

Assessing: Two Questions, Two Dimensions Each, Five Tools

Charting the optimum path for social engagement requires answering two questions for every shapeholder opportunity or challenge. Each question has two dimensions. The two questions are: first, "Is it legit?," and second, "Can I win?" The answers to these questions allow us to plot our action along the shapeholder decision matrix.

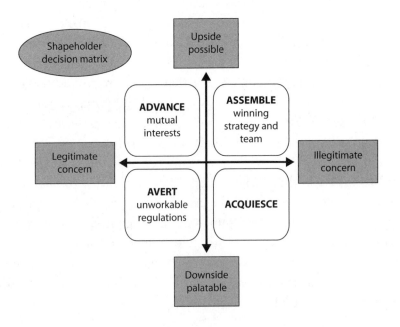

The two dimensions of the first question are accurately assessing whether each opportunity or challenge represents either a legitimate public policy request or a moral claim.

The two dimensions of the question of whether the company can win are whether it can capture an opportunity for collaboration if we seek to advance mutual interests or effectively withstand a challenge if we assemble to win. Otherwise, we would need to take other steps (avert or acquiesce) if an upside is not possible and the downside is palatable.

While determining whether an opportunity for collaboration can be achieved may be more straightforward, assessing whether a company can prevail in a confrontation with shapeholders requires extra tools. Five tools for getting a clearer picture of your chances for overcoming a shapeholder assault are public opinion polling, cost-benefit analysis, the Wilson-Lowi matrix, game theory, and confrontation analysis.

Question 1: Legitimate?

DIMENSION 1: POLICY

To accurately assess the legitimacy of claims and frame your response to them, you must understand the competing theoretical underpinnings for government intervention in commerce. Forces in society have struggled between those who believe that the market is the optimum allocator of resources and those who believe some form of collective response directed by government is preferable.

Keep in mind that, when assessing the legitimacy of claims, the operative viewpoint is not your own or that of your favorite economist. In the political arena, it is a matter of the perspective of the majority of people in the relevant jurisdiction when confronting challenges in a democratic political arena. When contesting issues in the arena of public opinion, the views of a significant segment of a company's customers willing to change consumption patterns can override the costs of conceding.

Political attitudes vary substantially by country. Edelman conducted a global poll that clarifies how attitudes on the role of business differ. They queried whether the "informed public" (with university degrees in the top quarter of wage earners) in countries agreed with Milton Friedman's view that "the social responsibility of business is to increase its profits." The poll's results revealed wide variances in views of the proper role of business.

Eighty-four percent of those polled in the United Arab Emirates agree with Friedman's statement, compared with fewer than a third in Spain. The Edelman poll places America in the middle, in support for Friedman's view. Europe is generally less supportive, while Asia is more supportive.[5] When determining the legitimacy of policy, it is essential to understand that activities that may be acceptable and profitable in Dubai may incite the democratic majority to find ways to stop the same activities in a country like Spain.

Perception is the reality that determines whether a matter is valid. Given that whether an organization can capture an opportunity or withstand an assault often trumps the debate over policy legitimacy, we will skip a detailed discussion of the legitimate policy role for political engagement in commerce that is widely available elsewhere.

DIMENSION 2: MORAL CLAIMS

Moral claims are particularly troublesome. When something is a moral issue, there is a more compelling argument that it must be addressed at all costs. How can a business determine whether an issue is a moral one or not?

One of Benjamin Franklin's sayings engraved in the sidewalks of the University of Pennsylvania's campus comes to mind: "He that teaches himself has a fool for a master." Using your personal ideas on right and wrong will mire you in endless debates. Rather, anchor moral assessments on publicly acknowledged standards.

The challenge companies face assessing whether something is a moral issue is that there are many different frameworks for morality. By what metric should we judge a corporate action as moral? Do we follow the utilitarian view and seek the greatest good for the most people? Or rights theory, and see individuals as ends in themselves? Or justice theory, and work toward social institutions that grant advantages to the naturally disadvantaged?"

Adding yet more complexity is that global companies operate in regions of the world where Western thought lacks credibility. Here the UN's Global Compact can act as a global standard. The Global Compact enunciates ten principles covering human rights, labor, environmental, and anticorruption standards. With more than 8,000 business signatories and 4,000 other organizations signing on from 170 countries, it reflects standards that cross cultural boundaries.[6]

Even beyond the defined theoretical or codified moral codes are the equally demanding, if less defined, codes of authenticity, fairness, and equality. These can be the most vexing for companies, especially when facing savvy stick activists looking for a pressure point.

AUTHENTICITY

PETA could not avail themselves of any traditional ethical standards in their quest since such standards do not apply to animals. Therefore, they chose to press the authenticity standard when suing Whole Foods based on the standards it uses for its premium-priced "humane meat" range, standards that PETA called "deceptive and misleading." Though PETA filed a lawsuit, this is likely only a vehicle to contest the matter in the arena of public opinion. The real jurors will be the consumers of this product line.[7]

FAIRNESS

Environmental groups are targeting bottled water. They sued the U.S. Forest Service, alleging that the agency allowed Nestlé Waters to draw water from a creek in the San Bernardino Mountains under a permit that expired more than twenty-five years ago. They appealed to the fairness principle in asking why Nestlé was allowed to profit from this water use while Southern California faced restrictions because of a drought.[8]

EQUALITY

The equality principle can drag a company onto the battleground in culture wars. Chick-fil-A is a privately owned company with several unique business practices drawn from its founder's Baptist faith. Its stores are closed on Sundays, Thanksgiving, and Christmas. When its owner affirmed his support for what he called "biblical marriage," Democratic mayors in Boston and Chicago declared his stores unwelcome in their cities. Our highly charged political environment holds the potential to put any private owner who is vocal about his or her views on social issues in the hot seat.[9]

What standard should companies consider? All of them. And more: one should consider what the public ethos will be in twenty years. I call this "global plus twenty." Why look so far ahead? Siemens, the largest engineering company in Europe, paid $1.6 billion in government fines in 2008 for activities that were legal and deductible for tax purposes in Germany just a few short years earlier.[10]

This extra aggressiveness in applying moral standards is warranted, given the penalties for crossing the ethical line, as the lasting memory of Nike's long-ago transgression demonstrates. It even applies to one's career. You don't want to be passed over for CEO for an action ten years from now that meets society's expectation then, but not the standards of twenty years from now when you have a shot at the top job. Private enterprises need to make a personal decision on either-or ethical decisions, such as the one faced by the owner of Chick-fil-A. For public companies and other decision makers, applying my global plus twenty standard captures more shapeholder moral claims but will give you greater credibility when you refute claims that do not pass widely acclaimed standards.

Question 2: Upside Possible?

DIMENSION 1: COLLABORATION

Capturing legitimate opportunities to collaborate requires developing a business case that defines benefits sought, actions required to achieve such benefits, a division of tasks among the partners, and methods of coordinating actions and correcting course as necessary. Insights on these more routine business skills are readily available elsewhere.

DIMENSION 2: CONFRONTATION

Accurately assessing whether a company can be successful in contesting an issue with shapeholders is particularly challenging. Both AT&T and Google, two of the world's most astute and politically active companies, had $6 billion stumbles because of miscalculations on this score.

AT&T'S $6 BILLION BREAKUP When AT&T set out to buy T-Mobile in 2011, they were so confident they would have regulatory approval that they agreed to pay a $6 billion breakup fee to Deutsche Telekom if they failed to get approval. The AT&T

government affairs organization is among the largest and most powerful forces in Washington. Achieving this was their top priority. They spent $16 million on lobbying and almost $2 million in campaign contributions.[11]

AT&T even delivered fifteen thousand cupcakes to the FCC during the previous Christmas holiday season with "military precision—a three-page spread-sheet, stamped 'AT&T Proprietary (Internal Use Only),' detailed how the desserts were to be deployed to each of the sixty-three commission offices: four dozen were assigned to the enforcement bureau, ten dozen to the wireless divisions, twelve cupcakes to each of four commissioners, and eighteen to the chairman."[12]

Despite these efforts, AT&T lost and found itself out $6 billion. They did not accurately assess the relative strength of their case for acquisition acceptance compared with the concerns raised by its competitors and competition advocates. They did not accurately game out the decision-making process.

GOOGLE'S $6 BILLION BREAKUP In what *Bloomberg Businessweek* called "Google's $6 Billion Miscalculation,"[13] Google chairman Eric Schmidt fumbled negotiations to settle an antitrust probe with the European Commission, allowing it to metastasize. He misjudged the likelihood of action during his negotiations with the EU competition authorities to resolve concerns that arose in 2012. Further misjudgments in 2013 and 2014, when these considerations should have concluded far more amicably, has caused continued management distractions to the time of this writing, a mushrooming of inquiries and accumulating restrictions on Google's operating model, not to mention a diminished reputation with European consumers.

So where did Google go wrong?

Business-Political Differences. Schmidt relied too much on his personal relationship with Joaquin Almunia, the EU commissioner for competition, forged during a private lunch in the Swiss Alps in December of 2012. It was helpful that Almunia largely discounted the anti-Google campaign that he believed was driven by Microsoft and was affronted by the fact that Microsoft's chief, Steve Ballmer, did not reach out to him personally like Schmidt. Yet, while two CEOs can perhaps rely on each other in business negotiations, it is a serious mistake to attribute that kind of latitude to any single political actor in a democracy, no matter his or her position or power. Almunia's proposal to the commission in January 2014, which was acceptable to Google, never even came up for a vote, as the matter spun quickly out of control.

Ignoring Political Timetables. While Schmidt went through three rounds of hardball negotiations, presenting a more conciliatory settlement each time, Almunia's term ran out and attitudes toward Google deteriorated. Had Schmidt begun negotiations by putting what was his third offer on the table at the beginning, he may have been able to reach a deal with Almunia.

Political Math. Those familiar with the political math of the European Union would see that there are multiple points of leverage. Commissioners are powerful. One can also leverage the weight of individual countries through the European Council. Agitation within the European Parliament, with its expanded powers under the Lisbon Treaty, adds a third point of entry for voices of opposition. Even within the commission, the European culture relies more on collaborative decisions than is common in the United States.

Failing to recognize that commissioners represent not only their designated role but also the interests of their countries, Google never met with Germany's commissioner Günther Oettinger, because he was in charge of the energy portfolio. When German media interests rose up in opposition to Almunia's proposal, it was Oettinger who led the charge.

Political Positioning. The investigation into Google's abuse of its search engine prominence to sell other services was launched by the U.S. Federal Trade Commission in 2011 and dropped at the beginning of 2013 without Google incurring serious harm.[14] Google had strong relationships with the administration of Barack Obama, in part because its employees collectively were his fourth-largest corporate donor in his 2008 campaign[15] and the second largest in 2012.[16] But Google's relationships with (and political understanding of) the European Union were weaker—and that should have made Schmidt more anxious to conclude negotiations.

Opponents' Political Positioning. Schmidt underestimated that Google's competitors had longer and deeper relationships in Europe; Microsoft had developed these relationships during its own extended antitrust battles. Even more important was opposition from European actors. Local telecom carriers were frustrated by low payments for carrying Internet traffic. European publishers were annoyed by Google's rising media influence and what they saw as its disrespect for copyright protection. Each applied pressure on political actors to stop Google.

Cultural Differences: Intervening Events. When privacy activist Edward Snowden erupted onto the scene on May 20, 2013, European views toward Google and other American tech giants soured. Snowden revealed that Google and others had reluctantly given U.S. spy agencies access to customer accounts. Given differing views of privacy on each side of the Atlantic, it was hard for Americans to understand the ferocity of public anger. This was particularly the case in one of Europe's most powerful capitals—Berlin—with its history under East Germany's oppressive Stasi intelligence service.

As the reins of the Competition Directorates-General passed to Margrethe Vestager in 2014, Google found itself facing a more challenging regulator and heightened public concern over privacy. The atmospheric shift sparked by Snowden got worse. Negotiations over a Transatlantic Trade and Investment Partnership with the United States frequently put digital issues center stage. Günther Oettinger, now the EU commissioner in charge of digital affairs, pushed forward to issue a new General Data Protection Regulation. The EU Court of Justice ruled in 2015 that the fifteen-year-old Safe Harbor pact that allowed data transfers across the Atlantic failed to protect European citizens from surveillance by the U.S. government.[17]

Making matters worse for Google were the quickly multiplying investigations. In addition to the antitrust investigation into Google's product search service, the company faced a further seven significant challenges. In May 2014 the EU Court of Justice ruled that EU citizens had a "right to be forgotten," at direct odds with Google's purpose to "organize the world's information and make it universally accessible and useful."[18] In October 2014 the European Union joined a French investigation into the sufficiency of Google's tax payments.[19] In April 2015 the European Union launched an antitrust investigation into Google's Android system[20] and Google Shopping.[21] In September of that same year, the U.S. Federal Trade Commission began their own investigation of the Android system.[22] In April 2016 the European Union formalized its objections regarding Android dominance,[23] the United States extended its Android probe,[24] and the *Wall Street Journal*[25] and Getty Images[26] filed formal complaints with the European Commission on Google scraping news reports and images for its own posting, depriving traditional news outlets of traffic. In July 2016 the European Union charged that Google's advertising business was imposing terms and conditions that hobbled rivals.[27]

As of January 2017 Google found itself in a far stickier wicket than it would have if it had better assessed what it would take to resolve EU concerns in 2013.

Besides understanding the differences between business and politics, the political math involved, the relative power position of your company and its coalition relative to opponents, cultural differences, and having a healthy concern that the tide may turn against you, there are five tools that companies ought to be familiar with as they assess the likelihood of an upside for companies with shapeholder interactions.

Tool 1: Public Opinion Polling

Remember, the two primary arenas shapeholders operate in are the arena of public opinion and the political arena. In either place, what the public thinks is paramount. When you are considering the decision making of public officials, even though an elected official or a board within an administrative agency is the ultimate decision maker, keep in mind that public opinion will be a major factor in the evaluation. A key consideration in assessing whether your company can win a face-off is "What does the public think?"

Just as a jeweler peers deep inside a diamond to determine its color and clarity, so must a company see attitudes about the company and the issues that surround it. What complicates finding the answers to this question?[28]

Ill-informed Public. Most people have spent little time thinking about issues of concern to businesses. Most are uninformed, unengaged, uninterested, and unconnected. This creates a risk but also an opportunity—the risk that an activist can wag the dog by establishing a fact that constitutes a captivating tail, but an opportunity in that defending against that attack can be done with a fact equally tangential to the operative factors relating to the issue. It is important to understand who knows what, where they stand on the issue, how intense their views are, and what could change their minds. These answers will change by geography and demography. My guess is that Google is now well versed on attitudes toward privacy around the world.

Fading Landline Usage. Traditional polling meant calling people at home when you had a chance of the respondent completing a full survey. Landline-only polling misses cell-phone households, which have different demographics. Pollsters find it difficult to conduct surveys over cell phones, because their caller ID function makes it easier to screen survey calls and people accessed on cell phones are more likely to be someplace where they don't want to be interrupted. While Internet polling is improving in quality, it also has a demographic bias—not everyone is on the Internet.

Opinion Leader Influence. Some people will be well informed on the issue, or at least they will think they are. Many of them can influence the debate, turn it in new directions, add new audiences, and in the end change views on questions of policy. They can filter how the issue is framed to the broader public—what ideas are advanced or suppressed, which facts get the focus. Many of these opinion leaders work for shapeholders—activists, bloggers, reporters, political leaders, associations, and think tanks.

Collaborating with a wide circle of opinion leaders active in areas of concern to the company keeps you informed and poised to advance your side of the story. For example, after the surge of attacks against Google in April 2016, the *New York Times* published an op-ed called "Europe's Web Privacy Rules: Bad for Google, Bad for Everyone" by Google's former associate general counsel, then at the Stanford Center for Internet and Society, and the executive director of the Reporters Committee for Freedom of the Press.[29]

Tool 2: Cost and Benefit Analysis of Those Advancing and Resisting an Action

Consider the cost-benefit analysis of each side in a shapeholder face-off to predict actions.[30] When considering cost and benefits, bear in mind that benefits may be measured in money or simply strong feelings over what is just and unjust. In the business world, efforts must be highly coordinated to be effective. In the nonmarket, unfocused disparate surges of activity aimed at the same target can be compelling. Finally, it is important to recognize that with the advent of service providers for shapeholders like

the Change.org petition platform that RAN used against the Girl
Scouts, the costs of activism are going down, elevating the likelihood of future action.

The financial benefits of Nike's labor practices are easy to see.
What about the other side? Clearly the AFL-CIO stood to gain if
Nike upped its labor standards, lessening the competitive threat
to American production. The union also benefited from allies
moved by moral outrage over human rights abuses. Relative to
these benefits, the costs of forming an affiliate and placing Jeff
Ballinger in Indonesia were minor. Their cost of disseminating
the AFL-CIO message was reduced by receptive publications
like *Harper's*. With proper analysis, Nike should have seen it
coming.

AT&T saw the benefit in its merger. Yet wouldn't that imply
that the cost to its peer rivals would be equally great, motivating
them to oppose it? Verizon's lobbying team is no slouch—with
or without cupcakes. Add to this the consumer activists who
oppose industry consolidation that drives higher prices, and we
wonder why AT&T was so confident that it agreed to such a
high breakup fee.

Among the many things Google missed in its face-off with the
EU was how commissioners Margrethe Vestager and Günther
Oettinger calculated their own political benefits. Taking a hard
line against the company made them heroes to Europeans (even if
they were villains in Silicon Valley boardrooms). Showing leniency
might have led to their electoral doom.

Shapeholders won't waste energy seeking change unless the
benefit they see outweighs their costs. This is why those who are
either the worst or the trendsetter in their industries are targeted
most often. The worst produce the biggest single-company benefit.
Even though activists don't achieve as much from getting industry
trendsetters to accept a new metric, the combination of changes
their actions trigger throughout an industry can aggregate to a
large benefit.

Tool 3: Wilson-Lowi Matrix: Concentrated Versus Distributed Effect

A tool for evaluating whether political efforts will achieve their outcomes was proposed by James Q. Wilson, building on the work of Theodore Lowi. The Wilson-Lowi matrix he created "categorized the nature of political competition on an issue as a function of the concentration or dispersion of the benefits and costs from an alternative . . . relative to the status quo. . . . The benefits or harm are concentrated if the per capita effects are high" and low if widely dispersed. The matrix has four possible outcomes.

Interest Group Politics: Concentrated Benefits Versus Concentrated Harm. In 2010 banks and retailers in the United States battled over whether to cap the costs of debit cards. Since there is concentration of benefits and harm among a handful of big banks and big retailers, the chance of action depended on whether one side could gain an edge over the other. The same was true in the AT&T versus Verizon / competition activists fight over T-Mobile.

Majoritarian Politics: Widely Distributed Benefits Versus Widely Distributed Harm. An example of this is health-care (Medicare) or

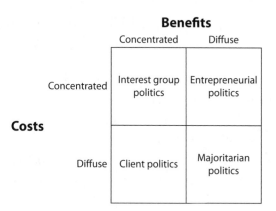

retirement security (Social Security) reform. Nearly everyone benefits somewhat. Nearly everyone is harmed somewhat. With so many people affected, the issue is entrenched, and it is unlikely anything will change. The difficulty of change here has contributed to the deficit and debt the United States and other established democracies face today.

Client Politics: Concentrated Benefits Versus Widely Distributed Harm. An example is subsidies for renewable energy. The benefits go to a relatively small number of producers, while the financial costs are disbursed across all taxpayers, making them imperceptible to any one taxpayer. Wilson assesses the likelihood of action is high. Those concentrated beneficiaries are motivated to aggressively push for action, while those paying for the subsidies have little incentive to act.

Entrepreneurial Politics: Widely Distributed Benefits Versus Concentrated Harm. Consider the repeal of oil and gas tax credits. Reflecting the flip side of client politics, the benefits for repealing these credits would be widely disbursed, while the harm would be concentrated among a few oil companies. The likelihood of action is low. A motivated minority actively engaged prevails against a majority for whom benefits are so widely dispersed that there is little motivation for anyone to advocate action. This is called *entrepreneurial*, because it would take a political entrepreneur to effect change. Even though President Obama sought to be the entrepreneur on this issue in 2011, no change came, confirming the difficulty of succeeding in these conditions.

America's Founding Fathers, with the tyranny of George III in mind, designed our government with checks and balances to prevent a concentration of power in a king. They were equally worried about the tyranny of the majority over the minority, so they discarded the idea of a direct democracy and instead created a republic to allow room for the educated discretion of representatives.

Eventually they added a Bill of Rights that further protected the minority from the majority.

Since they were inventing the modern republic at the time, I suppose our forbears are excused for not anticipating that a motivated few could tyrannize the apathetic many, so that organizations representing a mere fraction of the total population routinely trump the will of the majority, as we see with client and entrepreneurial politics.

Tools 4 and 5: Game Theory and Confrontation Analysis

A company would be wise, when assessing whether an opportunity can be captured or a challenge averted, to predict the outcomes of key decision makers and their motivations. Two tools can help us here—game theory and confrontation analysis. Both are, admittedly, complex. But when you make decisions in which billions of dollars hinge on the outcome (like AT&T), it is more than worth it.

Game theory uses a mathematical model to predict the most probable outcome of decision making among rational, self-interested agents in a given situation. These models require input of numerical assessments for each actor—position on the issue, intensity of interest in the issue, and capacity to influence other actors. The output is the most likely outcome.

Confrontation analysis (also known as *dilemma analysis*) is a structured method to analyze multiparty interactions. It evolved from game theory, but instead of trying to resolve a single game, it examines interactions among the players to redefine the game—and it acknowledges the role of emotions. Instead of predicting a single outcome, it assesses a series of interactions in sequence to identify and resolve dilemmas.

For each scenario, the parties communicate what they would like to see happen, their "position," and what will happen if they cannot agree, the "threatened future." These interactions produce dilemmas. The three most common dilemmas that block action are *persuasion*—failing to be persuaded by the argument of the other party; *trust*—not trusting the other party will follow through on promises; and *threat*—not believing the threat of adverse consequences.

To move past these dilemmas, parties must improve the persuasiveness of their arguments, provide assurances of their follow-through, or bolster the credibility of the threat as a consequence for not acting.

The accuracy of game theory and confrontation analysis depends on an intimate understanding of the players, the web of interests between them, the intensity of each actor's interest, and the actors' relative power to persuade. For companies making public affairs decisions involving large sums that depend on the outcome of decisions, it is well worth the effort and money to access people who can provide the insights available from both these methodologies.[31]

Warning! Avoid the False Consensus Effect

There is always a risk of falling prey to the *false consensus effect*. This is the tendency to overestimate how many people share one's view on a subject. Nearly everyone travels in circles where a higher than average percentage of the people they meet actually agree with them or are too polite to make clear their opposition. Yet most people's circles are only small pieces of the whole.

Once you have results from the assessment techniques, it is necessary to determine whether an issue is legitimate and should be addressed and whether activism to affect change represents an upside for the company. Now you are prepared to determine courses of action.

- Charting the optimum path for social engagement requires answering two questions for every shapeholder opportunity or challenge. Each question has two dimensions. The two questions are: first, "Is it legit?," and second, "Can I win?" The answers to these questions allow us to plot our action along the shapeholder decision matrix.
- The two dimensions of the first question involve accurately assessing whether each opportunity or challenge represents either a legitimate public policy request or moral claim.
- Policy legitimacy is a matter of the perspective of the majority of people in the relevant jurisdiction when confronting challenges in a democratic political arena.
- When considering the legitimacy of moral claims, it is best to consider all moral standards from the perspective of the public ethos in twenty years. I call this "global plus twenty."
- The two dimensions of the question of whether the company can win is whether it can capture an opportunity for collaboration if we seek to advance mutual interests or effectively withstand a challenge if we assemble to win. Otherwise, we would need to take other steps (avert or acquiesce) if an upside is not possible and the downside is palatable.
- Five tools help companies get a clearer picture of their chances for overcoming a shapeholder assault:

  1. *Public Opinion Polling.* A company needs to understand attitudes about the company and the issues that surround it—who knows what, where they stand, the intensity of their views, and what would change their minds.
  2. *Cost-Benefit Analysis.* It is important to assess the costs and benefits for both the company and the shapeholder coalition pressing the company to change to determine the likelihood of action and eventual success.
  3. *Wilson-Lowi Matrix.* Applying this matrix factors in the track record of smaller, concentrated interests prevailing over larger, but dispersed interests.

4. *Game Theory.* This mathematical model incorporates judgments of each actor's position on an issue and the intensity of actors' interest and capacity to influence others to determine the likely outcome of a dispute.
5. *Confrontation Analysis.* This method assesses a series of interactions in sequence to identify and resolve dilemmas. It pinpoints where parties must improve the persuasiveness of their arguments, provide assurances of their follow-through, or bolster the credibility of the threat as a consequence for not acting.

9

Avert

Dead ahead, through the pitch-black night, the captain sees a
 light on a collision course with his ship. He signals: "Change
 your course 10 degrees east."
Reply: "Change your course 10 degrees west."
"I'm a U.S. Navy captain! Change your course."
"I'm a seaman second class. Change your course."
"I'm a battleship! I'm not changing course."
"I'm a lighthouse. Your call!"

IN 1973 I WAS in the Pequot Lakes High School marching band.
Our band director told us that he wanted us to focus and look
straight ahead while marching—"even if an atomic bomb went
off"—to maintain parade discipline.

At a parade I was playing trombone in the front row. As we
moved down the street, a television cameraman squatted down in
front of me. Remembering my director's words, I marched straight
ahead and bowled the cameraman over. We won first place at the
parade, but the local television station ran footage of the second-
place band—for obvious reasons.

The next day in class, my director told me that although he
appreciated how strictly I followed directions, I could have maintained parade discipline by sidestepping the cameraman instead.
The moral of the story: sometimes it makes sense to change course
to avoid an inevitable collision.

My parade experience exemplifies the underlying logic of the
avert step when facing a legitimate request from shapeholders
that requires you to deviate from your preferred path. Doing so

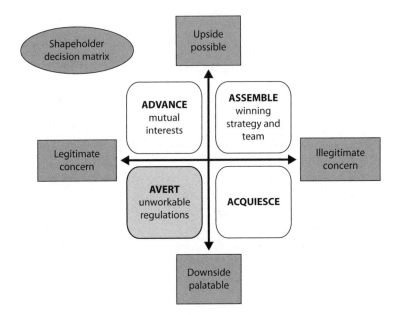

is preferable to ignoring the shapeholders' appeal and suffering consequences.

McDonald's Cage-Free Eggs Decision

Let us consider how McDonald's compromised with activists by deciding to use cage-free eggs, even though doing so offers no upside to McDonald's.

How little the public understands about even the most basic aspects of commercial operations is a challenge for every industry. Perhaps nowhere is this as true as in agriculture. During one of my congressional campaigns, my opponent confessed to a Farmfest debate audience that she grew up thinking milk came from the grocery store.

In 1916, 32 percent of the U.S. population lived on a farm. You either lived on a farm or had close relatives on a farm. With only

2 percent of the American population farming today, it's possible that someone really doesn't know where milk comes from.

Many a farm family ate animals they raised and butchered. Unless you are a practicing vegetarian or vegan, you are the beneficiary of those who butcher livestock to fill your freezer. What could be more inhumane than butchering? How do you judge an animal's rights short of that fateful end?

So now consider McDonald's decision to embrace cage-free eggs in the United Kingdom in 1998[1] and in the United States and Canada in 2015.[2] We begin with evaluating all questions against the company's purpose.

- *Align.* McDonald's purpose statement is disappointingly platitudinal: "Our purpose goes beyond what we sell. We're using our reach to be a positive force. For our customers. Our people. Our communities. Our world." That says everything and therefore nothing. Under its website's "Good Food" tab, it lists further attributes: "We promote choices. Real ingredients. Great taste. Transparency."[3] But what about the chickens?
- *Anticipate.* McDonald's failed to adequately anticipate that stick activists would enforce the company's pledge of "transparency." In 2011 Mercy for Animals took undercover videos in the barns of Sparboe Farms—one of McDonald's top egg suppliers. The conditions the videos portrayed became the subject of an *ABC News* investigation broadcast on 20/20, and the Food and Drug Administration cited Sparboe for "significant . . . and serious violations" of regulations regarding the production of eggs.[4] McDonald's immediately dropped Sparboe as a supplier, but this did not prevent Mercy for Animals from memorializing McDonald's suppliers' conduct on a website entitled mcdonaldscruelty.com.

The attacks on Nike two decades earlier should have put all branded companies on notice that they would be called to account for the conduct of their suppliers. The WikiLeaks State Department cable release the year before should have alerted companies, especially those highlighting their embrace of transparency, that activists would eventually reveal activities at the weakest links in their supply chains.

• *Assess: Legitimacy.* When assessing whether animal rights activists' concern over caged chickens is legitimate, let us consider from a moral perspective the associated benefits and costs of moving to cage-free production: What potential consequences arise for humans by raising cage-free chickens?

A scientific study commissioned by the Humane Society of the United States[5] did not conclude that chickens faced a higher mortality rate in a caged environment. Even so, they stated, "It *might* be worse to spend a long life confined to a restrictive, barren cage than a short life in an enriched, cage-free environment that offered a much greater degree of freedom to express natural behavior . . . the choice is *simple.*" Despite only being able to say cage-free *might* be better, the Human Society believes the choice to do so is *simple.* Such a decision is anything but simple. Cage-free eggs have a derivative effect that results in direct harm to humans. Cage-free production significantly increases the carbon footprint and capital required to produce an egg. This makes eggs less accessible to cost-conscious consumers and more difficult for social aid programs to afford when addressing hunger.

Raising flocks in barns that allow them freedom to roam requires significantly more land, steel, and air to heat in the winter and cool in the summer than does stacking chickens in cages. Additionally, because chicken feed is more likely to be spilled and intermixed with waste when feeding in open environments, more grain is required in cage-free conditions. These factors rack up expenses, which means that less food can be provided to consumers. All these factors (except the land) also elevate the carbon footprint of producing an egg.

When addressing the well-being of chickens, we must consider whether chickens can be left in the open or whether they should be enclosed to some degree when free of cages. Raising poultry in the open is impractical, given the vagaries of the weather and exposure to diseases encountered from the wild, as was illustrated by the avian influenza outbreak in 2015. Diseases carried by migratory birds—wild ducks and geese—infected domesticated flocks. Migratory birds infecting chickens and turkeys in the Midwest caused the extermination of almost 40 million birds and required the U.S. government to earmark nearly $400 million to compensate poultry farmers for disease testing, culled birds, and cleanup.[6] Incidents like these make a compelling case for keeping flocks in barns to ensure safe animals and safe food.[7]

We find a mix of moral benefits and harms in this decision. The decision to embrace cage-free eggs arises in legitimate moral issues. Not doing so might violate animal rights, but doing so will elevate carbon consumption and make it more expensive to feed the hungry.

To a farm kid, this is an easy decision—keep chickens caged. Yet McDonald's must base its decision on the wants of a society that knows little about farming but is increasingly fixated on the sources of its food.

• *Assess: Likelihood of Action.* Before deciding on a course of action, McDonald's must also consider the likelihood that activists will succeed in forcing the action they seek.

Consider the costs and benefits of Mercy for Animals pressing its case compared with what it would cost McDonald's to educate the public on the downside of cage-free practices. Factor in the obvious receptivity of the public and the media to concerns regarding animal abuse compared with the complexity of trade-offs. The scale clearly tilts in favor of the animal activists' success.

McDonald's must consider that the credibility of its claim to "good food" will be undermined far more by critical media concerning the conditions of chickens producing its eggs than the calculated cost of their carbon production. I have visited many of these barns, and I can confirm that they are better suited to exposés than to branding advertisements.

Corporate herd instinct strengthens the activists' hand. Starbucks, Nestlé, Aramark, and Burger King committed to go fully cage-free prior to McDonald's decision. The month after McDonald's announcement, Kellogg and TGI Friday's followed suit.[8]

When considering these three variables, we find ourselves in the equivalent of client politics under the Wilson-Lowi matrix. Animal rights activists would receive a concentrated benefit from the adoption of cage-free eggs. The costs regarding carbon and poverty are widely disbursed. It is unlikely that environmental or antipoverty activists will attack McDonald's for going cage-free, though it is certain that animal rights activists will if they don't. So the matrix suggests that the likelihood of success for animal rights activists is high. One can understand why McDonald's chose to embrace cage-free eggs—to avert a collision.

Companies in other industries where public awareness of underlying processes is scant may find themselves making similarly complex conclusions to avert actions that would hurt their operations.

You Can't Fight Something with Nothing

Too many companies try to blunt action on legitimate shapeholder concerns without providing an alternative response. These companies underestimate shapeholders. Activists working toward an authentic cause will keep at it until they have generated enough pressure to force action.

As a congressman, I had many companies in this position come to me, saying, "We don't want this to happen. It will hurt us." When I asked for their solutions, a shockingly high percentage had no answer. I cannot tell you how many times I advised companies opposing a bill that addressed a legitimate issue: "You can't fight something with nothing."

McDonald's faces more complex and costly sourcing because of its decision to go cage-free, but this decision was necessary given shapeholder demands. You can assume that something is eventually going to happen on legitimate issues: averting conflict enhances your political standing on the issue and enables you to shape what happens; not acting leaves you with little political credibility. Levi's action to avert attacks on Asian sourcing gave it a stronger voice in shaping sourcing standards.

Like McDonald's, companies in every industry must balance multiple variables to make similar decisions.

- Uber chose to settle lawsuits in 2016 about the employment status of its drivers by changing the policy for deactivating drivers. This was done to retain the drivers' status as independent contractors, an essential element of Uber's business strategy.[9] This decision followed a shift from a more confrontational approach to one that sought to negotiate agreements and bring the company into compliance with existing laws, even if it leads to lower profit margins.[10]
- After defeating a San Francisco ballot initiative to limit its activities in 2015, Airbnb issued a community compact outlining steps to work with municipalities and accommodate their concerns to avoid future costly referendums. This compact included Airbnb promising to pay its "fair share" of hotel and tourist taxes in cities in which they are established.[11]
- In an effort to mitigate the drive to limit the availability of soda, beverage companies, including Coca-Cola, PepsiCo, and Procter & Gamble, assembled to voluntarily implement calorie count labeling on individual servings of their products so purchasers could make informed, healthier decisions.[12]
- Hoping to avoid a ban on the sale of products like Sudafed that contributed to the methamphetamine drug scourge, Target moved them behind the counter, charting an alternative path legislatures accepted.[13]

Now we consider the fact that sometimes it makes sense to acquiesce to illegitimate demands when it is a fight the company cannot win.

KEY TAKEAWAYS

- Shapeholders working toward an authentic cause will keep at it until they have generated enough pressure to force action.
- You can't fight something (a legitimate issue) with nothing (inaction).
- When faced with a legitimate request that offers no upside for the company, address it in the manner most palatable to the organization, rather than have the worst case imposed by shapeholder pressure.

10

Acquiesce

I respect all men and women who, from high motives and with sanity and self-respect, do all they can to avert war.
—THEODORE ROOSEVELT

MY FATHER TOLD ME, "Your first loss is your best loss." If you have a losing hand, don't throw good money after bad money—take your hit early. You will lose less.

Even more difficult than making the decision to avert is the decision to acquiesce to illegitimate demands in cases where you cannot win or can only win with undue costs.

To acquiesce is never pleasant, but if you pay careful attention to earlier steps, you will find yourself in this position less often. Choosing this path means cutting your losses and living to fight another day.

Stanley Tool Stays Home

Let me share an example of acquiescence I witnessed firsthand during my early days in Congress—Stanley Tool's decision to jettison its plan to move its headquarters to Bermuda.

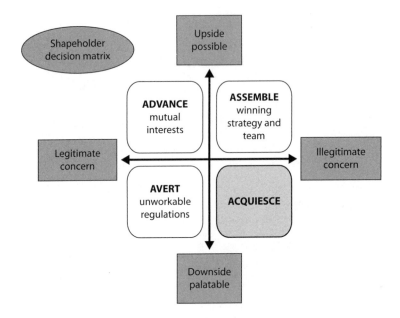

The United States, unlike other major advanced economies, taxes foreign earnings brought back to its shores. So American companies fight global competitors with one hand behind their backs. When Apple competes with Samsung in the mobile phone market or Caterpillar with Komatsu to determine who builds skyscrapers in tax-free Dubai, Apple's California-based and Caterpillar's Illinois-based workers are at a cost disadvantage, because their employers must pay U.S. domestic taxes on overseas earnings, while Samsung and Komatsu do not. To mitigate this disadvantage, companies can defer paying this tax until they bring the money back to the United States. That incentivizes them to invest in international markets.

This is like America shooting itself in the foot. It's extremely difficult for a one-armed, one-footed company to compete against multinational corporations whose governments don't impose similar burdens on their international business operations. The most outspoken CEO against this policy is Apple's Tim Cook, who lambasted the taxes as "made for the industrial age, not the digital age."[1]

Besides being a drag on American businesses, it's also one of the most misrepresented aspects of the tax code. President Barack Obama and others who oppose removing this provision demonize it by calling it a tax loophole that "encourages American companies to ship jobs overseas." The true effect is the opposite. It makes it more difficult for goods and services produced by American-domiciled companies to compete in a global marketplace.

Stanley Tool was concerned about this competitive disadvantage in 2002. Not only did it face a disadvantage against foreign-based competitors, but two of its American competitors—Cooper Industries and Ingersoll Rand—had already reincorporated overseas.

The company's plan to reincorporate in Bermuda, while leaving its primary operations in New Britain, Connecticut, narrowly won shareholder approval in May 2002. This sparked an overwhelming shapeholder firestorm.

Sued by two Connecticut officials and questioned by the Security and Exchange Commission, the company sought a second shareholder vote. The attorney general and the treasurer of Connecticut claimed the second election was flawed. The company's plan became such a big issue in a Connecticut congressional campaign in its local district and attracted so much national attention that on July 30, 2002, House majority whip Tom DeLay (R-TX) sent a letter to Stanley's CEO asking him to reconsider. Pressured by congressional leaders and protests by the AFL-CIO, in August 2002 the company decided to maintain its incorporation in the United States.[2]

Stanley Tool could not understand how it was legitimate for them to incur extra taxes not incurred by its competitors. Sometimes the optimum path for action by a company is to acquiesce, even if it does not assess the shapeholder request to be legitimate. The company had little chance of prevailing in an uphill battle with shapeholders, given the bright glare of national political attention, and decided it was not worth the costs and distraction needed to win.

Oftentimes it is wise for companies to suppress their desire to fight it out. The press likes conflict. Many of those opposing companies have the ear of the media—remember Mercy for Animal's ability to get on ABC's *20/20*.

Deciding when to assemble to win and when to acquiesce to illegitimate concerns requires careful analysis of the likelihood of shapeholder success. If your analysis of the costs of complying with a shapeholder demand versus fighting it and the likelihood of their activism succeeding leaves you in doubt, I suggest you acquiesce, if only because companies often overestimate their ability to win political contests, given their inexperience in such matters.

Let's consider a few more examples of organizations that found it necessary to acquiesce to shapeholder demands.

- After the president-elect, Donald Trump, threatened to slap a 35% tariff on Ford vehicles made in Mexico and sold in the United States, Ford chose to cancel plans for a new plant in Mexico, saying its decision was based on lower-than-expected demand for the smaller vehicles the plant was to produce.[3]
- Facebook and Mark Zuckerberg invited conservative leaders to its headquarters in Menlo Park, California, to address damaging allegations that Facebook steers people away from conservative viewpoints.[4]
- The Boy Scouts found it prudent to acquiesce on the issue of gay scouts and scoutmasters.[5]
- McDonald's decided to source all its milk for Swiss products from Switzerland rather than convince the Swiss that their milk is no better than milk from other countries.
- When outrage erupted over Starbucks's paltry tax payments in the United Kingdom, it "pledged to pay £20m in British corporation tax in 2013 and 2014 regardless of its profits."[6]

When you're getting run out of town, get out in front and turn it into a parade. Don't spend time complaining. Make it your idea. If your company chooses to acquiesce, it is important that you reach accommodation in a way that does not unduly limit future options. You should redirect feelings of frustration to resolving to engage in strategies that will reduce the likelihood that you will find yourself in this situation again. The path to closely follow is the seven steps to shapeholder success. The next step considers conditions in which companies and shapeholders share a common upside.

KEY TAKEAWAY

- It is not worth contesting illegitimate shapeholder contests when you cannot win. Harbor your strength for battles you must win.

Advance Common Interests

Coming together is a beginning. Keeping together is progress.
Working together is success.

—HENRY FORD

BUSINESSES FINDING WAYS TO advance mutual interests has
always been a cornerstone of progress. Sustained commercial success requires constantly scanning the landscape for such opportunities and aggressively pursuing them when you find them.

There is little evidence that J. P. Morgan had objectives beyond
fame and fortune when he bet his future on Thomas Edison's
new inventions to form what eventually became General Electric.
This risky gamble delivered both: in 1900 GE established the
nation's first laboratory dedicated to scientific research. It lever-
aged its own inventions and commercialized those of others to
revolutionize our lives by living up to its motto: We Bring Good
Things to Life.

Domestic life was simplified by its toaster (1905), electric range
(1910), refrigerator (1917), and clothes washer (1930). As it
evolved, GE became more deliberate about aligning its highly
profitable business model with delivering significant benefits for
society. GE's advances in radio and television helped us communicate with one another, its innovations in railroad and aviation

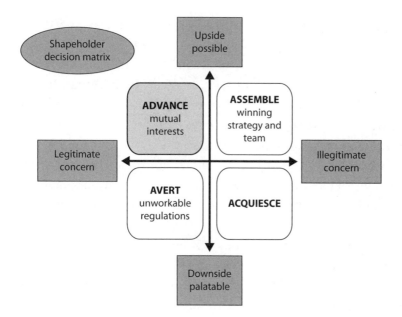

transportation bring us all closer together, and its enhancements of X-ray technologies help determine the correct treatment of our ills.

GE's current Ecomagination effort reflects the profoundly positive results that can flow from a company embracing a cause that is profitable and socially beneficial. The goal of Ecomagination is to "enable economic growth while avoiding emissions and reducing water consumption . . . and developing strategic partnerships to solve some of the toughest environmental challenges at scale to create a cleaner, faster, smarter tomorrow." Between 2005, when Ecomagination launched, and 2014, GE invested $15 billion in research and development, generating $200 billion in revenue from products and services related to the program. It reduced its greenhouse gas emissions by 31 percent and its use of freshwater by 42 percent. These are huge reductions. GE has set goals for further program results by 2020.[1]

Specific Ecomagination breakthroughs have included reducing the fuel burn and CO_2 emissions of its jet engines, applying aeroderivative technologies to create ultra-efficient power plants, enhancing the efficiency of wind turbines by injecting them with the industrial Internet so that they generate enough energy to power 27 million European households each year, making its train locomotives more efficient so they save $98 million in fuel expenses over 10 years, improving waste-water solutions to enable millions of gallons of water to be reused each day, and innovating technologies that can reduce streetlights consumption of electricity by 50–70 percent.[2]

GE's focus on the purpose of Ecomagination closely aligns with its differentiation in the marketplace. GE is leveraging its deep industrial heritage and technological expertise to unlock real-time insights that lead to better productivity. GE aims to be the leader in applying the industrial Internet, the Internet of Things for industrial applications. Its goal is achieving significant industrial productivity enhancements by marrying physical industrial assets with sensors connected to the Internet, sophisticated software, and complex predictive analytics. Taking a page from Apple, it has launched an "app store" for operators who develop apps that can significantly improve productivity. All these efforts mean more profits and more efficiencies that drive sustainable results for its customers and the planet.

In addition to its strategy of Ecomagination and a companion Healthymagination effort that focuses its lines of business on achieving sustainable objectives, GE supports targeted corporate social responsibility, or CSR, efforts that help communities while helping GE. One example of these efforts is its investment in a program in Nigeria to create a network of mentors, coaches, and teachers, including its four hundred-plus Nigerian employees, to foster a qualified workforce for power generation and health care in Africa. Biomedical engineering training provides students with advanced employable skills-training programs, Nigeria with a skilled workforce, and GE with the operators essential to health-care providers who use its medical technology.

GE's story is not unique but regrettably is still not universal. There are many companies, large and small, all over the world that are increasingly focused on aligning their energies and innovations toward bettering their businesses and society simultaneously by advancing common interests. In many ways, directing corporate energies toward social challenges holds greater promise of results at on a large scale than stand-alone government or NGO efforts.

Creating Shared Value

Americans are frustrated with gridlock in Washington and political leaders' unwillingness to move beyond partisan trench warfare to address the biggest problems we face—namely, the failure of our education system to provide workers with the skills they need to succeed in a rapidly changing economy; our mounting national debt; retiring baby boomers; rapidly escalating health-care costs; and reining in carbon emissions. The middle class is rising as the dominant voice in emerging markets, but they are impatient with substandard public services, endemic corruption, and government dysfunction.

A savvy businessperson sees problems as opportunities to profitably overcome challenges. When business and governments move beyond combative strategies to collaborative approaches, everyone can win. Businesses can profitably provide high-quality essential services to citizens at a lower cost than the government. When businesses evaluate every issue pressed on them by activist groups and consider whether they can address them profitably, previously unseen growth opportunities emerge.

Savvy business leaders can take the lead, pulling political leaders in tow. Companies themselves can chip away at these challenges by capturing opportunities for what Michael Porter and

Mark Kramer called creating shared value (CSV): "Policies and operating practices that enhance the competitiveness of a company while simultaneously advancing the economic and social conditions in the communities in which it operates" (6). Porter and Kramer write, "Creating shared value represents a broader conception of Adam Smith's invisible hand. It opens the doors of the pin factory to a wider set of influences. It is not philanthropy but self-interested behavior to create economic value by creating social value" (17).[3]

Porter and Kramer suggest that businesses miss out if they don't aggressively capture opportunities to create shared value. "The essence of strategy is choosing a unique positioning and a distinctive value chain to deliver on it. Shared value opens up many new needs to meet, new products to offer, new customers to serve, and new ways to configure the value chain. And the competitive advantages that arise from creating shared value will often be more sustainable than conventional cost and quality improvements" (16).

CSV is an evolution in thinking that moves beyond CSR; it is better for the company and society than pure altruism. Business leaders often view CSR as an expense item. During times of economic stress, it is considered nonessential to the company's strategy and is hastily trimmed back.

While CSR activities are supplementary to a company's primary business, CSV activities emerge from the core of the company, support the company's strategy, and offer opportunities to improve company profitability. This means that a company that organizes its good deeds around a CSV model is less likely to cancel them when times are tough. A company whose business model includes profitably addressing social challenges could expand in challenging times.

It is easy to slip into thinking that the way to effectively engage shapeholders is all about avoiding negative consequences. An "all-pain avoidance, no-gain surveillance" approach is shortsighted.

Capturing opportunities to create shared value offers not only a chance to add to a company's bottom line but significantly improves a company's standing with shapeholders. As with most things in life, success breeds success. Experience in recognizing shared value will open future opportunities.

Reconceiving Products and Markets

Porter and Kramer suggest that assessing "the social needs, benefits, and harms that are or could be embodied in the firm's products . . . will lead companies to discover new opportunities for differentiation and repositioning in traditional markets and recognize the potential of new markets they previously overlooked" (8). GE recognized the environmental effect of its many products and how increased efficiency made them more attractive to customers.

Since companies are more effective than governments or NGOs at moving consumers to embrace products and services that generate social benefits, society's gains are even better. Could the government have done a better job of focusing consumer attention on sustainable groceries than Whole Foods? Could the government have done a better job of prodding consumers to address obesity by exercising than Nike and Fitbit? Could the government have urged people to embrace the environmental benefits of cold water and concentrated detergents to wash their clothes more comprehensively than Procter & Gamble or Unilever? Each company reconceived product offerings to the mutual benefit of themselves and society, relying on strategic marketing to appeal to consumers.

Redefining the Value Chain

Businesses can also both benefit society and improve their performance by carefully evaluating every element of their value chain: resource use, procurement method, distribution, employee productivity, and location. "Walmart, for example, was able to address both [cost and sustainability objectives] by reducing its packaging and rerouting its trucks to cut 100 million miles from its delivery routes in 2009, saving $200 million even as it shipped more products."[4] When Procter & Gamble introduced Tide Ultra 2x, P&G's retail partners shipped more cheaply (less bulk), freed up shelf space for other products (since the new product took less space), and did so with a cleaner environmental footprint.

Enabling Local Cluster Development

Collaborative engagement to strengthen local clusters helps the businesses and community members situated within the cluster. Many of our major cities were built up around clusters of expertise. Minneapolis, Minnesota, rose to prominence as a milling town, providing flour to feed the nation. John S. and Charles A. Pillsbury and Cadwallader Washburn set up rival flour-milling businesses on each side of the Saint Anthony Falls in downtown Minneapolis. Both families worked collectively to start the Millers' Association, develop a system of elevators for storage, and serve their community in political office. They invested significantly in local institutions that bettered both the community and the operating environment for their businesses. Today, these efforts still provide research advancements, a highly qualified workforce, and a cultural environment that helps their unified manifestation as General Mills to attract and retain the best talent.

Enabling Industry Cluster Development

Companies also benefit from investing in industry clusters like the World Food Prize. Activities around this prize, though centered in Des Moines, Iowa, have worldwide impact. General Mills's involvement in this efforts helps fulfill its purpose to advance human development by improving the quality, quantity, and availability of food in the world. The University of Minnesota fostered by Pillsbury educated Nobel Prize winner Norman Borlaug, who also inspired the World Food Prize. Borlaug is regarded as the father of the Green Revolution, credited with saving over a billion people worldwide from starvation. The World Food Prize calls attention to what has been done to improve global food security and to what can be accomplished in the future, attracting scholars to the field and encouraging their pursuit of further technological breakthroughs, benefiting corporate sponsors and society alike.

Partnering with Social Enterprises, For-Benefit Enterprises, and Impact Investors

These organizations "generate earned income but give top priority to an explicit social mission."[5] Impact investors generate a measurable, beneficial social or environmental impact alongside a financial return. Businesses partnering with such enterprises can be critical to their successfully fulfilling a social purpose while also benefiting their business. Solar energy provider SolarCity benefited greatly from "a distribution partnership with DIRECTV to install solar panels alongside satellite dishes." This allowed DIRECTV to achieve its sustainability goals at a much lower cost while making affordable sources of sustainable energy available to its consumers.[6]

Imagining Mutually Beneficial Solutions to the Toughest Challenges

GE leveraging the power of imagination reflects the philosophy that finding solutions to tough challenges is just a creative thought away. Nearly all of our pressing challenges can be addressed by businesses adopting an enlightened view of their own capabilities and interests. To bolster this point, let's review a few of the creative strategies that companies have undertaken to create shared value with society, oftentimes, though not always, in collaboration with shapeholders.

Arts

Google's Cultural Institute makes masterpieces accessible to everyone. There are few things more enriching—and more costly—than traveling. By making major art collections and architectural masterpieces available in high-resolution detail to all with Internet access, the institute inspires young and old around the world. I have been to many of the buildings and collections profiled, but the institute has the added benefit of letting you see what is not readily accessible—for example, the costume room or close-ups of paintings on the ceiling. This service circumvents prohibitive costs of travel and makes cultural landmarks accessible by sharing their treasures more broadly. The benefit it delivers allows Google to change the conversation with many shapeholders who may be otherwise hostile to the company.

Compassion/Development

The company that produces London's famous "black cab" designed vehicles capable of transporting passengers in wheel chairs. Its benefits were widespread: it helped cement the vehicle's preferred position in the marketplace, the government did not have to fund a separate program to provide mobility for the handicapped, and those in wheelchairs received more readily available and dignified mobility.[7]

Facebook added a "Donate" button on the pages of nonprofits that allows people to contribute directly via the social network, improving fundraising efforts for worthy causes and enhancing the attractiveness of creating a Facebook page for nonprofits.[8]

Walmart partnered with the Nutritional Development Services of the Catholic Archdiocese of Philadelphia to deliver free meals in the summer to disadvantaged youth. This strengthened relations with its core customers—young mothers—while increasing foot traffic to its stores.

Frontier markets, sometimes newly emerging from war or civil strife, offer unique opportunities for those willing to accept a higher risk in exchange for the possibility of exceptional returns and the satisfaction of helping those in dire need. C. K. Prahalad highlighted this in *Fortune at the Bottom of the Pyramid*.[9] When governments struggle to provide basic services, an opportunity is created for enterprising private firms to assist them in elevating conditions for their citizens for mutual benefit.

Education

IBM helps schools develop learning content repositories and analytics to drive personalized instruction, while providing high-speed connectivity and mobility solutions for anywhere, anytime learning on any device.[10]

Microsoft's funding of programs to teach at-risk youth digital skills (including how to use Microsoft software) nurtures skills that can improve grades and expand career opportunities for students as they become smarter Microsoft users.

Siemens funds engineering programs around the world that teach students how to apply the technical applications that it markets to solve a wide range of social challenges. This strategy not only brightens student employment prospects but also provides the talent emerging countries need to use Siemens products to address concerns like clean water, affordable health care, and efficient transportation.

Environment

Tapping opportunities to conduct operations efficiently, save costs, and lighten one's environmental footprint have increasingly become standard operating procedure in all industries.

Google provides data-driven philanthropy to the World Wildlife Fund to develop animal-tagging technology that fights poaching and to the Smithsonian's Barcode of Life project to compile a DNA library to identify products from poached animals. These contributions turbocharge efforts to protect endangered species and advance digital search activity.[11]

Health Care

Besides the actions of Whole Foods to promote healthier foods and the efforts of Nike and Fitbit to promote exercise, there are many other corporate efforts to find ways to deliver better and cheaper health care.

IBM's Watson helps doctors apply findings from advanced analytics of the collective experiences its database encases to deliver more personalized care. Precision in diagnosing ailments and applying the optimum remedy for each individual patient and his or her unique circumstances holds the promise of better health care at reduced costs.[12]

Proteus Digital Health integrates a tiny sensor inside pills that works with a wearable device and mobile app that tracks whether prescriptions are being followed. Not following prescriptions costs $100 billion each year in excess hospitalizations alone.[13]

PhysIQ offers a predictive health analytics tool that creates a personalized baseline by collecting data from wearable devices, detects anomalies, and then alerts health-care providers if necessary.

Facebook added an organ donor sign-up option and greatly accelerated the number of people who did so, while connecting them with donor registries.[14]

Accenture and Philips demonstrated how a doctor wearing Google Glass in an operating room could use the display to monitor a patient's vital signs while performing surgical procedures. Augmented devices provide doctors with more degrees of freedom, portability, and unprecedented contextual information. Some hospitals are making plans to improve training by using cameras to stream and record live surgeries, as seen through the eyes—and smart glasses—of a surgeon.[15]

UnitedHealth Group's Optum Insight unit applies findings from analytics of its massive pool of data to help clinics lower costs and improve clinical outcomes.

Pharmacy and grocery retailers like CVS, Walgreens, and Tesco are finding ways to profitably deliver basic medical services closer to consumers at a lower cost.

Security and Promoting Freedom

Facebook established pages for the Amber Alert system in each state and territory in the United States, allowing people who like each page to be notified of missing children in their communities so they can notify their own friends to significantly extend the reach of the system.[16]

Facebook's "Safety Check" feature prompts you to mark yourself as safe if you are in an area where a catastrophe has occurred.[17]

Social media platforms empower individuals and social movements, both for good and for ill. They were famously pivotal in organizing young activists in the Arab Spring. Twitter, Facebook, and YouTube are contributing to social welfare by helping people advance their causes more effectively, while simultaneously expanding their appeal with global youth. Clearly social media is playing an important role in empowering those previously kept in the dark through a controlled press. These examples highlight social media's impressive power and revolutionary worldwide reach.

Twitter suspended more than 125,000 accounts since mid-2015 "for threatening or promoting terrorist acts."[18] As Facebook falls under increased pressure to address its role in facilitating communications and weapons sales by terrorists,[19] it too has stepped up efforts to counter their activities, including assembling a team promoting "posts that aim to discredit militant groups like Islamic State."[20]

Transportation

Toyota, the market leader in hybrid cars with its Prius model, convinced California to let the single-occupant Prius hybrids drive in the high-occupancy vehicles (HOV) lanes. This helped advance California's goal for more environmentally friendly transportation and clearly benefited Prius sales. After this spurred more hybrid sales, the state switched its law to make its HOV lanes available to fully electric cars and those that run on natural gas or hydrogen— but Prius hybrids carrying only one person can no longer drive in that lane.[21]

Barclays, the London-based international bank, agreed to pay £5 million annually for five years to sponsor a rent-a-bike program that launched in London in 2010. Doing so granted citizens an affordable and convenient form of transformation that improves their health and the health of the planet. As a result, Barclays affiliates itself with causes like better health and environmental sustainability in an innovative and constructive effort, while the government addresses urban congestion and meets sustainability goals at a negligible cost. Santander Bank took over the financing role for the program in 2015.[22]

Businesses should constantly survey their operating environment to find similar ways to partner with society and government. The opportunity to do so is another compelling reason why companies have an imperative to actively engage shapeholders. Doing so will better position them if they must contest an issue with shapeholders—our final step.

KEY TAKEAWAYS

- Sustained commercial success requires constant scanning of the landscape for opportunities to benefit your company while helping society and aggressively pursuing them when you find them.
- This is embodied in the idea of creating shared value (CSV) advanced by Michael Porter and Mark Kramer: "Policies and operating practices that enhance the competitiveness of a company while simultaneously advancing the economic and social conditions in the communities in which it operates."
- CSV is better for the company and society than pure traditional CSR approaches. Business leaders often view CSR programs as an expense item and cut them during challenging times when they are needed the most. Since CSV offers opportunities to improve company profitability, it is as likely to expand as contract during difficult times.
- Companies find CSV opportunities by reconceiving products and markets, redefining their value chains, participating in local community or industry cluster development, or partnering with social enterprises, for-benefit enterprises, and impact investors.
- Companies are hard at work on advancing shared value to bring the inspiration art provides to all, to compassionately address those in need, and to deliver social benefits in the areas of education, sustainability efforts, health care, security, and transportation.

12

Assemble to Win

We must all hang together, or assuredly we shall all hang separately.

—BEN FRANKLIN ON SIGNING THE DECLARATION
OF INDEPENDENCE

AMERICA'S PRODUCERS OF MOVIES and music like Sony, Viacom, and Time Warner risk a major loss of revenue with the advent of digitization, which facilitates easy transmission of digital copies to others, without compensation to the artists or their producers. What makes pirating particularly infuriating is the fact that foreign websites facilitate much of this illegal traffic. The Motion Picture Association of America (MPAA) projected that the movie industry brought in more export income than agriculture, aerospace, or automobiles. The MPAA also estimated that 13 percent of Americans had watched pirated TV shows or movies, which cost media companies billions in revenue and more than 100,000 jobs.[1]

To address this key business priority, lobbyist groups from Hollywood studios, recording industry giants, and major publishing houses worked for more than four years to build bipartisan support in Congress for a law to stop this theft. On October 26, 2011, Representative Lamar S. Smith (R-TX) presented a bill that was colloquially known as SOPA—the Stop Online Piracy Act.

SOPA and its sister bill in the senate, PIPA (the Protect Intellectual Property Act), introduced by Senator Patrick Leahy (D-VT), were designed to protect America's creative industries by making it easier for the government to prosecute foreign websites that disseminated copyrighted information. Although the U.S. government could shut down domestic websites that offered pirated content, they were limited in their ability to investigate foreign websites.

SOPA was intended to prevent U.S. companies from funding, advertising on, or linking to foreign piracy sites. It also would have given the U.S. Department of Justice the ability to block access to certain foreign sites by preventing users from typing in the Web address or searching for it through Google. Credit card processors could also be required to hold funds from companies that had proven piracy records.

Soon after the bill was introduced, Google, Wikipedia, Facebook, and other tech giants began speaking out against the ways this bill could curtail free speech rights.[2] Their protests culminated with an estimated 7,000 websites blacking out their services in protest on January 18, 2012. They mobilized people to flood Congress with complaints.[3] Two days later, the bill was put aside and effectively died.[4]

When you believe you are having a illegitimate demand imposed on you by other companies, industries, or shapeholders, you need to assemble to win.

Why, What, Where, Who, How, and When

SOPA illustrates how companies must take great care in determining what will prevail in a political skirmish. A useful tool is to think of this as the why, what, where, who, how, and when of engagement.

First, you must be clear on *why* you are assembling and what you will win.

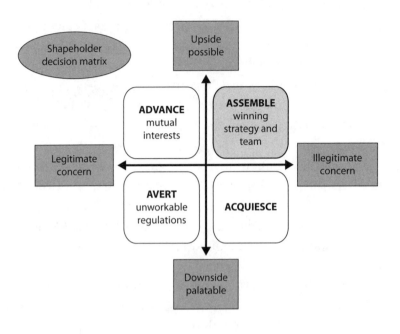

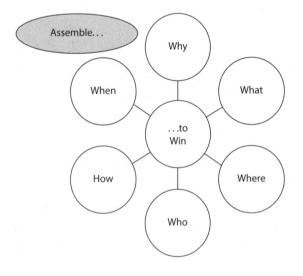

Then, whoever succeeds in establishing the top-of-mind question (the "what") in the decision makers as they consider the issue wins. You win when your question animates the debate and lose when you are forced to answer someone else's question. Messaging depends on choosing a question that can appeal to a wide enough audience and leads to the answer you seek.

You must also carefully select the arena *where* you would prefer to ask that question. Before which decision maker should you present your case?

Then you must focus on *who* is opposing your efforts, who you must assemble into a coalition, and who should be your public face. Assembling a winning team is much easier if the company has an ongoing process of seeking and attracting friends to common causes.

You must determine *how* to best deliver your message. What is the right mix of coalition partners and grass-roots supporters to reach key decision makers through strategic channels of communication? You must make your case in a convincing manner through targeted delivery and a coordinated surround-sound approach.

Finally, you must launch your effort at the opportune time *when* your key audiences and decision makers are most receptive or, if necessary, to meet fixed deadlines.

Traditional Media

Traditional media wanted to block foreign sites from facilitating the piracy of their digital products (why). Their question (what) was, "Should we let foreigners pirate our products?" They chose Congress as their arena for action (where). They assembled a wide mix of associations and unions representing the content providers as their coalition (who). Their primary method of message delivery was lobbying directly with members of Congress (how), and they acted once they had the support of key sponsors in each chamber (when).

When SOPA was proposed, it had strong industry support and bipartisan agreement in the House and the Senate. On the industry side, the MPAA, the Recording Industry Association of America, and the U.S. Chamber of Commerce strongly supported the bill. The House bill had the backing of thirty cosponsors. PIPA passed Leahy's Senate Judiciary Committee unanimously and had forty cosponsors.[5]

New Media

New media companies did not like the table that old media had set, so they turned it over. They sought to stop the bill (why) and blunted old media's attempt by engaging in the arena of public opinion (where). Their question (what) was, "Do you want the federal government to black out your Internet?" They built their coalition (who) from Internet companies, NGOs, and users. They encouraged these users to contact their members of Congress (how), pouncing as it was proceeding to expected passage (when).

The new media cohort included Google, Facebook, Microsoft, Intel, Reddit, Wikipedia, and thousands of other technology and content companies. Many of the sites that joined the protest, like Facebook and Wikipedia, were filled with user-generated content. These sites feared that the bill would give the government too much power to define a site as illegal and would force Internet companies to act as police, shutting down users and constantly monitoring postings.

Rather than quietly lobbying Congress, the Silicon Valley sites created viral campaigns to win public opinion. One of the first campaigns was called Don't Break the Internet, which focused on the ways that SOPA would effectively ruin free speech on Reddit, Twitter, Tumblr, and other online discussion groups. By late November 2011, more than 1 million people had emailed Congress on new media's behalf and made more than 87,000 phone calls.[6]

On January 18, 2012, the Internet companies made a united protest against SOPA. Wikipedia took its English-language content offline and left only a black sign with the words, "Right now, the U.S. Congress is considering legislation that could fatally damage the free and open Internet." Google covered its label with a black censor strip, though it kept its search capacity active.

In the end, more than 14 million people contacted lawmakers in protest of the bill. John P. Feehery, a former House Republican leadership aide, noted, "The problem for the content industry is they just don't know how to mobilize people. They have a small group of content makers—a few unions, whereas the Internet world—the social media world especially—can reach people in ways we never dreamed of before."[7]

This example illuminates how companies must take great care in determining the right mix of why, what, where, who, how, and when to prevail in a political skirmish.

In this chapter, we consider situations in which shapeholders make demands of a company that the company assesses to be illegitimate and the company determines it can win in contesting the demand. The approach we discuss also applies to positions that companies advance that are contested by other businesses or industries, as was the case in the new media versus old media scenario. Let us further consider the steps to success when assembling to win.

Why: Begin with the End in Mind

> The enlightened ruler lays his plans well ahead; the good general cultivates his resources.
>
> —SUN TZU

Every successful strategy begins with a well-articulated definition of success. Everyone on your extended team must be clear about the objective you are seeking.

What: The Question Is Always the Answer

When you come to a hill or a bank, occupy the sunny side.
—SUN TZU

Choosing the right communication strategy begins with selecting the optimum question. Those who control the question win. A company should first of all think of questions that generate the answers leading to the objectives they seek. It should also anticipate the questions opponents may advance. Then it should test public opinion of each question to determine which is its strongest option, which competing questions are the most formidable, and who wins face-offs between dueling queries. Which question you advance is determined by which one stacks up best against your adversaries' issue framing.

A key part of having your preferred question define the debate is directing all your energy toward justifying why your question is vital. Any time you spend answering the other side's question is counterproductive. Doing so bolsters the centrality of their question. To an outsider, it looks like the two sides are talking past each other as each tries to establish the supremacy of its competing question. I am sure you have sensed this when watching a political debate.

This is an important skill when learning to engage shapeholders. Political novices marshal significant company resources to make the case for their answers to an issue. They often waste time answering their own questions or the questions of their adversaries, while their opponents focus on establishing their preferred questions.

Novices walk away frustrated from encounters with experienced advocates, complaining that they didn't listen to them and didn't address the issue (as they see it). Businesspeople comfort themselves by portraying the politicians or activists they unsuccessfully engaged as incapable and incompetent.

Global Warming

Take the debate over whether to legislate cap-and-trade laws on carbon emissions in Congress in 2009—an issue of consequence to many companies, especially in the energy sector. President Obama and advocates for the bill sought to establish the question "Do you want to prevent global warming?" or "Do you want to stop the seas from rising?" Opponents of the legislation countered with an alternative question: "Do you want to kill the economy and millions of jobs?" During the prolonged recession the country had just experienced, President Obama's passionate promotion of cap-and-trade failed, because his question did not prevail over one relevant to economic circumstances. Pope Francis advanced a new question on carbon emissions: whether you want to violate "moral law written into human nature itself," in a manner that will most harm the "vast ranks of the excluded." This was a more compelling question in generating support for climate change action and helped ensure the success of the Paris summit in 2015.[8]

Affordable Care Act

In the battle over the passage of President Obama's health-care plan, the Affordable Care Act won necessary swing votes when it appealed to middle-class voters' concerns about rapidly rising health-care costs. The base of the Democratic Party was energized by the proposition of health-care access, the primary focus of the bill.

The bill's proponents astutely raised the question "Should we enact a bill to control health-care costs?" They titled their bill the Affordable Care Act (even though it was primarily an access-enhancement bill) and offered it as the answer to their own question. President Obama emphasized the necessity to control health-care costs, impressing on the American people that this was the focus of the bill. Opponents' efforts to dispute the bill's affordability benefits kept the attention on Obama's question and distracted attention from their own question: "Do you want to stop government takeover of your health care?" They failed to advance a competing question, and that prevented them from defeating the bill.

Big Gulp Ban

In 2012, the New York City Board of Health approved Mayor Michael Bloomberg's proposal to ban the sale of beverages larger than sixteen ounces, an action that became known as the "Big Gulp Ban." Bloomberg put forth the question "Do we want to do something about obesity?" The American Beverage Association (ABA) blocked the ban when the New York appeals court accepted ABA's question: "Can the court stand by while the city usurps the state legislature's constitutional powers?"[9]

Fight for $15

The Service Employees International Union supported the formation of Fight for $15 in late 2012. The SEIU assessed that advancing the questions "Can you live on less than $15 an hour?" and "Do you want to fight injustice?" were more appealing than the question "Do you want to join our union?" Opponents advanced the question "Do you want to kill jobs?" citing a report from the President Obama's Office of Management and Budget that his proposed $10.10 minimum wage, up from $7.25, would reduce employment by 500,000.[10]

Trade Promotion Authority

One of the toughest Congressional battles for business in 2015 was over whether the Republican-controlled Congress would grant the president's Trade Promotion Authority (TPA), so-called Fast-Track, which would require a yes or no vote on trade agreements without amendments. This legislation was essential if the Transpacific Partnership and Transatlantic Trade and Investment Partnership were to pass. Both were business priorities.

Opponents of this legislation, led by the AFL-CIO and other unions, advanced different messages to different segments. They got most Democrats to oppose the bill with the question "Do you want unions to support a primary challenger in your reelection?" They peeled off several conservative Republicans, sensitive about President Obama's string of executive orders, from supporting the bill with the question "Do you want to give this president more power?" Proponents of the bill, conscious of the economic angst that gripped the country, posited the question "Should China define the rules of trade instead of us?," instead of advancing a question focused on the benefits of trade. TPA passed.

Where: Optimum Arena to Ask the Question

> In country where high roads intersect, join hands with your allies. Do not linger in dangerously isolated positions.
> —SUN TSU

Where a question is asked matters. This begins with deciding whether to engage at the global, multilateral, national, state, or local level. When returning to my hometown in Pequot Lakes, Minnesota, while in Congress, I found few people knew what bills were on the floor. Everyone asked me how life was in Washington—what's it like to go the White House and work with the president? My brother David was on the local school board and was regularly pinned against the wall by someone with an issue they cared passionately about. Different people are engaged at different levels. Consider this when picking your battlefield.

You must also decide between the executive, legislative, and regulatory arenas; the arena of public opinion; and the courts. Ultimately you must decide which people are the decision makers who can answer your question and identify who influences those decision makers.

Global Warming

Proponents of climate change action initially focused on the UN Climate Summit in Copenhagen in 2009. Opponents focused on blocking action in the U.S. Senate. Given that the cap-and-trade legislation the president sought to use to achieve his obligations to the UN required congressional approval, the UN arena proved irrelevant, and in the U.S. Senate arena, the "economy and jobs" question proved decisive. Recognizing his weak hand, the president pivoted, committing to Paris summit goals in a manner that did not require congressional approval.

Debit Card Fees

Retailers pressed hard to enact legislation that would limit how much banks could charge for the use of debit cards. They really had no choice but to accept such cards as payment regardless of what banks charged for the cards' usage and felt that legislation was the best remedy. In the legislative venue, the retailers prevailed—they convinced Congress to act. It passed the Durbin Amendment, which required the Federal Reserve to limit fees as part of the Dodd-Frank financial reform legislation in 2010.[11]

The Federal Reserve's primary responsibility is for the safety and soundness of the banks. With this in mind, it chose to limit fees by far less than the retailers had hoped. The retailers challenged the Federal Reserve ruling, but the Supreme Court denied the petition in 2014, and the ruling stood.[12] Retailers won in the congressional arena, where they had the advantage, given banks' low approval with the public, but the Federal Reserve proved a more favorable arena for banks, tempering the retailers' victory.

AT&T

In 2011 AT&T attempted to address its bandwidth capacity shortage by buying T-Mobile, but was stopped in its tracks with a surprise challenge by the U.S. Department of Justice. Not only was it required to pay a multibillion dollar breakup fee, but it wasted precious time addressing this issue instead of keeping up with its archrival Verizon. This was in large part because AT&T focused its attention on regulatory questions and regulators, while it was politicians and political issues that scuttled the deal. This was due in part to the timing being off, because President Obama turned his attention to his 2012 reelection campaign unusually early.

Big Gulp Ban

Mayor Bloomberg chose as his arena the New York City Board of Health, while the beverage association chose state courts, where they blocked Bloomberg's win.

Fight for $15

Fight for $15 found success for their $15 an hour minimum wage in heavily democratic cities—Los Angeles, San Francisco, and Seattle—or with public workers in heavily democratic states like Massachusetts. Opponents chose to fight back in territory they assessed would be more receptive—state legislatures. In September 2015, Missouri passed legislation prohibiting St. Louis and Kansas City from setting a minimum wage, overriding a veto by Governor Jay Nixon.[13]

Trade Promotion Authority

While opponents of the measure found the threat of supporting a primary opponent effective in heavily Democratic house districts, the supporters of the bill rounded up just enough votes to win by attracting Democratic Senate supporters who weren't up for reelection in 2016, many of who were on the West Coast and had constituencies in port cities that better understood the importance of trade with Asia.

Chevron

Ecuador's National Court of Justice ruled that Chevron must pay $9.5 billion to plaintiffs in the country's rain forests over decades-old contamination. Chevron inherited the lawsuit in 2001 when it acquired Texaco.[14] Chevron was able to get the largest funder of the suit to pledge to give no more money and to turn over his entire stake in the judgment by suing him in Gibraltar, where he lives, alleging that he was knowingly funding a fraudulent suit.[15]

Who: A Coalition Big Enough to Win

Having collected an army and concentrated his forces, he must blend and harmonize the different elements thereof before pitching his camp.

—SUN TZU

Having established your optimum what and where, it is next important to answer three "who" questions:

1. *Opposition.* Who will form the opposing coalition? Understanding your opposition will help you understand who is available for your coalition and how big and broad your coalition must be to succeed.
2. *Coalition.* Who must be in your coalition to sway decision makers?
3. *Face.* Who should be the face of your message?

Coalition Building

• *Encourage Stakeholder Engagement.* Aside from the other reasons to establish excellent relations with stakeholders, these customers, employers, suppliers, and communities can also be pivotal influences on shapeholders. Companies should plan to keep stakeholders informed about shapeholder engagements and enlist stakeholder support in their case against shapeholder backlash. You don't want this demographic to go undecided, or worse, to oppose your efforts.

Ideally, your employees would advocate your position. Eric Eve, CEO of Ichor Strategies, shares a story of visiting a bank executive. As he approached the bank entrance he noticed protestors outside. When he was inside, meeting with an executive, he asked him, "Why doesn't the bank have counter-protestors?" His point was that, if two sides were presented, the media would feel compelled to cover both. Eve meant to suggest that there must be employees who believed in the bank's purpose and its benefit to the community who could be deployed to make the bank's case.

Felipe Noguera, a political consultant in Argentina during the presidency of Cristina Fernández de Kirchner, once said that the businesses in his country must organize protest rallies against measures that disrupted commerce. Certainly most of the people who turned out for those protests were stakeholders of companies affected by these measures.

• *Associations Are Vital Partners.* Not only is addressing common industry issues through an association more efficient, it is often more effective. When you speak as an industry, your voice is louder than it is as a company, because there are more of you and it confirms to the shapeholder that the industry is united on the matter.

Conflicts within industries are debilitating. Political leaders are presented with many issues where the industry view is set. But when the industry disagrees, politicians set the matter aside until the industry comes together.

Often a company belongs to a number of industry associations, providing it multiple options. Many associations pulling in the same direction are more likely to win.

• *Issue-Focused Campaigns.* Issue campaigns assemble a wide range of actors to advance or stop progress on a particular issue, administrative action, or piece of legislation. In the United States, they often are conducted through specialized funding vehicles (527s or 501(c)4s). Companies, associations, chambers, or advocacy organizations may all chip in to promote their common cause. One organization may take the lead or multiple entities may form a guiding committee with a public affairs firm assisting with strategy and/or execution.

• *Find Friends.* Business (and life) is a game of addition and multiplication—not subtraction or division. You should ally yourself with as many groups as possible that want to make progress on issues most important to your respective company. Scour the landscape to find activist organizations who share your interests and values.

Be prepared to accommodate differences so long as you can move together effectively toward common goals. Those that are most different from you are most valuable. As you become more adept at partnering with shapeholders, you will find that you and your new diverse partners can form a powerful combination. The more friends you have, the fewer enemies you face.

It is vital for businesses to engage any organizations that earnestly support the same goals. Doing so can help you blunt the spears of opponents. It is just as important to identify and avoid organizations that may overextend your external commitments. Just as you seek earnest partners, activists will also suss out whether you are truly committed to the effort at hand or just going through a PR exercise. While carrot activists can be highly valuable, disappointing them can hurt you. Be clear about your commitments and follow through.

• *Don't Fund Enemies.* "You can please some of the people, some of the time, but you can't please all of the people all the time." You should always seek cooperative relationships with activists and NGOs when you can, but you cannot buy peace by funding those who regard your company as their enemy or think you should be a regulated utility (unless, of course, you already are).

Some companies foolishly subscribe to the view that no one shoots the bartender when the drinks are on the house. Even though an unnamed company sponsored a more stick activist–oriented LGBTQ event and had a good track record on that score, the guest speaker at the event attacked the company for supporting child trafficking.[16]

The best way to get stick activists on your side is to collect carrot activist allies. You are less likely to be attacked and more likely to prevail if you have assembled a strong team of activist groups with whom you collaborate.

Royalist Watchdogs

The British royal family and London bobbies are a case in point of neutralizing professional protesters by expanding one's circle of friends. During the wedding of Prince William and Kate Middleton in 2011, officials had significant cause for concern—just months before the wedding, riotous protests turned violent over the government's decision to increase student fees for university education.[17]

I was surprised to learn that it is tradition for fans of the British monarchy to camp out in the parks surrounding Buckingham Palace preceding major events like the prince's wedding. Apparently British Prime Minister David Cameron camped out for the wedding of Prince Charles and Princess Diana. While the presence of these masses camped out in palace parks may seem like a risk to the unknowing, to those who understand the mentality of royalists, they offered the perfect shield against unruly conduct during the wedding ceremony.

If activists tried to disrupt the wedding day, they would quickly be subsumed and camouflaged by those who passionately support the British royalty. London authorities understand that using a percentage of the attention of the whole crowd significantly leverages the whole attention of a few policemen.

To achieve this, London police were individually assigned a specific part of the crowd. They built relations with them and screened them for potential threats. The chief of police, Prince William, and Prince Harry circulated unannounced through the crowds, tightening those bonds. Laying this groundwork meant a wedding without disturbance.[18]

Businesses would be wise to follow this example and build bridges with an ever-widening circle of businesses and activists who hold similar interests to insulate themselves from professional activists who have no intention of compromising.

Turning Down the Heat on Air Conditioning

The heating and air conditioning industry found out the hard way why you should build winning coalitions. President Clinton, prodded by the Appliance Standards Awareness Project,[19] implemented higher standards on their industry during his lame duck days. The industry's association sued.[20] In the end, they lost the lawsuit and spent millions to comply in the last months before the deadline.

The next time, they reached agreement with a wide group of activist groups and approached the administration together with new rules that were eventually accepted. Working together caused a far better outcome for the industry than their previous, more contentious approach, as it allowed more input from the industry and more time to prepare to implement the new standards.

Coalitions must include a diverse enough group to achieve the end you seek. Bringing in those who extend beyond your own reach is invaluable. Carrot activist groups likely connect with more politicians on the left than the average company.

Face of Coalition

How can you pick the right person or organization to serve as the face of your organization when addressing shapeholders? A couple of examples highlight the importance of this step.

- *Small-Town Broker for NYSE.* As the founder and chairman of the Economic Club of Minnesota, I sought an appointment to invite the NYSE-Euronext CEO to address the club. Even though I had been a financial officer for a New York Stock Exchange–listed company for a dozen years, a congressman, and a member of the U.S. House Financial Services Committee, I found that my chances of getting an appointment would be better if I worked through a small broker in Anoka, Minnesota, who runs a small shop and knew about and supported the NYSE. The NYSE responded to him, because they assessed that if they needed someone other than the CEO to be in front of a camera defending them from populist attacks, an informed small-town broker was a much better candidate in the eyes of the public than a hot-shot Wall Street type.

• *Fight for $15.* Unions have found that having front groups like Wake Up Walmart or Fight for $15 as their face in advancing political messages is more effective then flying their own flag.

How: Make Your Case

Gongs and drums, banners and flags, are means whereby the
ears and eyes of the host may be focused on one particular point.
—SUN TZU

Once you have chosen the optimum terrain and built a winning team, you must strategically decide how best to make your case. This requires three important elements, all of which must be executed with care and skill to achieve your desired outcome—compelling message, targeted delivery, and surround sound.

Actions taken by the oil and gas industry illustrate these three elements. A presentation by the top five oil company CEOs at a 2011 Senate Finance Committee reflected a tightly synchronized campaign to fend off attacks seeking to repeal tax credits to spur exploration for energy in the United States.[21]

- *Compelling Message.* The industry has been highly disciplined in staying on message. Obama won the presidency because he kept the focus on one word—change. When you are as easily demonized as the oil and gas industry, perhaps you need two. For them, the clear messages were (1) jobs and (2) (energy) supply, no matter what the location or who the messenger happened to be.
- *Target Delivery.* The oil and gas industry's message is designed to appeal to a coalition of anti–tax increase Republicans and oil patch Democrats. These senators, House members, and their staffs were the focus of the aforementioned combined messaging, explaining why there was a heavy focus on advertising in Washington, D.C., by the industry.
- *Use Surround Sound.* As I traveled around Washington, it was impossible to miss their message. The Natural Gas industry rented the ad space available at Capitol South, the subway stop closest to Congress, with messages of jobs and energy supply. In case their target audience took the bus, they covered a few buses with their message as well. Shell Oil captured the inside of the subway cars with a similar message. In the event these legislators walked or took the airplane, the oil and gas industry made sure you saw their message on bus stands and airport advertisements. They ran television advertisements on national cable news. In newspapers and magazines, you could not miss the many advertisements by Chevron.
- Culminating this highly coordinated campaign was the testimony given by the CEOs of the top five companies in Washington, D.C. As *Politico* reported, "One by one, the five CEOs essentially gave the same message: Raising industry taxes could hamper jobs and energy supply while exacerbating already high prices."[22]

Success in advocacy requires knowing your script and your audience. Whatever the outcome of the future votes on repealing tax credits for the oil and gas industry and regardless of whether you support their objective or not, the oil and gas industry shows the power of a targeted, surround-sound message.

Bankruptcy or Windfall?

How your message is delivered can mean the difference between bankruptcy and a $9 billion dollar windfall. Consider the fates of two companies that sought to convert spectrum airwaves for digital communications that the U.S. Federal Communications Commission allocated for satellites to more lucrative cell-phone use—LightSquared, funded by Philip Falcone's hedge fund, and Dish Network, a satellite TV operator. Both cases hinged on military officials' fears that opening up the spectrum to cell-phone use might impair sensitive satellite navigation systems.

Philip Falcone, a major political donor, seemed more concerned with quick action than addressing the military's concern. In 2011 he met with the White House and spectrum regulators, reportedly aggressively pushing for quick approval of his petition.[23] Two government witnesses reported pressure from the administration to minimize their regulatory concerns.[24] This made the matter highly partisan.

Falcone targeted his delivery and used surround sound. He advertised everywhere in Washington. But his delivery sparked opposition from the military, Republicans, and citizen watchdog groups. His request was denied. LightSquared later filed for bankruptcy.[25]

Dish Network's CEO Charlie Ergan took a different approach in 2012. He negotiated with the military and government agencies to ensure that his plan would *not* interfere with their priorities. Rather than seeking political favors, he went straight to relevant regulators, saying his goal was to "set up a competing wireless service that would benefit consumers and create jobs." This was a compelling message for regulators concerned with the dominant duopoly of AT&T and Verizon. Ergan obtained regulatory approval to use the spectrum, which was valued at $9 billion in 2012.[26]

When: Strike While the Iron Is Hot

> It is a military axiom not to advance uphill against the enemy,
> nor to oppose him when he comes downhill.
>
> —SUN TZU

Timing is everything in political contests. Your chances of success are greater the earlier you are in the life cycle of an issue. When advancing an issue, you must be in time with the rhythm of your targeted decision maker and pay close attention to what sets the mood of the moment at a particular time.

- *Global Warming.* Timing for efforts supporting action, including Pope Francis's, were geared to the UN Climate Change Conference in December 2015.
- *Affordable Care Act.* The timing of the push to pass this bill was influenced by the Democrats' control of the presidency and both chambers in Congress. The push for finalization was made more urgent by the electoral victory of Scott Brown to fill Senator Ted Kennedy's seat.
- *Fight for $15.* Timing for initiating this campaign was keyed to continuing economic angst among the public and the approaching 2016 U.S. presidential elections.
- *Trade Promotion Authority.* The timing of the Obama administration's push for the TPA was driven by the approaching finalization of negotiations for the Trans-Pacific Partnership. The other eleven countries were reluctant to put final proposals on the table until they knew the American president had this authority.

A Concurrent Approach Is Often the Key to Success

Up until now we have been covering situations with only one iteration of why, what, where, who, how, and when. In a competitive environment, we must often round these bases with *different* messages for *different* coalition segments if we want to succeed.

During my time in Congress, my FAST Lanes amendment was the only amendment to pass in the House of Representatives markup of the nearly $300 billion road bill in 2004.[27] This was not because the Bush administration wanted it—they opposed it. It was not because the Republican-led Transportation Committee wanted it—they also opposed it. It passed because I received support from three diverse groups—fiscal conservatives, those interested in increased infrastructure funding, and highway user groups like the truckers. Each required a separate who-what-how, all focused on the *where* of the House of Representatives.

To fiscal conservatives I asked, "Do you want to avoid a gas tax increase?" My bill provided new lanes funded by tolls, which reduced reliance on taxpayer funding. This segment was reached by a supportive op-ed in the small government–focused *Wall Street Journal*.[28]

To those after infrastructure spending, I asked, "Do you want to tap a new source of funding for road construction?" I reached this audience through an op-ed in the big government–focused (at the time) *Washington Post*.[29]

It was the truckers who took me over the top. They liked the feature in my bill that prohibited tolls on existing lanes, which they abhorred. The key to winning their approval was speaking on satellite trucker radio shows to guide truckers to a website, where they could enter their zip codes to determine who represented them in Congress, and to the House switchboard, which could direct their calls to their members. One congressman told me that he had more than 1,000 truckers call his office to tell him to vote for the Kennedy Amendment.

Rounding out the bases with three separate audiences allowed me to overcome opposition and pass my amendment with the help of thirty-three Democrats.

This completes our review of the seven steps for shapeholder success. I am confident that following them will provide great rewards to your career and company. Now let's take our discussion from the company level to the concerns of all who rely on a robust free enterprise system.

KEY TAKEAWAYS

Successfully engaging in political skirmishes requires astutely selecting why, what, where, who, how, and when. You must:

- Be clear on why you are assembling and what you will win.
- Establish the top-of-mind question (the "what") in the decision makers as they consider the issue wins. Do not answer someone else's question. Choose a question that appeals to a wide audience and leads to the answer you seek.
- Carefully select the arena where you would prefer to ask that question.
- Focus on who is opposing your efforts, who you must assemble into a coalition, and who should be your public face.
- Determine the right mix of coalition partners and grass-roots supporters to reach key decision makers through strategic channels of communication. Make your case through targeted delivery and a coordinated surround-sound approach.
- Launch your effort at the opportune time when your key audiences and decision makers are most receptive or, if necessary, to meet fixed deadlines.

13

Pope Francis, a CEO Worth Emulating

THE 2016 OSCAR AWARDS ceremony, among the most secular of events, concluded with awardees giving a nod to Pope Francis, confirming the profound influence of his surprising papacy. If you think of Francis as the CEO of a major global enterprise, there is much that commercial leaders can learn from him when it comes to engaging the world.

Academy Award for Best Actor recipient Leonardo DiCaprio appealed for action on climate change, expressing concern for the "billions and billions of underprivileged people who would be the most affected by this,"[1] framing the issue the way Francis introduced it in support of the 2015 climate summit in Paris.

Michael Sugar, the producer awarded the Oscar for the best picture, concluded his remarks by saying, "Pope Francis, it's time to protect the children and restore the faith."[2] Sugar's appeal to the pontiff reflected the view that Francis was responsive to social concerns and was capable of changing the course of events.

When even the most earthly of institutions calls for action to "restore the faith," it is clear that Francis has effectively engaged society and steered the Roman Catholic Church on a path that leads nonbelievers to consider it a force for good.

The failure to imitate Francis's effective engagement permits businesses to be portrayed as a force for ill. We have already addressed the imperative for businesses to incorporate social concerns into their organizational strategies. It is equally essential for businesses to collectively respond to disruptive currents in broader society.

In pursuit of a mutually beneficial purpose, business leaders must do more than ensure their organizations align with society's values. They must also ensure that free enterprise delivers benefits for the many, not just the few.

Currents Unleashed by Technology and Globalization

Technology and globalization have unleashed strong currents that have led many to question whether market economies are delivering on their promise.

• *Economic Impact.* By embracing the beneficial trade effects of David Ricardo's theory of comparative advantage, amplified by the efficiencies emanating from Moore's law that computing power will get progressively less expensive, the United States and the rest of the world have grown accustomed to getting more for less.

The result has lowered the costs of many products and services, permitting paychecks for those in advanced economies to buy more, while making once out of reach offerings—like phone and banking services—newly accessible to billions in the most remote corners of the world. While the benefits of lower costs have been widespread, the impact on income growth has been uneven.

The rapid spread of digital technologies simultaneously eliminates, creates, alters, and moves jobs. Those designing and optimizing computerized systems are replacing the jobs of those who sorted and delivered mail; built, sold, and fed fax machines; and sold, designed, and published advertising in traditional media outlets. Predictions of a jobless future only heighten worker anxiety.[3]

Apple, Facebook, and Google are in an amenities bidding war to attract top talent to their Silicon Valley campuses. This digitally driven creative destruction creates economic tsunamis in one industry after another: as the tech savvy prosper, those without such skills are left in their wake.

Putting computing power in the hands of billions has improved the efficiency with which even the most traditional tasks can be performed. It helps African fishermen determine which port will offer them more for the fish they just caught, workers in Bangalore to scrutinize documents for a lawsuit in Boston, and health-care professionals in Kolkata to diagnose CAT scans from a hospital in Cleveland. These changes have propelled many out of poverty in emerging markets but have shifted the income growth of low-skilled workers in advanced economies into neutral and, at times, reverse.

• *Social Currents.* The joint effect of technological advances and globalization has caused a divergence of social expectations that has increased friction within and between countries. Expectations are rising in emerging markets, as a growing middle class becomes increasingly intolerant of bearing the cost of corruption and settling for substandard services. In advanced economies, the middle class feels squeezed by the dual impacts of automation and the need to compete with emerging markets for a slice of complex and opaque global supply chains. As tech-savvy talent and those who enable their output thrive, the middle class struggles to keep up.

• *Political Currents.* A black-and-white approach by business would say "too bad, not my problem." A more enlightened view suggests that shapeholders can and are making these concerns an important matter for businesses to consider. As angst increases around the world, so have the twin forces of digitization and globalization empowered the disaffected. The less that grid-locked politicians accomplish, the more society looks to business for answers.

Economic pressures on the middle class in rich countries may be from technological and globalization tides that cannot be reversed—but these are not on the ballot. Concerned citizens rebel against the closest political issues they can find—immigration and trade liberalization—and candidates they perceive as supporting either. Voters in emerging democracies rebel against a status quo they rightly see as corrupt and self-serving.

Buffeted by economic pressures, agitated by increasingly loud and shrill voices, and mistrustful of their government leaders, citizens turn inward and respond to those who promise appealing elixirs long disproven.

These trends are troubling for businesses and the ideals of the Roman Catholic Church alike. While many multinationals appear shell-shocked, Pope Francis engages the public in a way that has strengthened the church while upping the pressure even more for flat-footed enterprises.

While Francis Fascinates, Business Blunders

On March 13, 2013, Argentine cardinal Jorge Mario Bergoglio became the supreme pontiff. He not only deftly responded to the seismic shifts shaking the world but set off a few earthquakes of his own. His success in altering the perception of the church he leads and in setting the terms of debate can be seen through our lens, the seven steps to shapeholder success.

• *Align.* Some businesspeople might suggest that aligning authentically to fulfill a purpose that benefits society and the bottom line of your enterprise is easier for an organization whose bottom line is saving souls—but that betrays an understanding of capitalism's unmatched, though often overlooked, track record in lifting people from misery. After all, it was the embrace of capitalist principles in China and India that lifted hundreds of millions of people out of poverty in the last forty years.

Cardinal Borgoglio made his purpose clear from the outset. Even though he is the first Jesuit pope, he adopted the name of the founder of the Franciscan order—Francis of Assisi. Saint Francis was famous for his concern for the poor and his love of nature, which perfectly aligns with the pope's intent to be a champion for the poor and the planet. Pope Francis authentically adopted the spirit of Saint Francis with his no-frills approach to the papacy, including forsaking the Apostolic Palace to live in the Vatican guesthouse.

Businesspeople are likely to view Pope Francis's comments as representing "a caricature of market economies";[4] yet one cannot deny that he has been effective in advancing his purpose, calling attention to the consequences of our economic actions on the environment and the least among us.

In contrast, most business leaders can, at best, communicate in "caricatures" when addressing the plight of the needy. Their gig is market economics. If business leaders were half as good at advocating for the benefits of the market as Francis is at highlighting the needs of the poor, we would not have a vacuum of economic understanding that demagogues on the left and right fill with ill-informed prescriptions that hurt citizens and businesses alike.

• *Anticipate.* It was not hard for Francis to recognize the challenges the church faced; the prolonged sexual abuse scandal has, for years, been debilitating to the church's reputation. Francis also saw the opportunity to address the economic angst that preoccupied the moment. Unlike politicians who appealed to people's darker instincts or offered utopian largesse, Francis saw an opportunity to call on our better angels, asking us to elevate our concerns for the needy and for our shared home.

Businesses as a whole not only failed to foresee how economic angst would unfavorably shape the makeup of the governing authorities that set the rules of commerce, but they also never anticipated how standing by while corruption tarnished the brand of free enterprise would inform the viewpoints of world leaders.

Francis's view of capitalism is shaped by cowardly business-people unwilling to sacrifice marginal gains to confront the corruption-fueled suffering their silence facilitates. The World Economic Forum ranks Francis's Argentina as the third worst country in corporate ethics, 138 out of 140 countries considered.5 Businesses complain about the corruption they encounter, but when government agencies press them to publicly make their case to spur reform, these companies nearly always decline. Businesses fail to anticipate the costs of letting corruption fester.

• *Assess.* Francis rightly assessed that concerns over the church's poor performance in responding to sexual abuse scandals were legitimate and understood the dual obligation to mitigate damage to those who suffered and the church's reputation was urgent. He also correctly assessed that speaking out strongly for those being left behind by economic and environmental trends was a legitimate concern shared by both the church and many in society.

Businesses fail to grasp that it is in their best interests to ensure that the fruits of free enterprise are dispersed widely, that disruptions caused by technology and globalization are mitigated, and that corruption is promptly confronted. They underestimate the cost that neglecting these imperatives will impose on them. Because of that neglect, the business community's positive priorities, like the continued expansion of trade liberalization, stalled. Consequences have mushroomed: excessive regulations, inefficient government attempts at redistribution pressuring the need for higher taxes, and corruption that limits opportunities in emerging markets.

• *Avert.* Pope Francis recognized that the church's response to its sexual abuse scandal undermined its credibility to address the needs of the disadvantaged. Being merciful to priests put innocent people at risk. Francis averted further harm to both the church's credibility and those who suffered by taking concrete steps to enact change.[6] While his efforts are still a work in process, Francis set up a sex abuse commission comprised primarily of laypeople and acted on their recommendation to set up a tribunal to hold guilty clergy accountable.[7]

Businesses must recognize that, if they are to forestall populist action that would be economically disastrous for their companies and countries, they must address the causes of economic uncertainty. They must combat market-distorting corruption, not just by avoiding corrupt conduct, but by challenging it head-on, even if doing so risks their short-term economic prospects in any particular country.

It is in business's best interests to join Pope Francis in being concerned by the uneven distribution of wealth in modern markets. The failure of those who benefit most from disruptive technologies and globalization to ensure opportunities for those caught in their turbulent wake has fueled public discourse against market solutions like the Trans-Pacific Partnership that offer economic, environmental, and social benefits for both companies and citizens.

To avert the embrace of policies that would be disastrous for the wealthy and needy alike, business leaders must do more to address underlying sources of economic uncertainty by cultivating continuing education, financial literacy, healthy lifestyles, and retirement saving. Companies must be attuned to how collaborating with NGOs, impact investing, and for-benefit companies can advantage their operations and more effectively address social needs.

• *Advance.* Francis championing the concerns of the less fortunate was not only true to his purpose of focusing on the poor and the planet like his namesake, but also benefited society, as it aided in the church's efforts to preach a gospel of love.

Businesses would benefit from action ensuring that the benefits of free enterprise are more widespread and corruption is confronted. Not only would they avoid debilitating political backlash, they would also expand their customer base.

Francis Models Assembling to Win

Francis was not content to just have the church directly address the needs of the poor and the planet. He assembled to engage in the arena of public opinion to prod individuals and governments alike to pay more attention to those needs. He deftly managed the right mix of why, what, where, who, how, and when.

The feeble attempts to promote free enterprise by commercial actors—individually by any specific business leader, company, organization, or chamber, or collectively globally—have been unfocused, tactical, and sporadic. It is in the interest of free enterprise to follow Francis's lead by strategically assembling to win on matters most important to markets and amply and fairly delivering benefits.

• *Why.* Public engagement is most effective when you have a clear answer for "why" you are engaging and succeeds when your "why" is aligned with your social and organizational purpose. For Francis, everything is focused on the least among us and the home we share, which bolsters his effectiveness.

Companies could be equally effective if they embraced capitalism's unmatched ability to generate and equitably distribute wealth, yet their behavior reveals the opposite. An accumulation of evidence suggests that corporations are not earnest in addressing distortions in the conduct of free enterprise in international markets and are busy erecting further barriers in America, leading the *Economist* to lament that in the United States, Adam Smith's invisible hand seems oddly idle.[8] We must reawaken the competition that propels and distributes capitalism's benefits.

American companies have consolidated their industries, allowing them to increase their market shares and cut costs. An analysis by the *Economist* suggests that two-thirds of the 900 sectors they analyzed in America concentrated themselves between 1997 and 2012, with the weighted average share of the top four firms in each sector rising from 26 to 32 percent.[9]

Signs that this consolidation is fostering monopolies is reflected in near-record corporate profits relative to the size of the economy in 2016, return on equity for U.S. firms is now 40 percent higher in America than overseas, the share of profits going to workers declined in the last decade, and investors believe merger cost savings will drop to the bottom line and not benefit consumers.[10] These self-serving corporate actions squeeze the working class from both ends, resulting in lower wages and higher costs.

Small companies are disadvantaged by America's corporate tax code, which has the highest rate of any industrialized country yet is riddled with carve-outs only large companies can afford to uncover. They are further disadvantaged by not being able to afford professional help in navigating increasingly arcane regulations that have been imposed in recent years. The proliferation of occupational licensing has raised additional obstacles for competition. In 2016, 29 percent of professions required permits, up from 5 percent in the 1950s.[11] It is little wonder that America in 2016 experienced the lowest rate of small-company creation since the 1970s.[12] With small businesses as the primary source of job growth, workers again lose out.

For companies to warrant less disdain, they must accept more antitrust oversight, be sincere in pushing to simplify regulations, be skeptical about licensing schemes, and direct their lobbying efforts toward leveling the playing field, not tilting it. The test of a company's sincerity in the United States is whether it supports comprehensive tax reform in which all companies and industries forfeit their special benefits to lower the rate for all, especially the small businesses essential to propelling needed job growth.

• *What.* Francis set forth the question "Are we conducting our Church, economic, civil and environmental affairs in a manner that discharges our duties to help those most in need?" This question directed his focus on the church's approach to sexual abuse to those who suffered. It salvaged an inept global effort to promote climate change action from less animating questions like "Do you want the seas to rise?" to more compelling questions like "How can you, in good conscience, not act when most all those disadvantaged by rising seas are the poorest people on the planet?"

Businesses seem fixated on a question of "What is best for business?" instead of "What delivers the most sustainable and equitably distributed prosperity for all?" Few outside the corporate C-suite truly care about the first question; only if commercial activities are an adequate answer to the second question will their license to operate be renewed. Businesses' seeming preoccupation with the first question is indicative of their incorporating shareholders and perhaps stakeholders into their strategies, but not shapeholders.

• *Where.* What is most revolutionary about Francis's approach to engagement is his changing the venue of where issues are debated and decided. The United States and its allies reshaped the world order after World War II, setting up the global governance institutions of the United Nations, World Bank, International Monetary Fund, and the predecessor to the World Trade Organization. Yet all were dominated by Word War II's Allied powers, the victors of the war.

The consequence of this great powers global governance system was that there was no urgency to address the fact that Argentina has a corrupt business climate. Argentina is not a permanent member of the Security Council with a blocking veto. It is inconsequential in the governance of the World Bank or IMF. The newly minted G-20 group of nations, of which it is a part, has not yet shown that it can effectively enact policy. The general view was that nations and companies could safely ignore Argentina without macro-level governance challenges.

The irrelevance of Argentina was long the case in the governance of the Church as well: every pope for the last 1,300 years has been European,[13] but with Francis's appointment, everything changed. Now he is calling commerce in every country to task, in great part because of what has been allowed to pass as free enterprise in Argentina—a result of businesses' timidity in pushing back against corruption.

Francis's voice is amplified by economic angst—concern that as the economy has become global, there is no effective watchful eye to ensure that commerce benefits all. The Dickensian abuses of the United Kingdom during the Industrial Revolution largely resulted from businesses rising to a national scale, while political power remained local. The politicians responded to the public outcry over the abuses of that time by creating more national regulatory authorities to provide checks on excesses and imbalances in negotiating positions.

People demand a global economic watchdog if we are to integrate the world's economies. Pope Francis is filling that void. In his 2015 address to the United Nations, Francis suggested that without "interventions on the international level, mankind would not have been able to survive the unchecked use of its own possibilities."[14]

The Roman Catholic Church has always viewed itself as having a global mandate.[15] In the broad sweep of history, the church has inserted its voice into political and commercial affairs, in great part to fill a void, not because it bullied its way into a crowded field. It was only after the fall of Rome in the fifth century that the Church took on widespread secular duties. The absence of acceptance or awareness of global regulatory provisions on a scale equal to that of global commerce has created a similar vacancy that Francis is entering.

It is in companies' best interest to join Francis in filling this vacuum. There is more going on to ensure a level playing field than most know. Businesses would benefit if workers understood the degree to which enforcements by organizations like the World

Trade Organization (WTO) should give them more confidence that the rules of commerce are fair and beneficial to their jobs.

Properly understood, the international trade regime currently in place, fostered in great part through American leadership, has a strong track record of cutting living costs, raising living standards, settling disputes, reducing trade tensions, stimulating economic growth and employment, cutting the cost of doing business internationally, encouraging good governance, helping countries develop, giving the weak a stronger voice, supporting the environment, and contributing to peace and stability.[16]

When was the last time the average citizen heard about his or her nation receiving beneficial judgments by the WTO appellate body that forced another nation to remedy their unfair practices? The United States has a strong track record of winning appeals, as do many other countries, including some judgments against unfair practices by the United States. When was the last time the average worker watched an advertisement or documentary either promoting any of these benefits or exposing the cover-up that is keeping them from being known?

Actions by nations to turn inward may momentarily placate segments of their population, but in doing so they will exacerbate concerns in other countries. Conservative general dislike for global governance and the unions imposing resistance to trade on liberal politicians has left this favorable narrative out of political discourse. It may not be in the interests of any political faction to promote the benefits to workers of global trade disciplines, but it is in the interests of responsible businesses to do so. If they really believed in free enterprise, they would stop outsourcing the task of extolling its benefits to government entities.

The WTO is by no means perfect. More attention to improving its effectiveness and a little less focus on manipulating its results could greatly enhance its beneficial impact. There are also domains where global standards could be beneficial. Google, Facebook, and Twitter have already had to forgo the Chinese market because they did not marshal global action on standards for Internet privacy. China may never listen to America alone on this topic, but the country will have a harder time ignoring a global consensus. Minimal global standards for digital privacy and openness (which countries could agree to exceed) would be as beneficial to commerce as it may be threatening to tyranny. Both are good reasons to press for them.

• *Who.* In many cases, Francis has been the primary spokesperson for the church. The coalition he yields is not just faithful Catholics, but those of many religious persuasions, with a special appeal to those who feel left behind by the modern economy.

The audiences of Francis's advocacy efforts have varied based on the topic. In relation to the sexual abuse scandal, he influenced the actions taken by Church leadership and regained the confidence of parishioners and the public. With regard to the impact of environmental and economic policy on the poor, he targeted secular governing authorities and the conduct of businesses.

When defending free enterprise, it is those closest to what drives your enterprise who will be your most effective spokespersons. A CEO can easily capture media attention, but passionate stakeholders and shapeholders are more likely to convince skeptics.

Honeywell's CEO David Cote and other executives should be commended for creating the Fix the Debt organization and campaign that rightly points out that inaction regarding America's debt has many harmful consequences. Fix the Debt is wise not to prescribe a specific solution or even indicate whether the debt should be reined in through spending cuts or tax increases.

Fix the Debt has been unable to overcome the myriad opponents who condemn its efforts.[17] This may in great part reflect the resistance to modern-day CEOs addressing society's most pressing issues in a populist political environment.[18] Focusing more energy on making company employees the face of the effort and concentrating more attention on educating the general public on the benefits of reining in national debt will probably be needed to spark action. This is undoubtedly more costly and time-consuming, but nevertheless it is a likely requirement for the success of Fix the Debt's mission to advance fiscal responsibility.

Businesses have fared little better in promoting trade liberalization. Knitting the world closer together economically over the last half century has significantly advanced the prosperity of nations and peaceful relations among them. But as nations struggle to reignite growth and respond to growing pressures to address income inequality, many are turning inward and embracing zero-sum thinking. There seems to be more attention to tilting the playing field toward local players than harnessing the tried and true uplift of more open markets.

No candidate for U.S. president in 2016 supported the Trans-Pacific Partnership or the Transatlantic Trade and Investment Partnership agreements that would help level the global playing field with significant economic and geopolitical benefits for both American workers[19] and the other nations involved.[20] The organizations supporting trade do little more than connect executives of companies that benefit from trade with legislators before key votes. Almost nothing is done to win converts to the benefits of trade. Efforts to fund and reform trade-adjustment assistance and job retraining have long been too meager, allowing opposition to trade to surge.[21]

Collectively and individually, businesses are dramatically under-investing in strategically engaging with the public or adequately incorporating the perspectives of shapeholders on matters of the utmost importance to the future of their companies, a vibrant free enterprise system, and the planet. The coalitions we are assembling in support of the principles of free enterprise are dangerously inadequate.

• *How.* While Francis has use of communication channels unique to popes such as encyclicals to carry his message, he has also taken advantage of other communications vehicles. In an effort to better connect the church with millennials, Francis joined Twitter.[22] More recently he has embraced Instagram.[23]

Yet the most impactful way Francis gets his message out is through travel, using locations as a springboard to constantly bring the needs of the poor to the eyes of the world. Understanding that tangible messages are often the most impactful, Francis has practiced what some call "a culture of encounter," meeting people suffering injustice where they are.[24]

In Bolivia, he visited a notorious prison, not only to highlight the need to address overcrowding, an unresponsive justice system, and the lack of training opportunities, but also to affirm the dignity of all prisoners.[25] In Nairobi, Kenya, he visited a slum to point out the inequality and injustice of what he called a "new form of colonialism" that exacerbates the "dreadful injustice of urban exclusion."[26] On Holy Thursday, Francis went to a refugee center outside Rome to wash and kiss the feet of not only Catholic, but also Orthodox, Hindu, and Muslim refugees.[27] A month later, he visited a Greek refugee camp and brought back three families of Syrian refugees on the papal plane.[28]

Just as Francis makes the case for the plight of the poor in tangible ways on a continual basis, so must business make the case for free enterprise on a year-in, year-out basis, making the palpable benefits of open markets and the real costs of market distortions visible to everyday citizens.

Corporate promotion of free enterprise should begin at home by educating employees on what is at stake. Former U.S. trade representative Carla Hills advocates listing the portion of an employees' pay that was funded by exports on their paystubs. Sadly, business engagement on this front is usually limited to engaging legislators, and then only when specific legislation is up for a vote.

There are ample opportunities to combat the corruption that undermines the legitimacy of free enterprise. It begins with prosecuting the corruption that the company faces and accepting the retribution this might generate.

• *When.* Effective public engagement requires careful timing. While Francis was consistent in promoting his concern for the poor and the planet, he skillfully timed his engagements, publishing *Laudato si'* in concert with the 2015 Paris climate summit, visiting the Mexican border to highlight a humane approach to immigration during a time of great debate on the subject during the U.S. presidential primaries in 2016, and washing the feet of Muslims and visiting a Greek refugee camp as Europe wrestled with how to address refugees from the Syrian war.

In a similar way, businesses must always conduct themselves in a manner that testifies to the benefit of markets, yet be prepared to join together to ward off attacks on capitalism's efficacy or to advance the reach of its benefits, as with trade agreements that remove barriers to trade. Like Francis, businesses must be prepared to aggressively insert themselves into the debate during the heat of public battles through the voices of their CEOs and their informed employees and shapeholder partners.

Printing in Color

Free enterprise is only embraced when it is formulated and communicated so it is seen as delivering widespread benefits to the many, not just the few. Two proof points that current efforts by business to do so are woefully inadequate are: (1) the fact that the public's economic anxiety has spawned populist politicians on both ends of the spectrum critical of pro-growth policies and (2) the resonance of Francis's condemnation of the impacts of capitalism.

In a world in which shapeholders are increasingly setting the standards to which businesses are forced to comply—either through legislative mandate or public opinion—this call to action is not so much based on a moral precept as on practical reality.

My hope is that I have convinced you that long-term success means ensuring others share your victory, that you appreciate the value in understanding what motivates others, that you will seek to embrace a full-spectrum view, and that you will always seek the common ground between your priorities and social concerns. I hope I have illustrated the power of shapeholders and that embracing the seven steps to effectively engage them opens up new ways for your company to succeed by addressing social challenges in a way that also benefits your operations. My hope is that you are attuned to how best to compete—and collaborate.

Notes

Preface

1. Pew Research has done excellent work on political polarization in the United States. I recommend both their 2014 analysis showing how adherents of the two parties are drifting away from one another ("Political Polarization in the American Public," Pew Research Center, June 12, 2014, www.people-press.org/2014/06/12/political-polarization-in-the-american -public) and their more recent analysis of how animosity toward the oppo- site party has increased ("Partisanship and Political Animosity in 2016," Pew Research Center, June 22, 2016, www.people-press.org/2016/06/22 /partisanship-and-political-animosity-in-2016).

2. "Congress and the Public," Gallup, www.gallup.com/poll/1600/congress -public.aspx.

Introduction: From the Heart of a Businessman

1. Chris Mooney and Steven Mufson, "How Coal Titan Peabody, the World's Largest, Fell Into Bankruptcy," *Washington Post*, April 13, 2016, www.washingtonpost.com/news/energy-environment/wp/2016/04/13 /coal-titan-peabody-energy-files-for-bankruptcy.

2. "Remarks of President Barack Obama—State of the Union Address as Delivered," January 13, 2016, www.whitehouse.gov/the-press-office/2016 /01/12/remarks-president-barack-obama-%E2%80%93-prepared-delivery -state-union-address.

3. Milton Friedman, "The Social Responsibility of Business Is to Increase Its Profits." In *Ethical Theory and Business*, 8th ed., edited by Tom L. Beauchamp, Norman E. Bowie, and Denis G. Arnold (New Jersey: Pearson, 2009.), 55.

4. Anupreeta Das and Emily Glazer, "Republicans and Democrats Agree: We Hate Wall Street," *Wall Street Journal*, January 13, 2016, www.wsj.com /articles/republicans-and-democrats-agree-we-hate-wall-street-1452681567.

5. Adam Grant, *Give and Take: Why Helping Others Drives Our Success* (New York: Penguin, 2014), 16.

6. C. K. Prahalad, *Fortune at the Bottom of the Pyramid: Eradicating Poverty Through Profits* (Upper Saddle River, N.J.: Prentice-Hall, 2006).

7. Otto Bettmann, *The Good Old Days—They Were Terrible* (New York: Random House, 1974), 34.

8. Project Loon, "Balloon-powered Internet for Everyone," www.solve forx.com/loon.

9. David Barron and Erin Yurday, "Anatomy of a Corporate Campaign: Rainforest Action Network and Citigroup (A)," (Case No.P42A, Stanford Business School, Stanford, CA, 2004).

10. "Martin Shkreli, A Provocateur in the Pharmaceutical Wars," *Financial Times*, September 25, 2015, www.ft.com/intl/cms/s/0/47e0c998-62ae-11e5 -9846-de406ccb37f2.html#axzz3mZX8IAGC.

11. Erika Kelton, "14.7 Billion Reasons Why Volkswagen Should Have Welcomed Whistleblowers," *Forbes* June 29, 2016, www.forbes.com/sites /erikakelton/2016/06/29/14-7-billion-reasons-why-volkswagen-should-have -welcomed-whistleblowers/#c2e58b762bca.

12. Yoko Kubota, "Mitsubishi Used Improper Fuel-Economy Tests for Some Cars Since 1991," *Wall Street Journal* April 26, 2016, www.wsj.com /articles/mitsubishi-used-improper-fuel-economy-tests-for-some-cars -since-1991-1461657990.

13. Peter Campbell, "Anger as Starbucks Boss Says: We May Not Pay UK Tax for Up to Three Years," *Daily Mail*, December 1, 2014, www.dailymail .co.uk/news/article-2856284/Starbucks-chief-reveals-coffee-giant-not-pay -normal-tax-three-years.html.

14. Susan Berfield, "Avon's Ugly China Bribery Probe Ends with a $135 Million Settlement," *Bloomberg News*, May 1, 2014, www.bloomberg.com /news/articles/2014-05-01/avon-s-ugly-china-bribery-probe-ends-with-a -135-million-settlement.

15. Jeff Kingston, "Tepco Executives Get a Taste of Citizens' Wrath," *Japan Times*, March 26, 2016, www.japantimes.co.jp/opinion /2016/03/26/commentary/tepco-executives-get-taste-citizens-wrath /#.VxuGa6ODGko.

16. The term has multiple antecedents, including John Mackey and Raj Sisoda's *Conscious Capitalism*, in which they write, "The paradox of profits is that, like happiness, they are best achieved by not aiming directly for them"; John Mackey and Raj Sisoda, *Conscious Capitalism: Liberating the Heroic Spirit of Business* (Boston: Harvard Business Press, 2014) Kindle version, loc. 1029.

1. Shapeholders

1. Amy Mitchell, Jeffrey Gottfried, and Katerina Eva Matsa, "Facebook Top Source for Political News Among Millennials," Pew Research Center, June 1, 2015, www.journalism.org/2015/06/01/facebook-top-source-for -political-news-among-millennials.

2. Bernie Woodall and David Shepardson, "Chided by Trump, Ford scraps Mexico factory, adds Michigan jobs," http://www.reuters.com/article /us-usa-trump-autos-idUSKBN14N1To

3. Scott Plous, *The Psychology of Judgment and Decision Making* (New York: McGraw-Hill, 1993), 233, http://psycnet.apa.org/psycinfo/1993 -97429-000.

4. Alexis de Tocqueville, *Democracy in America*, December 28, 2015, http://bit.ly/1ROj7JQ.

5. Globalise Resistance, "About," www.resist.org.uk/category/about.

6. Guy Taylor, "Turning Gadflies Into Allies," *Harvard Business Review*, February 2004.

7. "Live: Six Greenpeace Climbers Scale Shell's Arctic-bound Oil Rig," Greenpeace, www.greenpeace.org/usa/live-six-greenpeace-climbers-scale-shells -arctic-bound-oil-rig.

8. Reuters, "North Carolina Business Leaders Join the Call to Repeal Transgender Bathroom Law," *Fortune*, April 20, 2016, http://fortune.com /2016/04/20/north-carolina-business-bathroom-law.

9. Delroy Alexander, Greg Burns, Robert Manor, Flynn McRoberts, and E. A. Torriero, "The Fall of Andersen," *Chicago Tribune*, September 1, 2002, www.chicagotribune.com/news/chi-020901031sep01-story.html.

10. Ameet Sachdev, "Arthur Andersen Conference Center May Go up for Sale," *Chicago Tribune*, February 22, 2013.

11. Alexander et al., "The Fall of Andersen." My personal memory of Arthur Andersen being referred to as the "gold standard" and "Marine Corps" of the profession is confirmed in this article. This article also details Harvey Kapnik's separate audit and consulting practices; Ken Brown and Ianthe Jeanne Dugan, "Arthur Andersen's Fall From Grace Is a Sad Tale of Greed and Miscues," *Wall Street Journal*, June 7, 2002. Arthur Andersen being referred to as the "conscience of the accounting industry" is from this article, which also details the pressure on partners to boost profits.

12. Howard Schultz, *Onward: How Starbucks Fought for Its Life Without Losing Its Soul* (New York: Rodale, 2011).

13. Conservation International, "Mission," http://www.conservation.org /about/Pages/default.aspx#mission.

14. Schultz, *Onward*, 20.

15. "Stop Mattel Destroying Rainforests for Toy Packaging," Greenpeace, www.greenpeace.org/international/en/campaigns/forests/asia-pacific /barbie.

16. Meghan E. Irons, "Menino Expands Sugary Drink Ban," *Boston.com*, April 8, 2011, www.boston.com/news/local/massachusetts/articles/2011/04 /08/city_properties_added_to_boston_ban_on_sugary_drinks.

2. Social Activists

1. "Project O.R.A.N.G.S.," *Sourcewatch*, www.sourcewatch.org/index .php/Project_O.R.A.N.G.S.; "Girl Scouts and Palm Oil," Rainforest Action Network, www.ran.org/girl-scouts-and-palm-oil; Rhett Butler, "In Girl Scouts vs. Kellogg's Over Palm Oil, Rainforests and Orangutans Win," *Mongabay.com*, https://news.mongabay.com/2014/02/in-girl-scouts-vs-kelloggs-over-palm -oil-rainforests-and-orangutans-win.

2. Upton Sinclair, *The Jungle* (New York: Doubleday), 1906.

3. Saul Alinsky, *Rules for Radicals* (New York: Vintage, 1989), 1.

4. Greenpeace About page, www.greenpeace.org/international/en/about.

5. Greenpeace Home page, www.greenpeace.org/international/en.

6. Sasha Goldstein, "Golden Corral Dumpster Video Shows Food Stored Outside by Garbage in Hot Florida Sun," *New York Daily News*, July 9, 2013, www.nydailynews.com/news/national/golden-corral-fire-meat-stored -dumpster-article-1.1393620.

7. Ravi Balakrishnan, "O&M Ex-employee Sofia Ashraf Takes on Unilever's Kodaikanal Plant for Alleged 'Environment Pollution,'" *Economic Times*, August 4, 2015, http://economictimes.indiatimes.com/articleshow

/48337436.cms?utm_source=contentofinterest&utm_medium=text&utm_campaign=cppst.

8. Tushar Kaushik, "Never Thought 'Kodaikanal Won't' Video Could Make Unilever Settle: Rapper Sofia Ashraf," *New Indian Express*, March 9, 2016, www.newindianexpress.com/states/tamil_nadu/Never-Thought-Kodaikanal -Wont-Video-Could-Make-Unilever-Settle-Rapper-Sofia-Ashraf/2016/03/09 /article3318386.ece.

9. "Duke Announces 2015 Closing of Beckjord Coal Plant," Greenpeace, July 20, 2011, www.greenpeace.org/usa/duke-announces-2015-closing-of -beckjord-coal-plant.

10. Laura Kenyon, "Success: Barbie and Mattel Drop Deforestation," Greenpeace, October 5, 2011, www.greenpeace.org/international/en/news/Blogs /makingwaves/success-barbie-and-mattel-drop-deforestation/blog/37176.

11. Jeff Swartz, "Timberland's CEO on Standing Up to 65,000 Angry Activists," *Harvard Business Review*, September 2010.

12. "Fight for 15/Fast Food Forward," Worker Center Watch, http:// workercenterwatch.com/worker-centers/fast-food-forward-fight-for-15.

13. Robert Mackey, "Indian Rapper Calls Out Unilever to a Nicki Minaj Beat," *New York Times*, July 31, 2015, www.nytimes.com/2015/08/01 /world/asia/indian-rapper-calls-out-unilever-to-a-nicki-minaj-beat.html?_r=0.

14. Mark Kennedy, "Taylor Swift's Apple Approach Lives Up to Her Name," *Huffington Post*, June 23, 2015, www.huffingtonpost.com/mark-r -kennedy/taylor-swifts-apple-appro_b_7648136.html.

15. "CI Through the Years," Conservation International, http://s3 .amazonaws.com/conservation/timeline/index.html?__utma=221478794 .1092585271.1398800437.1399652325.1400122766.14&__utmb=221478794 .1.10.1400122766&__utmc=221478794&__utmx=-&__utmz=221478794 .1398800437.1.1.utmcsr=(direct)|utmccn=(direct)|utmcmd=(non.

16. "CI Through the Years: Celebrating Our Shared Success," Conservation International, www.conservation.org/publications/Documents/CI_25yrTimeline _FINAL.pdf.

17. Karen McVeigh, "Canada Mining Firm Compensates Papua New Guinea Women After Alleged Rapes," *Guardian*, April 3, 2015, www .theguardian.com/world/2015/apr/03/canada-barrick-gold-mining -compensates-papua-new-guinea-women-rape.

18. Alina Selyukh, "Zuckerberg Tells Facebook Staff to Stop Crossing Out 'Black Lives Matter,'" NPR, February 26, 2016, www.npr.org/sections /alltechconsidered/2016/02/26/467985384/zuckerberg-tells-facebook -staff-to-stop-crossing-out-black-lives-matter.

19. David P. Barron, "(P52A) Wal-Mart: Nonmarket Pressure And Reputation Risk (A)" (Case No.P52A, Stanford Graduate Business School, Stanford, CA, 2009).

20. Robert Barnes, "Supreme Court Blocks Massive Sex-Discrimination Suit Against Wal-Mart," *Washington Post*, June 20, 2011, www.washington post.com/politics/supreme-court-blocks-massive-sex-discrimination -suit-against-Walmart/2011/06/20/AGCQ81cH_story.html.

21. David P. Barron, "Anatomy of a Corporate Campaign: Rainforest Action Network and Citigroup (B)" (Case No.P42B, Stanford Business School, Stanford, CA, 2004).

22. Cyrus Farivar, "Protesters Show Up at the Doorstep of Google Self-Driving Car Engineer," *Ars Technica*, January 21, 2014, http://arstechnica .com/business/2014/01/protestors-show-up-at-the-doorstep-of-google-self -driving-car-engineer.

23. "Wal-Mart Calls for Minimum Wage Hike," *CNN Money*, October 25, 2005, http://money.cnn.com/2005/10/25/news/fortune500/walmart_wage.

24. Erica L. Plambeck and Lyn Denend, "The Greening of Wal-Mart," *Stanford Social Innovation Review*, Spring 2008, http://ssir.org/articles/entry /the_greening_of_wal_mart.

25. For more on the competition between standard-setting bodies, see Gregory Unruh and Richard Ettenson, "Winning in the Green Frenzy," *Harvard Business Review*, November 2010.

26. For more on the Chevron Forum on Development at the Center for Strategic and International Studies, see the CSIS website: www.csis.org.

27. Ed Pilkington and Suzanne Goldenberg, "ALEC Facing Funding Crisis from Donor Exodus in Wake of Trayvon Martin Row," *Guardian*, December 3, 2013, www.theguardian.com/world/2013/dec/03/alec-funding -crisis-big-donors-trayvon-martin.

28. Office of the First Lady, the White House, "First Lady Michelle Obama Announces Unprecedented Collaboration to Bring Physical Activity Back to Schools," press release, February 28, 2013, www.whitehouse.gov /the-press-office/2013/02/28/first-lady-michelle-obama-announces-unprecedented -collaboration-bring-ph.

29. Justin Gillis and Nicholas St. Fleur, "Global Companies Joining Climate Change Efforts," *New York Times*, September 23, 2015, www.nytimes.com /2015/09/23/science/global-companies-joining-climate-change-efforts.html? _r=0.

30. For more on the RED campaign, see Youngme E. Moon, Michael I. Norton, and David Chen, "(PRODUCT) RED (A)" (Harvard Business School Case 509-013, Boston, MA, July 2008; revised February 2009), www.hbs .edu/faculty/Pages/item.aspx?num=36241.

3. The Media

1. Brian Stelter, "As TV Ratings and Profits Fall, Networks Face a Cliffhanger," *New York Times*, May 12, 2013, www.nytimes.com/2013/05/13/business/media/tv-networks-face-falling-ratings-and-new-rivals.html.

2. "Today's Washington Press Corps More Digital, Specialized," Pew Research Center, December 3, 2015, www.journalism.org/2015/12/03/todays-washington-press-corps-more-digital-specialized.

3. Kerem Oktem, "Why Turkey's Mainstream Media Chose to Show Penguins Rather than Protests," *Guardian*, June 9, 2013, www.theguardian.com/commentisfree/2013/jun/09/turkey-mainstream-media-penguins-protests.

4. "Erdogan Calls People Onto Streets on CNN Turk Via Mobile Phone, Says 'Will Overcome' Coup," *RT*, July 16, 2016, www.rt.com/news/351373-erdogan-cnn-turk-coup-announcement.

5. For more on the impact of WikiLeaks on the GMO debate, see "WikiLeaks Cables Reveal US Sought to Retaliate Against Europe Over Monsanto GM Crops," *Democracy Now*, December 23, 2010, www.democracynow.org/2010/12/23/wikileaks_cables_reveal_us_sought_to.

6. Dan Cancian, "Panama Papers: HSBC and Coutts Reportedly Set Up More than 2,000 Offshore Companies," *International Business Times*, April 5, 2016, www.ibtimes.co.uk/panama-papers-hsbc-coutts-reportedly-set-more-2000-offshore-companies-1553208.

7. Patrick O'Connor, "Political Operatives Find Demand for Their Skills in Business World," *Wall Street Journal*, May 1, 2016, www.wsj.com/articles/political-operatives-find-demand-for-their-skills-in-business-world-1462136874.

8. Josh Ong, "SmartNews, A Top News-Reading App in Japan, Comes to the US," Next Web, October 1, 2014, http://thenextweb.com/apps/2014/10/01/smartnews-top-japanese-news-reading-app-japan-comes-us/#gref.

9. Rich Lowry, "Dan Rather's Big Lie Hits the Screen," *New York Post*, October 12, 2015, http://nypost.com/2015/10/12/dan-rathers-big-lie-hits-the-big-screen.

10. Hannah Malach, "'Blackfish' to Be Celebrated at Live Concert Event in Hollywood," *Hollywood Reporter*, June 30, 2016, www.hollywoodreporter.com/news/blackfish-be-celebrated-at-live-907669.

11. Nick Danger, "Fact-Checking Michael Moore," *Blog Critics*, July 2, 2004, http://blogcritics.org/fact-checking-michael-moore.

12. "Mark Kennedy," Internet Movie Database, www.imdb.com/name /nm2422389.

13. Lesley Gaines-Ross, "Reputation Warfare," *Harvard Business Review*, December 2010, https://hbr.org/2010/12/reputation-warfare/ar/1.

14. Cass R. Sunstein, "How Facebook Makes Us Dumber," *Bloomberg View*, January 8, 2016, www.bloombergview.com/articles/2016-01-08/how-facebook -makes-us-dumber.

15. For more on the Edelman Trust Barometer 2015, see www.edelman .com/2015-edelman-trust-barometer.

16. Jeanne Whalen, "'Dr. Drew' Was Paid by Glaxo," *Wall Street Journal*, July 3, 2012, www.wsj.com/articles/SB10001424052702303933404577505 032006855076.

17. Jim Sciutto, "Exclusive: China Warns U.S. Surveillance Plane," *CNN Politics*, September 15, 2015, www.cnn.com/2015/05/20/politics/south-china -sea-navy-flight.

18. "On Metro, Rail Enthusiasts Fill Communications Void for Riders," *Washington Post*, April 30, 2016, www.washingtonpost.com/local /trafficandcommuting/on-metro-rail-enthusiasts-fill-communications- void-for-riders/2016/04/30/375017dc-0c90-11e6-a6b6-2e6de3695b0e _story.html.

19. "Using Multiple Communication Channels to Increase Message Exposure," *Beyond PR* (blog), *PR News Wire*, January 16, 2013, www.prnewswire .com/blog/using-multiple-communications-channels-to-increase-message -exposure-5922.html.

4. Politicians

1. U.S. Department of State, "State Sponsors of Terrorism," www.state .gov/j/ct/list/c14151.htm.

2. Adam Thomson, "Chaos in Paris as French Taxi Drivers Protest Over Uber," *Financial Times*, June 25, 2015, www.ft.com/cms/s/0/9b0cb574-1b2c -11e5-8201-cbdb03d71480.html#axzz4G5Ago1nU.

3. Sam Schechner, "French Prosecutors Don't Demand Prison Time for Uber Executives in Criminal Trial," *Wall Street Journal*, February 12, 2016, www.wsj.com/articles/french-prosecutors-dont-demand-prison-time-for -uber-executives-in-criminal-trial-1455297094.

4. Anne Sylvaine-Chassany, "Uber Found Guilty of Starting 'Illegal' Car Service by French Court," *Financial Times*, June 9, 2016, www.ft.com/cms /s/0/3d65be7a-2e22-11e6-bf8d-26294ad519fc.html#axzz4DQJKVVvU.

5. Robert Williams, "Uber Faces Permit Pressure in France," *Financial Times*, July 6, 2016, www.ft.com/cms/s/0/5bb6139a-436f-11e6-9b66-0712b3873ae1 .html#axzz4G5Ago1nU.

6. David Gauthier-Villars, Stacy Meichtry, and Eyk Henning, "France Holds Court on Alstom Deal," *Wall Street Journal*, April 28, 2014, www.wsj .com/articles/SB10001424052702303939404579529100203071122.

7. Lisa Beilfuss, "GE Completes Alstom Power Acquisition," *Wall Street Journal*, November 2, 2015, www.wsj.com/articles/ge-completes-alstom-power -acquisition-1446477255.

8. Tom Squitieri, "Trafficant Expelled After Final Jabs in House," *USA Today*, July 24, 2002, http://usatoday30.usatoday.com/news/washington /legislative/house/2002-07-24-traficant_x.htm.

9. Susan Schmidt and James V. Grimaldi, "Ney Sentenced to 30 Months in Prison for Abramoff Deals," *Washington Post*, January 20, 2007, www .washingtonpost.com/wp-dyn/content/article/2007/01/19/AR2007011900162 .html.

10. Charles R. Babcock and Jonathan Weisman, "Congressman Admits Taking Bribes, Resigns," *Washington Post*, November 29, 2005, www. washingtonpost.com/wp-dyn/content/article/2005/11/28/AR2005112801827 .html.

11. Cullen Browder, "Ballance Completes Federal Sentence," *WRAL*, July 7, 2009, www.wral.com/news/local/politics/story/5410095.

12. Dave Cook, "Former Rep. William Jefferson Sentenced to 13 Years in Prison," *Christian Science Monitor*, November 13, 2009, www.csmonitor .com/USA/Politics/2009/1113/former-rep-william-jefferson-sentenced-to -13-years-in-prison.

13. Jacob R. Straus, "Honest Leadership and Open Government Act of 2007: The Role of the Clerk of the House and Secretary of the State," Congressional Research Service, Washington, D.C., July 22, 2008, www.fas.org /sgp/crs/secrecy/RL34377.pdf.

14. To amend title 18, United States Code, to prohibit former Members of Congress from engaging in certain lobbying activities, H.R.4658, 109th Congress, www.congress.gov/bill/109th-congress/house-bill/4658?q=%7B %22 search%22%3A%5B%22mark+kennedy%22%5D%7D.

15. Michael Hiltzik, "The Revolving Door Spins Faster: Congressmen Become 'Stealth Lobbyists,'" *Los Angeles Times*, January 6, 2015, www.latimes .com/business/hiltzik/la-fi-mh-the-revolving-door-20150106-column.html.

16. Robert Kelner and Raymond La Raja, "McCain-Feingold's Devastating Legacy," *Washington Post*, April 11, 2014, www.washingtonpost.com /opinions/mccain-feingolds-devastating-legacy/2014/04/11/14a528e2-c18f-11e3 -bcec-b71ee10e9bc3_story.html.

I voted against McCain-Feingold.

17. Kos, "The NRA Won in Colorado. This Time," *Daily Kos* (blog), September 11, 2013, www.dailykos.com/story/2013/9/10/1238004/-The-NRA -won-in-Colorado-This-time.

18. Lauren French, "Dems Still Steamed Over Labor's Trade Tactics," *Politico*, June 18, 2015, www.politico.com/story/2015/06/democrats -angry-labor-trade-deal-attacks-119154.

19. "Rep. Scott Peters Stands for American Leadership, Prosperity for Working Families," June 12, 2105, https://scottpeters.house.gov/media-center /press-releases/rep-scott-peters-stands-for-american-leadership-prosperity -for-working.

20. "Lights Out for the Incandescent Light Bulb as of Jan. 1, 2014," *Fox News*, December 31, 2013, www.foxnews.com/tech/2013/12/31/end-road -for-incandescent-light-bulb.html.

21. Noah Buhayar, "Who Owns the Sun?," *Bloomberg Businessweek*, January 28, 2016, www.bloomberg.com/features/2016-solar-power-buffett-vs-musk.

22. Bill McGee, "How Much Do Taxpayers Support Airlines?," *USA Today*, September 2, 2015, www.usatoday.com/story/travel/columnist/mcgee /2015/09/02/how-much-do-taxpayers-support-airlines/71568226.

23. Niraj Chokshi, "The United States of Subsidies: The Biggest Corporate Winners in Each State," *Washington Post*, March 18, 2015, www .washingtonpost.com/blogs/govbeat/wp/2015/03/17/the-united-states -of-subsidies-the-biggest-corporate-winners-in-each-state.

24. Mike Maciag, "Which Companies Get the Most Federal Subsidies?," *Governing*, March 17, 2015, www.governing.com/topics/finance/gov-companies -receiving-largest-federal-subsidies.html.

25. Matt Flegenheimer, "$1 Million Medallions Stifling the Dreams of Cabdrivers," *New York Times*, November 14, 2013, www.nytimes.com/2013/11/15 /nyregion/1-million-medallions-stifling-the-dreams-of-cabdrivers.html.

26. Constance Gutske, "Farm to Market: Taking Stock of the Agricultural Land Grab," CNBC, January 21, 2016, www.cnbc.com/2016/01/21/getting-your -plot-of-american-farmland-.html.

27. Buhayar, "Who Owns the Sun?"

28. M. R., "Airline Subsidies in the Gulf: Feeling the Heat," *Gulliver* (blog), *Economist*, March 6, 2015, www.economist.com/blogs/gulliver/2015/03 /airline-subsidies-gulf.

29. Josh Chin, "China Gives Police Broad Powers Over Foreign Nonprofits," *Wall Street Journal*, April 28, 2016, www.wsj.com/articles/china-passes-law -clamping-down-on-foreign-ngos-1461853978.

30. Eva Dou and Daisuke Wakabayashi, "Apple Suspends Online Book and Movie Services in China," *Wall Street Journal*, April 22, 2016, www

.wsj.com/articles/apple-suspends-online-book-and-movie-services-in-china
-1461297947.

31. Eva Dou and Alyssa Abkowitz, "Alibaba-Disney Partnership Is Frozen in China," *Wall Street Journal*, April 26, 2016, www.wsj.com/articles/alibaba
-disney-partnership-frozen-in-china-1461645337.

32. James T. Areddy, "Shanghai Disneyland Draws Crowds—and It's Not Even Open Yet," *China Real Time Report* (blog), *Wall Street Journal*, May 1, 2016, http://blogs.wsj.com/chinarealtime/2016/05/01/shanghai-disneyland
-draws-crowds-and-its-not-even-open-yet.

33. Don Clark, "Microsoft Unveils Plans for China Joint Venture," *Wall Street Journal*, December 17, 2015, www.wsj.com/articles/microsoft-unveils
-plans-for-china-joint-venture-1450328708.

34. Jim Wolf, "U.S. Lawmakers Seek to Block China Huawei, ZTE U.S. Inroads," *Reuters*, October 8, 2012, www.reuters.com/article/us-usa-china
-huawei-zte-idUSBRE8960NH20121008.

35. Eva Dou, "IBM Allows Chinese Government to Review Source Code," *Wall Street Journal*, October 16, 2015, www.wsj.com/articles/ibm-allows-chinese
-government-to-review-source-code-1444989039.

36. Laura Saunders, "Top 20 Percent of Earners Pay 84 Percent of Income Tax," *Wall Street Journal*, April 10, 2015, www.wsj.com/articles/top-20-of
-earners-pay-84-of-income-tax-1428674384.

37. Jenice Robinson, "Who Pays Taxes in America in 2015?," April 9, 2015, http://ctj.org/pdf/taxday2015.pdf.

38. Pew Research Center, "Beyond Distrust: How Americans View Their Government," www.people-press.org/2015/11/23/beyond-distrust-how-americans
-view-their-government/.

39. Pew Research Center, "Beyond Red vs. Blue: The Political Typology—Fragmented Center Poses Election Challenges for Both Parties," www.people
-press.org/files/2014/06/6-26-14-Political-Typology-release1.pdf.

40. Congressional Management Foundation, *Setting Course: A Congressional Management Guide*, 14th ed. (Washington, D.C.: CMF, 2014), www.congress
foundation.org/publications/setting-course.

5. Regulators

1. "Over-regulated America," *Economist*, February 18, 2012.

2. Jon Kamp, "Health Insurers Call for Stronger Rules," *Wall Street Journal*, April 15, 2015, www.wsj.com/articles/health-insurers-call-for-stronger
-rules-on-medical-devices-1429129995.

3. Alexandra Berzon, "Why Chemical Firms Are Seeking More U.S. Regulation," *Wall Street Journal*, December 17, 2015, www.wsj.com/articles/trade-groups-for-chemical-firms-in-a-twist-seek-more-u-s-regulation-1450348202.

4. Danielle Douglas, "France BNP Paribas to Pay $8.9 Billion to U.S. for Sanctions Violations," *Washington Post*, June 30, 2014, www.washingtonpost.com/business/economy/frances-bnp-paribas-to-pay-89-billion-to-us-for-money-laundering/2014/06/30/6d99d174-fc76-11e3-b1f4-8e77c632c07b_story.html.

5. "The Oncoming Train Crash," *Wall Street Journal*, October 25, 2015, www.wsj.com/articles/the-oncoming-train-crash-1445806695.

6. "Big Banks Finalise $6bn-Plus Settlements on Foreign Exchange," *Financial Times*, May 11, 2015, https://next.ft.com/content/4e3eca04-f7cb-11e4-9beb-00144feab7de.

7. Ted Johnson, "'House of Cards' Receives Maryland Tax Credit," *Variety*, April 25, 2014, http://variety.com/2014/biz/news/house-of-cards-maryland-filming-1201164393.

8. Pat Garofalo, "Maryland TV Tax Credits Are a Real House of Cards," *US News & World Report*, December 2, 2014, www.usnews.com/opinion/blogs/pat-garofalo/2014/12/02/house-of-cards-and-veep-tax-credits-not-worth-it-for-maryland-study-finds.

9. Hal S. Scott, *Connectedness and Contagion: Protecting the Financial System from Panics* (Cambridge, MA: MIT Press, 2016).

10. Robert J. Samuelson, "Will Dodd-Frank Prevent the Next Panic?," *Charleston Gazette Mail*, August 1, 2016, www.wvgazettemail.com/daily-mail-syndicated-columnists/20160801/robert-j-samuelson-will-dodd-frank-prevent-the-next-panic.

11. "How About Shutting Them All Down?," *Economist*, May 31, 2010, www.economist.com/blogs/democracyinamerica/2010/05/deepwater_horizon_1.

6. Align with a Purpose

1. Thanks to Brian Mattes from the Vanguard Group for sharing with me the analogy that reputation is like a crystal vase.

2. Mark Sweney, "BP Falls Out of Index of top 100 Brands After Deepwater Horizon Oil Spill," *Guardian*, September 15, 2010.

3. Sarah Kent, "BP to End Controversial Sponsorship of the Tate Britain," *Wall Street Journal*, March 11, 2016, www.wsj.com/articles/bp-to-end-controversial-sponsorship-of-tate-britain-1457695181.

4. Alan Neuhauser, "Judge Approves $20B Settlement in 2010 BP Oil Spill," *U.S. News and World Report*, April 4, 2010, www.usnews.com/news

/articles/2016-04-04/judge-approves-2ob-settlement-in-2010-bp-deepwater
-horizon-oil-spill.

5. Sarah Kent, "BP Results Still Hurt by Gulf of Mexico Spill," *Wall Street Journal*, April 26, 2016, www.wsj.com/articles/bp-reports-first-quarter-pretax
-loss-1461651961.

6. Alan Neuhauser, "BP Oil Spill Behind Die-Off of Baby Dolphins," *U.S. News and World Report*, April 12, 2016, www.usnews.com/news/blogs/data
-mine/articles/2016-04-12/bp-deepwater-horizon-oil-spill-behind-die-off
-of-baby-dolphins.

7. "Deepwater Horizon: Mark Wahlberg in Disaster Movie Trailer Video," *Guardian*, March 29, 2016, www.theguardian.com/film/video/2016/mar/29
/deepwater-horizon-mark-wahlberg-in-disaster-movie-trailer-video.

8. Mark Kennedy, "Pursuing Purposeful Profit," in *Sustainable Development: The Millennium Development Goals, The Global Compact and The Common Good*, ed. Oliver F. Williams (South Bend, Ind.: University of Notre Dame Press, 2014).

9. Chip and Dan Heath, *Made to Stick: Why Some Ideas Survive and Others Die* (New York: Random House, 2007).

10. "VW Loses $26 Billion in Market Value in 2 Days," *KHQ*, September 22, 2015, www.khq.com/story/30091348/vw-loses-26-billion-in-market-value-in
-2-days

11. "Sustainability 2014 At a Glance," Volkswagen, www.volkswagenag.com
/content/vwcorp/info_center/en/publications/2015/04/sustainability-2014-at
-a-glance.bin.html/binarystorageitem/file/Volkswagen_Sustainability2014
_at_a_glance.pdf.

12. "From Risk to Opportunity: How Global Executives View Sociopolitical Issues," *McKinsey Quarterly*, September 2008.

13. Samsung About page, accessed 13 August 2015, www.samsung.com
/us/aboutsamsung.

14. "Values and Philosophy," Samsung, www.samsung.com/us/aboutsamsung
/samsung_group/values_and_philosophy.

15. Sources of company purpose statements (accessed 13 August 2015): ABB, http://new.abb.com/about; Cargill, www.cargill.com; Cisco, http://csr.cisco.com; Disney, https://thewaltdisneycompany.com/citizenship; UnitedHealth Group, www.unitedhealthgroup.com/SocialResponsibility/Default.aspx; US Bank, www
.usbank.com/community/index.html.

16. Christina Passariello, "Unpacking the Apple-Met Museum Fashion Collaboration," *Wall Street Journal*, October 20, 2015, www.wsj.com/articles
/unpacking-the-apple-met-museum-fashion-collaboration-1445372039.

17. Jeff Cobb, "December 2015 Dashboard," *Hybrid Cars*, January 6, 2016, www.hybridcars.com/december-2015-dashboard.

18. Examples of highlighting your purpose statement on your website include: ABB, http://new.abb.com/about; Cargill, www.cargill.com; Ecolab, www.ecolab.com; Pfizer, www.pfizer.com.

19. Mark R. Kennedy, "Advertising Purpose During the Super Bowl," *Huffington Post*, April 4, 2015, www.huffingtonpost.com/mark-r-kennedy /advertising-purpose-durin_b_6598246.html.

20. Lord Browne bravely admitted to this mistake, and his reflections on effectively engaging with society as reflected in his book *Connect* are worth reading.

21. For more on Uber, see "Uber Cab Rape Case," *Times of India*, December 9, 2014, http://timesofindia.indiatimes.com/Uber-cab-rape-case/specialcoverage /45427828.cms.

22. Mickey Rapkin, "Uber Cab Confessions," *GQ*, February 27, 2014, www.gq.com/story/uber-cab-confessions.

23. Mike Hughlett, "General Mills Recalls Some Gluten-Free Cheerios," *Star Tribune*, October 10, 2015, www.startribune.com/general-mills-recalls -gluten-free-cheerios-because-it-has-some-flour-with-gluten-in-it/330757841.

7. Anticipate

1. Jeffrey M. Jones, "Americans' Views of Oil and Gas Industry Improving," Gallup, accessed 22 December 2015, www.gallup.com/poll/184784/americans -views-oil-gas-industry-improving.aspx?version=print.

2. Cary Funke and Lee Rainie, "Public and Scientists' Views on Science and Society," Pew Research Center, January 29, 2015, www.pewinternet.org/2015 /01/29/public-and-scientists-views-on-science-and-society.

3. Robert Levine, "The 'Right-to-Be-Forgotten' and Other Cyberlaw Cases Go to Court," *Bloomberg Businessweek*, June 23, 2016, www.bloomberg .com/news/articles/2016-06-23/the-right-to-be-forgotten-and-other-cyberlaw -cases-go-to-court.

4. David Brooks, "The Coming Political Realignment," *New York Times*, July 1, 2016, www.nytimes.com/2016/07/01/opinion/the-coming-political-realignment .html?r=0.

5. Quorum Home page, www.quorum.us.

6. James Kanter, "European Regulators Fine Microsoft, They Promise to Do Better," *New York Times*, March 6, 2013, www.nytimes.com/2013/03/07 /technology/eu-fines-microsoft-over-browser.html.

7. Sarah Hsu, "Multinationals in China Feel the Heat," *Diplomat*, August 20, 2015, http://thediplomat.com/2014/08/multinationals-in-china-feel-the-heat.

8. "Carrefour to Be Fined Up to $80,000 for Mis-pricing: Xinhua," *Reuters*, December 16, 2012, www.reuters.com/article/us-china-carrefour-fine -idUSBRE8BF09C20121216.

9. Jungah Lee, "Samsung, LG Display Fined by China for Fixing LCD Panel Prices," *Bloomberg*, January 4, 2013, www.bloomberg.com/news/articles/2013 -01-04/samsung-lg-display-fined-by-china-for-fixing-lcd-panel-prices.

10. "China Says to Punish Audi, Chrysler for Monopoly Behaviour," *Reuters*, August 6, 2014 http://uk.reuters.com/article/uk-china-autos-antitrust -investigation-idUKKBN0G604T20140806.

11. "Activists Pushing Starbucks to Use Only Non-GMO, Organic Milk," *Fox News*, October 6, 2014, www.foxnews.com/leisure/2014/10/06/activists -pushing-starbucks-to-use-only-non-gmo-organic-milk.

12. Kevin Whitson, "Thousands Join Activist's Call For Starbucks to End Leases at These Locations," *Western Journalism*, May 31, 2016, www .westernjournalism.com/thousands-join-activists-call-for-starbucks-to-end -leases-at-these-locations.

13. "Inclusion at Starbucks," Starbucks, www.starbucks.com/responsibility /community/diversity-and-inclusion.

14. Narjas T. Zatat, "Feminist Activists Are Boycotting Starbucks Over This Sign at a Coffee Shop in Saudi Arabia," *indy100*, http://indy100 .independent.co.uk/article/feminist-activists-are-boycotting-starbucks-over -this-sign-at-a-coffee-shop-in-saudi-arabia—byxPnnpMGAl.

15. These observations were shared with me by Ken Cohn, then vice president of public and government affairs for ExxonMobil.

16. For more on the Firestone/Bridgestone and Ford controversy, see Thomas Sullivan and Michael Lelyveld, "After Job 1: Actions and Reactions in the Ford/Firestone Recall" (BAB113-PDF-ENG, Boston, MA: Harvard Business School Publishing, revised February 1, 2005).

17. Shan Li, "McDonald's Launches Campaign to Answer Pink Slime, Other Rumors," *Los Angeles Times*, October 13, 2014, www.latimes.com /business/la-fi-mcdonalds-ad-campaign-20141013-story.html.

18. More on Coca-Cola's disclosure of NGO contributions: Mike Esterl, "Coca-Cola Has Spent Millions on Health Research, Fitness Programs," *Wall Street Journal*, September 22, 2015, www.wsj.com/articles/coca-cola-spent-nearly -120-million-on-research-health-programs-since-2010-1442919600?mod=pls _whats_news_us_business_f.

19. "Association Newsmakers: Using Data to Enhance Your Industry's Reputation," CEO Update video, www.ceoupdate.com/articles/news/association -newsmakers-using-data-enhance-your-industrys-reputation.

20. George Horn, "M and A Due Diligence Failures: FCPA and Goodyear," *National Law Review*, March 1, 2015, www.natlawreview.com/article/m-and -due-diligence-failures-fcpa-and-goodyear.

21. U.S. Department of Justice, "Foreign Corrupt Practices Act," www.justice .gov/criminal-fraud/foreign-corrupt-practices-act.

22. Ned Levin, "J.P. Morgan Hired Friends, Family of Leaders at 75% of Major Chinese Firms It Took Public in Hong Kong," *Wall Street Journal* November 30, 2015, www.wsj.com/articles/j-p-morgan-hires-were-referred-by-china-ipo-clients -1448910715.

23. Trace International, "TRACE's 2014 Global Enforcement Report," *PRNewswire*, June 3, 2015, www.prnewswire.com/news-releases/traces -2014-global-enforcement-report-300093073.html. The 2014 Global Enforcement Report by the NGO Trace International shows that from 1977 to 2014, the United States had 184 enforcement actions, or 70 percent of the total 269 enforcement actions concerning alleged bribery of foreign officials taken to date. The United Kingdom had the next highest total of enforcement actions, with 27 total enforcement actions from 1977 to 2014.

24. More on Edelman's Trust Barometer at www.edelman.com/insights /intellectual-property/2015-edelman-trust-barometer.

25. Adriana Nina Kusuma and Neil Chatterjee, "Indonesia Lashes Citi Over Embezzlement, Debtor Death," *Reuters*, May 6, 2011, www.reuters.com /article/us-indonesia-citigroup-idUSTRE7451J120110506.

26. For more on the ouster of United's CEO, see Ed Crooks and Gina Chon, "How a Traffic Jam on a New York Bridge Led to a CEO's Ousting," *Financial Times*, September 9, 2015, www.ft.com/intl/cms/s/0/1229dbf8-570c -11e5-a28b-50226830d644.html#axzz3nVA2Ks6F.

27. For more on Walmart's corruption scandal, see Elizabeth Harris, "After Bribery Scandal, High-Level Departures at Walmart," *New York Times*, June 4, 2014,

28. Aruna Viswanatha and Devlin Barrett, "Wal-Mart Bribery Probe Finds Few Signs of Major Misconduct in Mexico," *Wall Street Journal* www.wsj.com/articles/Walmart-bribery-probe-finds-little-misconduct-in -mexico-1445215737.

29. Johann Bhurrut and Kirana Soerono, "Educating the Next Genera-tion in Vietnam," Cargill, September 3, 2015, www.cargill.com/connections /educating-the-next-generation-in-vietnam/index.jsp.

30. Paul Kiernan, "Brazil's Petrobras Reports Nearly $17 Billion in Asset and Corruption Charges," *Wall Street Journal*, April 22, 2015, www.wsj .com/articles/brazils-petrobras-reports-nearly-17-billion-impairment-on -assets-corruption-1429744336.

31. Will Connors and Luciana Magalhaes, "How Brazil's 'Nine Horsemen' Cracked a Bribery Scandal," *Wall Street Journal*, April 6, 2015, www.wsj .com/articles/how-brazils-nine-horsemen-cracked-petrobras-bribery-scandal -1428334221?alg=y.

32. Michael E. Miller and Fred Barbash, "U.S. Indicts World Soccer Officials in Alleged $150 Million FIFA Bribery Scandal," *Washington Post*, May 27, 2015, www.washingtonpost.com/news/morning-mix/wp/2015/05/27/top-fifa -officials-arrested-in-international-soccer-corruption-investigation-according -to-reports/.

33. Jose de Cordoba and Juan Forero, "U.S. Investigates Venezuelan Oil Giant," *Wall Street Journal*, October 21, 2015, www.wsj.com/articles/u-s -investigates-venezuelan-oil-giant-1445478342.

34. Etco About page, www.etco.org.br/about-etco.php.

35. Center for Political Accountability About Us page, http://political accountability.net/about/about-us.

36. "Beginner's Guide," Good Jobs First, http://www.goodjobsfirst.org/

37. C. J. Ciaramella, "Union Smear Machine Revs Up," *Washington Free Beacon*, December 21, 2012, http://freebeacon.com/politics/union-smear-machine -revs-up.

38. H. J., "What Is Brazil's 'mensalão'?," *The Economist Explains* (blog), *Economist*, November 18, 2013, www.economist.com/blogs/economist-explains /2013/11/economist-explains-14.

39. Mark Kennedy, "Entre a Sombra e a Luz," *Epoca*, http://lobby.epoca .globo.com/entre-a-sombra-e-a-luz.shtml.

40. Lauren Ingeno, "The Politics Surrounding the U.S. Dietary Guidelines," *GW Today*, October 5, 2015, https://gwtoday.gwu.edu/politics-surrounding -us-dietary-guidelines.

8. Assess

1. Research Associate Jane Palley Katz prepared this case under the supervision of Professor Lynn Sharp Pain. Levi Strauss & Co.: Global Sourcing (B) (Harvard Case) 9-395-128, revised March 10, 1995.

2. Research Associate Jane Palley Katz prepared this case under the supervision of Professor Lynn Sharp Paine. Levi Strauss & Co.: Global Sourcing (B) (Harvard Case) 9-395-128, revised March 10, 1995.

3. Jeffrey Ballinger, "The New Free-Trade Heel: Nike Profits Jump on the Backs of Asian Workers," *Harper's*, August 1992. http://harpers.org /archive/1992/08/the-new-free-trade-heel/.

4. Debora L. Spar and Jennifer Burns, "Hitting the Wall: Nike and International Labor Practices" (700047-PDF-ENG, Boston, MA: Harvard Business School Publishing, September 6, 2002). For more on Levi and Nike, David Baron's cost-benefit analysis, and the Wilson-Lowi matrix, see David P. Baron, *Business and Its Environment* (Upper Saddle River, N.J.: Pearson, 2010), 159.

5. "Milton Friedman Goes on Tour," *Economist*, January 27, 2011, www.economist.com/node/18010553.

6. For more on the UN Global Compact, see www.unglobalcompact.org/what-is-gc/participants.

7. Ellen Brait, "PETA Lawsuit Claims Whole Foods Is Duping Shoppers with 'Humane Meat,'" *Guardian*, September 22, 2015, www.theguardian.com/us-news/2015/sep/22/peta-lawsuit-whole-foods-humane-meat-duping-shoppers.

8. Geoffrey Mohan, "Nestle Drawing Millions of Gallons of California Water on Expired Permit, Suit Claims," *Los Angeles Times*, October 13, 2015, www.latimes.com/business/la-fi-nestle-water-lawsuit-20151013-story.html.

9. William McGurn, "The Chick-fil-A War Is Back On," *Wall Street Journal*, September 24, 2012, www.wsj.com/articles/SB10000872396390444180004578016683484879960.

10. Siri Schubert and T. Christian Miller, "At Siemens, Bribery Was Just a Line Item," *New York Times*, December 20, 2008, www.nytimes.com/2008/12/21/business/worldbusiness/21siemens.html.

11. Tony Romm, "Lobbying a Bust in AT&T Bid," *Politico*, December 20, 2011, www.politico.com/story/2011/12/at-ts-lobbying-turned-back-in-t-mobile-bid-070701; Michael J. de la Merced, "T-Mobile and AT&T: What's $2 Billion Among Friends?," *New York Times*, December 20, 2011.

12. Heidi Moore, "AT&T and T-Mobile: The Popping of the Cupcake Bubble?," *Marketplace*, September 1, 2011, www.marketplace.org/topics/business/easy-street/att-and-t-mobile-popping-cupcake-bubble.

13. Brad Stone and Vernon Silver, "Google's $6 Billion Miscalculation on the EU," *Bloomberg Businessweek*, August 6, 2015, www.bloomberg.com/news/features/2015-08-06/google-s-6-billion-miscalculation-on-the-eu.

14. Richard Waters and Tim Bradshaw, "U.S. Clears Google's Core Search Business," *Financial Times*, January 3, 2013, https://next.ft.com/content/61124f52-55d4-11e2-9aa1-00144feab49a.

15. "Barack Obama (D): Top Contributors, 2008 Cycle," Open Secrets, www.opensecrets.org/pres08/contrib.php?cid=N00009638&cycle=2008.

16. "Barack Obama (D): Top Contributors, 2012 Cycle," Open Secrets, www.opensecrets.org/pres12/contrib.php?id=N00009638&cycle=2012.

17. Natalia Drozdiak and Sam Schechner, "EU Court Says Data-Transfer Pact with U.S. Violates Privacy," *Wall Street Journal*, October 6, 2015, www.wsj

.com/articles/eu-court-strikes-down-trans-atlantic-safe-harbor-data-transfer
-pact-1444121361.

18. Rory Cellan-Jones, "EU Court Backs 'Right to Be Forgotten' in Google Case," *BBC News*, May 13, 2014, www.bbc.com/news/world-europe -27388289.

19. Sam Schechner, "Google's Tax Setup Faces French Challenge," *Wall Street Journal*, October 8, 2014, www.wsj.com/articles/googles-tax-setup-faces -french-challenge-1412790355.

20. European Commission, "Antitrust: Commission Opens Formal Investigation Against Google in Relation to Android Mobile Operating System," fact sheet, April 15, 2015, http://europa.eu/rapid/press-release_MEMO-15-4782 _en.htm.

21. "EU Accuses Google Shopping of Search 'Abuse,'" *BBC News*, April 15, 2015, www.bbc.com/news/technology-32315649.

22. David McLaughlin, "Google Said to Be Under U.S. Antitrust Scrutiny Over Android," *Bloomberg Technology*, September 25, 2015, www.bloomberg .com/news/articles/2015-09-25/google-said-to-be-under-u-s-antitrust-scrutiny -over-android-iezf41sg.

23. "Android Attack," *Economist*, April 23, 2016, www.economist.com /news/business/21697193-european-commission-going-after-google-againthis -time-better-chance.

24. Jack Nicas and Brent Kendall, "FTC Extends Probe Into Google's Android," *Wall Street Journal*, April 26, 2016, www.wsj.com/articles/ftc -extends-probe-into-googles-android-1461699217.

25. Natalia Drozdiak, "News Corp Files Formal Complaint to EU Over Google," *Wall Street Journal*, April 18, 2016, www.wsj.com/articles/news-corp -files-formal-complaint-to-eu-over-google-1460972405.

26. Natalia Drozdiak, "Getty Images Lodges Complaint Against Google with EU Antitrust Watchdog," *Wall Street Journal*, April 27, 2016, www.wsj .com/articles/getty-images-lodges-complaint-against-google-with-eu-antitrust -watchdog-1461747443.

27. Nicholas Hirst, "Margarethe Vestager vs Google (round 3)," *Politico*, July 14, 2016, www.politico.eu/article/margrethe-vestager-vs-google-round-3 -antitrust-battle-search-mobile-and-advertising.

28. Megan Thee-Brenan, "How the Rise of Cellphones Affects Surveys," *New York Times*, July 10, 2014, www.nytimes.com/2014/07/11/upshot/-how -the-rise-of-cellphones-affects-surveys.html.

29. Daphne Keller and Bruce D. Brown, "Europe's Web Privacy Rules Bad for Google, Bad for Everyone," *New York Times*, April 25, 2016, www .nytimes.com/2016/04/25/opinion/europes-web-privacy-rules-bad-for-google -bad-for-everyone.html?_r=0.

30. David Baron, a professor from Stanford Business School, has developed a framework for determining the costs and benefits of acting on an issue or facing the potential consequences of not acting.

31. Thanks to Professor Luis Raul Matos of George Washington University's Graduate School of Political Management for educating me in game and drama theory.

9. Avert

1. "Animal Welfare Charity, Compassion in World Farming, Explains How McDonald's Switch to Free-Range Eggs Over 15 years Ago is Good for Hens and Good for British Farmers," McDonald's Corporation UK, accessed 22 December 2015, www.mcdonalds.co.uk/ukhome/whatmakesmcdonalds/articles/good-egg.html.

2. Stephanie Strom, "McDonald's Plans a Shift to Eggs from Only Cage-Free Hens," *New York Times*, September 9, 2015, www.nytimes.com/2015/09/10/business/mcdonalds-to-use-eggs-from-only-cage-free-hens.html?_r=0.

3. "Our Ambitions," McDonald's Corporation, accessed 22 December 2015, www.aboutmcdonalds.com/mcd/our_company/our-ambition.html.

4. Cynthia Galli, Angela Hill, and Hillrym Momtaz, "McDonald's, Target Dump Egg Supplier After Investigation," *ABC News*, November 18, 2011, http://abcnews.go.com/Blotter/mcdonalds-dumps-mcmuffin-egg-factory-health-concerns/story?id=14976054.

5. Humane Society of the United States, "Understanding Mortality Rates of Laying Hens in Cage-Free Egg Production Systems" (Farm Animals, Agribusiness, and Food Production Paper 3, 2010), http://animalstudiesrepository.org/acwp_faafp/3.

6. Kelsey Gee, "Egg Prices Jump as Bird Flu Spreads," *Wall Street Journal*, May 21, 2015, www.wsj.com/articles/bird-flu-outbreak-decimates-egg-laying-flocks-1432237046.

7. Aamer Madhani, "Avian Flu Crisis Grows for Poultry Producers Throughout USA," *USA Today*, April 21, 2015, www.usatoday.com/story/news/2015/04/21/poultry-turkey-avian-flu-crisis/26100287.

8. Arin Greenwood, "More Major Companies Vow to Transition to Cage-Free Eggs," *Huffington Post*, October 29, 2015, www.huffingtonpost.com/entry/kelloggs-cage-free-eggs_56327c1fe4b00aa54a4d7536.

9. Mike Isaac and Noam Scheiber, "Uber Settles Cases with Concessions, but Drivers Stay Freelancers," *New York Times*, April 21, 2016, www

.nytimes.com/2016/04/22/technology/uber-settles-cases-with-concessions -but-drivers-stay-freelancers.html.

10. Douglas Macmillan and Lisa Fleisher, "How Sharp-Elbowed Uber Is Trying to Make Nice," *Wall Street Journal,* January 29, 2015, www.wsj.com /articles/hard-driving-uber-gives-compromise-a-try-1422588782.

11. Mike Isaac, "Airbnb Pledges to Work with Cities and Pay 'Fair Share' of Taxes," *New York Times,* November 11, 2015, www.nytimes.com/2015/11/12 /technology/airbnb-pledges-to-work-with-cities-and-pay-fair-share-of-taxes .html?_r=0.

12. www.ameribev.org/files/332_FINAL %20ABA %20CLEAR %20ON %20CALORIES-%20(Calorie %20Label %20Initiative %20and %20Style %20Guide).pdf.

13. Tom Scheck, "Target Stores to Clamp Down on Cold Medicines Used to Make Meth," Minnesota Public Radio, April 18, 2005, http://news .minnesota.publicradio.org/features/2005/04/18_scheckt_target.

10. Acquiesce

1. Tim Bradshaw, "Apple Chief Tim Cook Rounds on Outdated US Tax Code," *Financial Times,* December 20, 2015, https://next.ft.com/content /c7fc1e3a-a786-11e5-955c-1e1d6de94879.

2. Dan Ackman, "Stanley Works Stays Home," *Forbes,* August 2, 2002, www.forbes.com/2002/08/02/0802topnews.html.

3. Berkeley Lovelace, Jr., "Ford CEO: Main Reason for Canceling Mexico Plant Was Market Demand, Not Trump," http://www.cnbc.com/2017/01/03 /ford-ceo-main-reason-for-canceling-mexico-plant-was-market-demand-not -trump.html.

4. Jessica Guynn and Roger Yu, "Conservative Groups Encouraged by Meeting with Facebook's Zuckerberg," *USA Today,* May 20, 2016, www.usatoday.com /story/money/2016/05/18/conservatives-stress-thought-diversity-facebook /84550870.

5. Greg Toppo, "Boy Scouts of America Ends Ban on Gay Scout Leaders," *USA Today,* July 27, 2015, www.usatoday.com/story/news/2015/07/27/boy-scouts -gay-leaders/30752987.

6. Ashley Armstrong, "How Starbucks Woke Up and Smelt the Coffee on Tax and Technology," *Telegraph* (U.K.), July 20, 2015, www.telegraph .co.uk/finance/newsbysector/retailandconsumer/11749690/How-Starbucks -woke-up-and-smelt-the-coffee-on-tax-and-technology.html.

11. Advance Common Interests

1. Steve Heller, "Could General Electric Company Be a 'Rule Breaker' in Disguise?," *Motley Fool*, October 10, 2015, www.fool.com/investing/general /2015/10/10/could-general-electric-company-be-a-rule-breaker-i.aspx.

2. More on GE's Ecomagination initiative can be found at www.ge.com /about-us/ecomagination and www.gesustainability.com/2014-performance /ecomagination.

3. Michael E. Porter and Mark R. Kramer, "Creating Shared Value," *Harvard Business Review*, January–February 2011, 62–77.

4. Ibid., 9.

5. For more on for-benefit corporations, see Heerad Sabeti, "The For-Benefit Enterprise," *Harvard Business Review*, November 2011, https://hbr .org/2011/11/the-for-benefit-enterprise.

6. SolarCity's collaboration with DIRECTTV drawn from Jean Case, "A New Inning For Impact Investing," *Forbes*, August 11, 2015, www.forbes .com/sites/jeancase/2015/08/11/new-inning-impact-investing/2.

7. Thanks to Lord Jamie Borwick, previously the firm's CEO, for sharing these insights.

8. Matthew Schwartz, "Check Out How Facebook Just Made CSR and Cause-based Communications Easier," *PRNews*, December 17, 2013, www.prnewsonline.com/water-cooler/2013/12/17/facebooks-donate-now -appeals-to-nonprofit-pr.

9. C. K. Prahalad, *Fortune at the Bottom of the Pyramid: Eradicating Poverty Through Profits* (Upper Saddle River, N.J.: Prentice-Hall, 2006).

10. "IBM—Education Industry—Teaching and Learning—Technology Solutions—United States," IBM, accessed September 1, 2016, www-935.ibm .com/industries/education/learning.html.

11. Mohana Ravindranath, "Google Awards Grants to Boost Innovation in Nonprofit Sector," *Washington Post*, December 9, 2012, www.washingtonpost .com/business/on-small-business/google-awards-grants-to-boost-innovation -in-nonprofit-sector/2012/12/09/8d18bb80-4086-11e2-a2d9-822f58ac9fd5 _story.html.

12. "Easy Analytics—IBM Watson Analytics," IBM, accessed 1 September 2016. https://www.ibm.com/analytics/watson-analytics/us-en/.

13. Cost of not taking medicine as prescribed: Katy Colletto and Eden K. Pudberry, "What the Doctor Ordered: Prescription Adherence with Transparency" (white paper, Castlight Health, San Francisco, March 2013), http:// content.castlighthealth.com/rs/castlighthealth/images/Prescription-Adherence -with-Transparency-White-Paper-Pharma.pdf.

14. Noemi Pollack, "Facebook Takes CSR to Another Plane," *Strategy and Musings* (blog), www.pollackblog.com/?p=1348.

15. "Strategy, Consulting, Digital, Technology and Operations," Accenture, accessed 1 September 2016, www.accenture.com/t20150914T131203__w__/us-en/_acnmedia/Accenture/Conversion-Assets/Microsites/Documents20/Accenture-Healthcare-Technology-Vision-2015-Infographic.pdf#zoom=50.

16. Emily Babay, "Facebook Partners with Agencies on Amber Alerts," *Washington Examiner*, January 13, 2011, 8.

17. Alex Fitzpatrick, "Facebook Safety Check: How the 'I'm Safe' Feature Works," *Time*, November 19, 2015, http://time.com/4120326/facebook-safety-check-feature.

18. "Twitter Suspends 125,000 'Terrorism' Accounts," *BBC News*, February 5, 2016, www.bbc.com/news/world-us-canada-35505996.

19. C. J. Chivers, "Facebook Groups Act as Weapons Bazaars for Militias," *New York Times*, April 6, 2016, www.nytimes.com/2016/04/07/world/middleeast/facebook-weapons-syria-libya-iraq.html?hp&action=click&pgtype=Homepage&clickSource=story-heading&m&_r=0.

20. Natalie Andrews and Deepa Seetharaman. "Facebook Steps Up Efforts Against Terrorism," *Wall Street Journal*, February 11, 2016, www.wsj.com/articles/facebook-steps-up-efforts-against-terrorism-1455237595.

21. John Voelcker, "California Yanks Prius Perks: No More Hybrid HOV-Lane Access," Green Car Reports, last modified July 8, 2010, www.greencarreports.com/news/1046928_california-yanks-prius-perks-no-more-hybrid-hov-lane-access.

22. "Santander Cycles," Transport for London, accessed September 1, 2016. https://tfl.gov.uk/modes/cycling/santander-cycles.

12. Assemble to Win

1. Amy Schatz, "What Is SOPA Anyway?" *Wall Street Journal*, January 18, 2012.

2. Hayley Tsukayama and Cecilia Kang, "SOPA Opposition Goes Viral," *Washington Post*, November 22, 2011.

3. Jonathan Weisman, "In Fight Over Piracy Bills, New Economy Rises Against Old," *New York Times*, January 18, 2012.

4. Jonathan Weisman, "After an Online Firestorm, Congress Shelves Anti-piracy Bills," *New York Times*, January 20, 2012.

5. Weisman, "In Fight Over Piracy Bills, New Economy Rises Against Old."

6. Tsukayama and Kang, "SOPA Opposition Goes Viral."

7. Weisman, "In Fight Over Piracy Bills, New Economy Rises Against Old."

8. Marshall Shepherd, "How Pope Francis Is Changing the Climate Change Conversation," *Forbes*, November 16, 2015; Tony Dokoupil, "Pope Francis Issues Radical Call for Climate Change Action," MSNBC, September 25, 2015.

9. Joseph Ax, "Bloomberg's Ban on Big Sodas Is Unconstitutional: Appeals Court," *Reuters*, July 30, 2013.

10. Jonathon M. Trugman, "Raising Minimum Wage Would Cost a Million People Their Jobs," *New York Post*, November 14, 2015; Mark Peters, "States Push Back Against Cities' Minimum-Wage Boosts," *Wall Street Journal*, September 25, 2015; U.S. Chamber of Commerce, "Workforce Freedom Initiative," www.uschamber.com/workforce-freedom-initiative; "Fight for 15/Fast Food Forward," Worker Center Watch, www.workercenterwatch.com/worker-centers/fast-food-forward-fight-for-15; Fight for $15 Home page, www.fightfor15.org.

11. Tim Chen, "What the Durbin Amendment Means for You," *U.S. News and World Report*, July 12, 2011.

12. Richard A. Roth, "Supreme Court Won't Hear Challenge to Fed's Debit Card Rules," *Banking and Finance Law Daily*, January 20, 2015.

13. Peters, "States Push Back Against Cities' Minimum-Wage Boosts"; "Workforce Freedom Initiative," U.S. Chamber of Commerce; "Fight For 15/Fast Food Forward," Worker Center Watch; Fight for $15 Home page.

14. Mercedes Alvaro, "Ecuador Seeks Suspension of Chevron Arbitration Hearing," *Wall Street Journal*, November 15, 2013.

15. Roger Parloff, "Key Funder of Ecuadorians' Suit Against Chevron Quits," *Fortune*, February 16, 2015.

16. Hillary Lehr, "Rainforest Action Network on Cargill's Pinkwashing Attempt Backfires At Fancy Luncheon," *Understory* (blog), Rainforest Action Network, October 31, 2011, http://rainforest00.soup.io/post/187603725/Cargill-s-Pinkwashing-Attempt-Backfires-At-Fancy

17. Heidi Blake, "Student Tuition Fee Protest Turns Violent as Tory Headquarters Evacuated," *Telegraph*, November 10, 2011.

18. Thanks to Baron Jamie Borwick for sharing his insights on this.

19. "Coalition Calls on President Clinton to Improve Air Conditioner Efficiency," Appliance Standards Awareness Project, January 3, 2001, www.appliance-standards.org/content/president-clinton-please-dont-drop-ball%E2%80%A6-air-conditioning-standards

20. Matthew L. Wald, " Clinton Energy-Saving Rules Are Getting A Second Look," *New York Times*, March 31, 2001.

21. Steven Mufson, "Senate Committee Puts Big Oil Execs in the Hot Seat," *Washington Post*, May 12, 2011.

22. Darren Goode, "Dems, Oil Execs Face Off at Hearing," *Politico*, May 12, 2011.

23. Fred Schulte and John Aloysius Farrell, "Emails Show Wireless Firm's Communications with White House as Campaign Donations Were Made," Center for Public Integrity, September 14, 2011, www.publicintegrity.org /2011/09/14/6458/emails-show-wireless-firms-communications-white-house -campaign-donations-were-made.

24. Eli Lake, "White House's Testimony 'Guidance,'" *Daily Beast*, September 19, 2011; Jenny Strasburg, Greg Bensinger and Amy Schatz, "Lawmakers Target Falcone," *Wall Street Journal*, October 6, 2011.

25. Linda Sandler and Todd Shields, "LightSquared Bankruptcy Debt Doubles as FCC Weighs Wireless OK," *Bloomberg Technology*, July 28, 2015.

26. Anton Troianovski, Shalini Ramachandran, and Sarah Portlock, "Dish Network Wins a $9 Billion Spectrum Prize," *Wall Street Journal*, December 12, 2012.

27. Freeing Alternatives for Speedy Transportation (FAST) Act. H.R. 1767, 108th Cong. (2003).

28. "Life in the Fast Lane," *Wall Street Journal*, June 18, 2003.

29. Mark Kennedy, "The FAST Way to Get Traffic Moving," *Washington Post*, July 23, 2003.

13. Pope Francis, a CEO Worth Emulating

1. Leonardo DiCaprio, accepting the Academy Award for Best Actor (speech, 88th Academy Awards ceremony, Los Angeles, February 28, 2016), YouTube, www.youtube.com/watch?v=AOoP56eXtzM.

2. Michael Sugar, accepting the Academy Award for Best Picture (speech, 88th Academy Awards ceremony, Los Angeles, February 28, 2016), You-Tube, www.youtube.com/watch?v=UtREJJF1PUo.

3. "Automation and Anxiety," *Wall Street Journal*, June 25, 2016.

4. Francis X. Rocca, "Pope Blames Markets for Environment's Ills," *Wall Street Journal*, June 18, 2015.

5. *Global Competitiveness Report 2015–2016*, "Argentina," World Economic Forum, http://reports.weforum.org/global-competitiveness-report-2015-2016.

6. Jason M. Breslow, "The Vatican After Francis: Has the Pope Met His Mandate for Change?" *Frontline*, September 24, 2015, www.pbs.org/wgbh/frontline /article/the-vatican-after-francis-has-the-pope-met-his-mandate-for-change.

7. Ibid.

8. "Too Much of a Good Thing," *Economist*, March 26, 2016.

9. Ibid.

10. Ibid.

11. "The Problem with Profits," *Economist*, March 26, 2016.

12. Ibid.

13. Josh Levs and Holly Yan, "Francis Is the First Non-European Pope in Nearly 1,300 Years," CNN, March 14, 2013, www.cnn.com/2013/03/14 /world/europe/pope-non-european.

14. Pope Francis, "Address to the United Nations" (speech, New York, September 25, 2015), www.popefrancisvisit.com/schedule/address-to-united -nations-general-assembly.

15. Stephen Nakrosis, "5 Encyclicals That Had an Impact on the World," *Wall Street Journal*, June 18, 2015.

16. "10 Things WTO Can Do," World Trade Organization, www.wto.org /english/thewto_e/whatis_e/10thi_e/10thi00_e.htm.

17. Allison Kilkenny, "Seniors and Vets to Crash 'Fix the Debt' Party Hosted by Honeywell CEO," *Nation*, February 11, 2013.

18. "David Cote," Fix the Debt, www.fixthedebt.org/david-cote.

19. Robert Z. Lawrence, "TPP Benefits for Workers Far Outweigh Costs" (Trade and Investment Policy Watch, Peterson Institute for International Economics, Washington, D.C., April 18, 2016).

20. Joshua P. Meltzer, "The Trans-Pacific Partnership Is a Win for All Parties," *Future Development* (blog), December 9, 2015, www.brookings.edu/blog/future -development/2015/12/09/the-trans-pacific-partnership-is-a-win-for-all-parties.

21. "Trade in the Balance," *Economist*, February 6, 2016.

22. Erin Griffith, "Inside the Pope's Social Media Plan to Win Over Millennials," *Fortune*, September 15, 2015.

23. Liam Stack, "Get Ready, Internet. The Pope Has Joined Instagram," *New York Times*, March 19, 2016.

24. Daniel Burke, "Pope Francis' History-Making South American Excursion," CNN, July 13, 2015, www.cnn.com/2015/07/12/living/pope-francis-week-latin -america.

25. Anna Matranga, "Pope Francis Visits Notorious Prison in Bolivia," *CBS News*, July 10, 2015, www.cbsnews.com/news/pope-francis-visits-notorious -prison-in-bolivia.

26. Murithi Mutiga and Harriet Sherwood, "Pope Francis Criticises 'New Colonialism' in Emotive Kenya Speech," *Guardian*, November 27, 2015.

27. "Pope Francis Washes Feet of Refugees for Easter Week," *Al Jazeera*, March 25, 2016.

28. Jim Yardley, "Pope Francis Takes 12 Refugees Back to Vatican After Trip to Greece," *New York Times*, April 16, 2016.

Index